Kranz

Harney County, Oregon, and Its Range Land

Harney County, Oregon,

and Its Range Land

by
George Francis Brimlow

UNDER SPONSORSHIP OF

THE HARNEY COUNTY HISTORICAL SOCIETY,

BURNS, OREGON

BY THE PACIFIC

BINFORDS & MORT, *Publishers,*

PORTLAND, OREGON

Printed in the United States of America
by
The Metropolitan Press, Portland, Oregon

GENERAL WILLIAM SELBY HARNEY

Few soldiers had a more piquant and honorable career than the man for whom, in Oregon, were named the lake, valley and county of irreducible fascination.

William Selby Harney was born into a Southern family of sedate standing in Haysboro, near Nashville, Tennessee, August 22, 1800. He was the youngest of eight children of Thomas and Margaret Harney. His father was a merchant and land surveyor. After attending an academy in Haysboro, William tried to concern himself with the wishes of his mother. To steer him toward a career in the navy, she had him taught privately in navigation. The army, however, was his own choice. He entered it on February 13, 1818, accepting an appointment as a second lieutenant in the First Infantry.

He thirsted for action and kept his ambitions constantly primed, yet with controlled aims built on sound moral bases. With audacity and uninhibited courage, he fought in the Black Hawk War of 1833.

In that year, also, the sparkling soldier of lengthy stride and clifflike shoulders married Mary Mullanphy of St. Louis. Three children were born to them. Later, he and his wife separated. She died in the early 1860s.

By 1836, Harney was a lieutenant colonel in the Florida war. In many Indian campaigns in Florida, he proved repeatedly his ability as a soldier and leader. His bravery earned him the brevet of colonel in 1840.

General Winfield Scott, however, distrusted Harney's "judgment and impetuosity" as ranking cavalry officer under him — that of colonel of the Second Dragoons. At the beginning of the Mexican War, the field commander had doubts as to his being able to manage the outspoken Tennesseean. He attempted to turn Harney's command over to another. Harney defied Scott and was court-martialed. Not to be harassed and, with forthright determination coupled by aid from influential friends, Harney blithely appealed to superiors in Washington.

Scott was the recipient of a mild reprimand. Graciously, he

accepted the colonel's apology and restored him to his command. Harney lost no time in displaying brilliancy and courage in the battle of Cerro Gordo. Enemy fire from the heights of El Telegrafo was ruinous, but victory was gained as Harney, at the head of General Smith's brigade, led the upward charge. Promotion fully earned, he was brevetted brigadier general on April 8, 1847.

He played a zealous part in defeating the Sioux on the Platte River in 1855. The actual rank of brigadier general came to him when he assumed command of the Department of Oregon in 1858. While in this capacity, Harney garrisoned San Juan Island in the dispute over possession, in July, 1859. The isle, claimed vehemently by Great Britain, stirred up international diplomacy. The equally vehement American officer was recalled from his command. He was vindicated by 1873 when Emperor William of Germany, as arbiter, sustained the claims of the United States to the island.

After his recall from Oregon, Harney served as commander of the Department of the West at St. Louis until May, 1861. Meanwhile, he had been virtually kidnapped by premature Confederates and taken to Richmond, Virginia. Though a native of Tennessee, he stubbornly refused to aid the Southern cause on the brink of war. He denounced secession publicly but was lulled into an armistice by Sterling G. Price and Stonewall Jackson, still proclaimed as Unionists. It was his big mistake to promise to take no military step as long as states kept peaceful. Southerners soon got the jump on Yankee troops.

Harney, relieved, was deprived of an active command during the Civil War and went on the retired list in 1863. Notwithstanding, he was brevetted major general for his many years of distinguished service.

The part he played in opening eastern Oregon to settlement, with the all-important ventures by his troops into the Harney basin, belongs fittingly in other pages of this work.

In 1885, the General married his nurse, Mrs. Mary Elizabeth St. Cyr. He lived quietly in the South, at Pass Christian, Mississippi, and at St. Louis. Later, he went to Orlando, Florida. There, at the scene of his early triumphs as an inspired soldier in Florida and its Everglades, he died on May 9, 1889. Harney County, Oregon, had been created only some two months previously.

General Harney was buried in the western section of Arlington National Cemetery, his grave marked by a monument of dark gray polished Quincy granite, twenty-five feet in height. There, too, Mary Elizabeth Harney was laid to rest after her death on October 22, 1907.

On May 17, 1889, an editorial in *The Oregonian* of Portland, edited by the esteemed Harvey W. Scott, contained this tribute:

General Harney is still remembered by a number of old residents of Portland, who enjoyed his hospitality at Vancouver Barracks. He was a man of tall and powerful physique, and was a famous athlete and a keen sportsman. He had large influence over the Indians, who were greatly impressed by his superior stature, bodily strength and courage, and he always kept his word with them. Although he joined the army at an early date, when it was the rule for officers in the West to ride hard and drink deep, he must have led a temperate life to have reached the great age of eighty-nine. Like General William Jenkins Worth, he most cordially hated General Winfield Scott. General Harney is probably the last survivor of the regular army officers who were captains as early as the Black Hawk War of 1833, and lieutenant-colonels in the Florida War of 1836.

In dealing fairly with the vanquished and in fondness for the ways of the frontier, Harney may be likened to the doughty campaigner General George Crook, known as Three-stars to Indians of the plains. Each man, timely, donned the common garb of a hunter to trudge many miles in quest of game. At a camp fire in the Oregon country they found ofttimes the harvest of their greatest pleasure.

PREFACE

ALONG WITH OTHER STATES of our West, Oregon is quickening its efforts toward recording a fully rounded story of the live-stock industry. In the seemingly limitless expanse east of the Cascade Mountains in Oregon, the raisers of cattle, horses and sheep in great numbers labored against many odds.

In passage of time much of eastern Oregon's grazing empire gave way to him who plowed the sod for growing of grain. And the forests yielded to inevitable demands and needs. Although Harney County and the region encircling it have, agricul-turally, remained predominantly a kingdom for live stock, the stockmen join forces with lumbermen and protectors of wildlife. Once severely isolated, the county approximating the State of Maryland in size now feels daily the throb of the outer world.

To tell of the development of Harney County and its re-lationship to affairs of state and nation is the chief purpose of this work. Long has it been the vision and sincere resolve of Archie McGowan, president of the Harney County His-torical Society, to set forth accurately a goodly portion of that which should become a part of a broader history. He and the late Isaac Burpee, former directors of the Oregon Histori-cal Society, and fellow workers, lent constant aid and inspira-tion.

All sources for this book are printed herein, obviating the acknowledgments. Of necessity in a fresh work, the digging for material was deep and the gathering of it wide. The research extended from historical facilities in California, Nevada and the Pacific Northwest to those in Washington, D. C., and at the Widener Library of Harvard University. Su-perintendent Lancaster Pollard and staff of the Oregon His-torical Society have given stout assistance in the tasks relating to publication. To scores of individuals as well as to the numer-ous institutions fullest gratitude is offered.

It is hoped that the story of Harney County and its range land will provide the reader the vitality and historical per-spective in the degree intended.

GEORGE FRANCIS BRIMLOW.

Blue River, Oregon.

CONTENTS

CONTENTS (CONTINUED)

TABLE OF ILLUSTRATIONS

PHOTO CREDITS

The author and publishers wish to thank the following persons and organizations for permission to reproduce the illustrations in this book:

Mrs. R. D. Baker for picture of Walter (Bill) Brown.

Mart Brenton for the pictures of Peter French dated 1872, for that of the pioneer group in 1870, for that of the cowboy group at the "P" ranch, for that of the first county officials of Harney County in 1889, for that of the Red Front Feed and Livery stables, for that of the coming of the railroad to Burns, for that of the pioneer school group at Egan.

Birdie Dave, niece of Sarah Winnemucca, for the picture of Sarah taken in Boston in 1883.

Ray Erickson for the picture of the Trumpeter Swans at Malheur Refuge and that of the Mule Deer at "P" ranch.

Bill Hedrich, Hedrich Blessing Studio, for the picture of the Edward Hines Lumber Co.

T. Allen Jones for the picture of John Devine and Jeff Billingsley in 1890.

Mrs. Maggie Levens for the picture of Mrs. William Hanley.

Mrs. W. W. Miller for the pictures of branding on the Pine Creek ranch in 1920's and that of Drewsey, Oregon.

John Scharff for the pictures of the homestead cabin, about 1885, and that of the "P" ranch in the 1890's.

Henry H. Sheldon for the picture of Kiger Gorge in the Steens Mountains, for that of the cattle round-up, and that of the old Merion Horton Ranch.

Smithsonian Institution for the picture of General William S. Harney.

Mrs. Blanche Turner for the pictures of the early day freight team, that of the town of Harney on July 4, 1890, for that of early day branding irons, and that of the poker game at Egan.

Valley Flying Service, Inc., for pictures of Edward Hines Lumber Co., Hines, Oregon.

Mrs. Ella Voegtly for the picture of the Voegtly Building.

War Department for the picture of Camp Harney dated 1872.

(Copy courtesy Oregon Historical Society).

Harney County, Oregon, and Its Range Land

Chapter I

THE PREHISTORIC AGES

HEDGED as the history of a small segment of country may be, it should be traced to its roots. With its sixteen sister counties and parent Grant County, Harney shares the story of eastern Oregon.

In early geological time, eastern Oregon was not as dry as at present. Parched sagebrush areas, especially Fort Rock Valley, once had marshes inhabited by the red men. Here, many relics and signs of their ways of life have been found. In the sageland the Indians left numerous groups of pictures. By use of signs, denoting the ingenuity and advancement over red men of other regions because of trail markings in hard ground or shifting sand, the desert Indians depicted much in pictographs.

The Paleo-Indian of Oregon in due course left lasting impress. Signs of his association are found in geological phenomena including volcanism, best illustrated in Summer Lake and Fort Rock Valley. Paleo-Indian is, says Dr. L. S. Cressman, "a true representative of *Homo sapiens*."

Pumice from final explosions in forming of Crater Lake hide knives and other evidence of early man in eastern Oregon. Caves near Paisley in Summer Lake Valley provide best stratigraphic evidence of ancient human life for the geologist and paleontologist. The life was contemporary with fauna of Pluvial or Early Post-pluvial period. Date of early man's existence here is estimated as far back as 15,000 years, final eruption of Mount Mazama (birth of Crater Lake) from 5000 to 10,000 years ago. The great eruption of Mount Mazama, forming the caldera holding Crater Lake, scattered pumice "over some 5000 square miles to the north and east of Crater Lake." Sediments bearing telltale pollen are found on the pumice.

Glacial drifts and formation of lake indentures, with periodical advances and recessions, affected climate and growth of plant and animal life. Increase and decrease of moisture, with

1

wind work, tell of drying lake beds and erosion, with desert country adapting itself gradually to limited plant and animal sustenance. Chester Stock, scientist, says:

Perhaps nowhere in North America . . . does a representative portion of the past history of mammalian life unfold so clearly and impressively as in the John Day region of north-central Oregon. Here, in at least five out of seven or eight readily recognizable and superimposed formations occur the skulls, teeth, jaws, or skeletal elements of extinct mammals. Complete and articulated skeletons are found much less often. But whether complete or not, these are the remains of once living creatures that date from several distinct stages in geological time.

Millenia have since passed while the fossil mammalian material, undergoing changes, has been preserved. The most productive ground for the explorer in the John Day deposits is between Spray and Picture Gorge. Varying species number more than a hundred, including flesh-eating saber-toothed cats and lines of dogs; herbivores, like camels and horses; omnivores (peccaries and giant pigs) , along with rodents, rabbits, "and an opossum." Far distant is any resemblance to animals now living. Pigs had teeth like those of cud-chewers. Dogs were bearlike.

Other remains disclose such mammals of long ago as the rhinoceroses and tapirs. Of most popular interest are specimens of the primitive horse (Miohippus) . From Stock's study, this horse "stood about six hands at the withers, on both front and hind feet there were three well-developed toes, and its grinding teeth were short-crowned, as they are in a browsing mammal." Evolution of the horse kept pace with changes of earth and environment.

Formations, folding and eroding, followed by "upswelling of basic lavas," destroyed mammals, and layers of basaltic material encased the remains.. Volcanism, with resultant ashes, the silt and successive changes in climate eventually made plant life possible again, the region becoming habitable for animals and man.

In the last stage before arrival of recent time, life-history in the John Day area is traced in terrace deposits along present running streams. Remains here are meager, comprising "only extinct species of elephants and an equine essentially similar to the modern horse," says Stock.

Although, in the second decade of the nineteenth century, Peter Skene Ogden found no living buffalo in the Harney region, he reported abundance of bleached bones and weathered skulls. These surface remains, however, did not indicate past herds as large as those which thundered over the Dakota prairies. Few, if any, remains were further noticed until our present generation.

Vernon Bailey of the United States Biological Survey discovered, in the bed of Malheur Lake in an extremely dry season, 40 bison skulls. The lake had kept its secret sealed for generations. Doubtless the buffalo, stampeded by fear of foes, preying beast or Indian hunters, broke through ice and were trapped. Or there might have been death-dealing drought, when all but a small portion of waters evaporated and the buffalo died of thirst, bunched in a last stand for survival.

Nature and science, rolling away the stones of dark ages, will continue to reveal long-buried secrets.

Chapter II

EARLY RED MEN

LONG BEFORE WHITE MEN pressed against red men, the Shoshones dominated much of the Great Basin country. This included semi-arid plains, deserts, and mountains lying between the Rockies and the Sierra Nevada and Cascade ranges of California and Oregon. Crude picture-writing in caves and on sheltered rocks is not chronological but does reveal important happenings.

Pictography, according to Richard P. Irwin, is "that form of thought writing which seeks to convey ideas by means of pictures, signs or marks more or less suggestive or imitative of the object or idea in mind." Pictographs are paintings, and petroglyphs are marks which have been carved, pecked or cut. Another form on rock occurs where the writing has been pecked and the scoring painted afterward.

Generally, rock writing follows the linguistic areas, as with the branches of the great Shoshonean family. Usually, petroglyphs have been made by abrasion, with pecking stones to fit the hand, and are only on rocks. Pictographs are commonly found on walls, under rock shelters or in caves. Sometimes the paint may be just water and coloring matter, which oxidizes, penetrates the rock, to become part of it, and cannot be removed unless cut away. Some of the rock writing in Oregon and Idaho may have been done within the last hundred years.

Colors had significance — red signifying danger; white, honor, and so on. Shoshoni used vegetable colors on skins and garments but in pictographs employed mineral matter, especially iron, which yields browns, reds and greens. Talc or white clay gave white color, also burned gypsum and lime for white. Oil, such as bear oil, is mixed with pigments, then dissolved in a thin gum or resin obtained from pine and fir trees. The mixture, put on a rock, hardens and glazes, and the bright color, if weather-shielded somewhat, will hold for hundreds or thousands of years.

In the Shoshoni pictographs, only the victorious party does the recording in zeal for boasting of deeds of valor. They do

4

not depict a defeat or adversity. In the writings, John E. Rees, Idaho scholar, asserts, "there is no background, no proportionate sizes, and no perspective view, and . . . they will make a few marks here and there and imagine that it looks like a dog or a man, etc. There is always a central thought and the other pictures are built around it to elucidate it."

The Bannocks were considered the bravest Indians of the region, using the dragon-fly as their totem (guardian spirit), beautiful, powerful in flight, eater of insects, a dragon of the air. Shoshoni and Bannocks came from a union of a brave coyote and a fair young girl, in "coyote cult" legend. The related Utes or Paiutes, like other Indians, thought it insulting to be called an animal (many had "bad" meanings), but they also have their stories of the Good Coyote. The Good One aided them.

Although the name Bannock is in common usage, scholars also recognize "Bannack." Origin of the word still remains obscure. The late R. Ross Arnold contended the appellation was derived from the Shoshone word *bampnack*, "to throw backward," in the manner of sweeping a lock of hair from the forehead. The common noun *bannock* is of Scottish origin, referring to a kind of unleavened bread or to a wooden roller used in making bannocks. Other terms include "Banak."

In physique, Bannocks bore close resemblance to the Shahaptian Nez Perces. Generally, men and women were of sturdy build, tall, well proportioned. Once mounted, they hunted warily for food and used hides for clothing, moccasins and tepees. Ultimately separated into Northern and Southern bands, disease and headlong clashes with adversaries took heavy toll of the Bannocks. In due course, because of kinship and mutual grievances, they weaned many Paiutes from customary solidity of character and complacency.

Widely dispersed were the Western Shoshones, Northern and Southern Paiutes, divisions of the Shoshonean linguistic family, at the start of the historic period. "The Northern Paiutes," says Julian H. Steward, anthropologist, "spread throughout western Nevada and penetrated eastern California and southeastern Oregon. The Shoshoni came to occupy the territory from Death Valley, California, through central Nevada and southern to western Wyoming."

Peculiarly enough, Paiutes of Walker River and Pyramid Lake reservation in Nevada, many of them later living in Harney basin, spoke a language closely allied with the Bannocks' speech. They, sometimes designated as Paviotso, considered the Bannocks to be their cousins. In early days the Paiutes had been called *Say-do-carah*, "conqueror" or "enemy." The commonly accepted idea of the source of Pahute — *pah*, "water," and *Ute*, or *pai*, "true," is not applicable to all the tribes so called.

The Paiutes were rather short in stature, heavy-set, and lighter than many Indians in complexion. With longer faces and more eager for learning and display than the Washoes, the Paiutes treated them haughtily. Although Paiutes made successful invasions against weaker tribes in California, later they followed peaceful, well-worn trails for food. In tribal parties of 10 to 40 families, they harvested seeds and nuts. If hunting were poor, they ate insects. Out of available material they built, season after season, new lodges on familiar camp sites. Old wickiups, along with debris, were left untouched.

What the buffalo was to the Bannock or Crow, so was the rabbit to the primitive Paiute. The meat yielded food and the skins, fur inside, were sewed together to make clothes, robes and blankets. Annual mud-hen drives were held, the fowl losing its wild and bitter taste in the drying for winter eating. Water was poured in holes to drown out ground squirrels, considered a special treat for the spring. The skin, left on while roasting, was removed easily before serving, baring tender and juicy meat.

"Que-wees comin'! Que-wees comin'!" This Paiute cry is heard today, as of old, when fish run in the spring. Habits cling.

Pine nuts, or nuts of the pinon pine, are ground by a heavy stone upon another, to make flour. The highly prized flour makes delectable dishes for special occasions. Thick soup or gravy created from it gives an appealing aroma. The steaming kettle is placed in the center of the floor. Pan bread, fried in a skillet, and like a huge pancake, is passed from hand to hand. Chunks are broken from the tough disk and dunked in the gravy-soup. It is relished noisily and with satisfactory smacks.

Paiutes, like Crows, have mourned their dead at great

length, older ones wailing in burial grounds day after day.
Upon demise of a Paiute, the family moved the tepee (later
a house) , getting away from the fatal spot. Earthly goods, including pictures and ornaments, were buried in a big bonfire.

Modern Paiutes have run away from whirlwinds, said to be
crooked winds which were evil enough to cast a spell of inevitable death. Faith in a Great Spirit as well as in the white
man's God has been recognizable. Likewise, the white doctor
and the Indian medicine man may both serve well. At child-
birth, Paiute women prefer female attendants. Quite shy in
such ordeals, the Indian mothers have been reluctant to ask
for a white doctor unless they faced peril.

How proud the mother in care of the child! Often she went
to great length in decorating elaborately the cradles, or baby
boards, with sun shades. If the infant slept, the board lay flat
on the floor. If awake, the infant's board was tilted against
the wall and brown eyes could see everything.

With the coming of the white men, came many changes for
the red men. Creativeness, such as the art of basket-weaving,
withered away; yet there survived many strong habits and
deeply instilled beliefs.

Chapter III

ENTRANCE OF THE FUR-HUNTERS

HARNEY BASIN TODAY is a cattle country supreme. What made it so invites the inquirer into endless byways. Doubtless its most stirring period was from the time Grant County was created in 1864 until that parent wished godspeed to Harney County in 1889. Back of that, however, lies a colorful story.

Black cattle of the Spaniards appeared on the Pacific Northwest Coast before the close of the eighteenth century, reported at Nootka Sound in 1792. Twenty-two years later, the ship *Isaac Todd* landed cattle at Fort George, the former Astoria, and the five head led to establishment of the cattle industry in the Columbia River valley. With the arrival, in 1824, of Dr. John McLoughlin as chief factor for the Hudson's Bay Company in the territory west of the Rocky Mountains, Fort Vancouver, on the Columbia across from the mouth of the Willamette, replaced Fort George as headquarters. Chosen by Governor George Simpson as a promising agricultural site, Vancouver soon became self-supporting. The company had twenty-seven head of cattle there in 1825. The herd was allowed to grow, none being killed for beef until 1836.

The interior of eastern Oregon, fascinatingly etched by volcanism, now baffled men of French, Scotch and English blood. They tried to probe 200,000 square miles of tree-springing mountains, cupped lakes, clear streams, grassy valleys, seas and walls of lava, shelves of ore, flats of alkali, and floors of sand spangled with sagebrush, rabbit brush and juniper.

In the heart of it all, a hundred miles north to south, yawned a basin half that distance in width, destined to bear the name of Harney. The northern half of Harney County is a distinctive geographic unit, in which the streams flow toward Malheur and Harney lakes, with no outlets. The pine-covered Blue Mountains rise on the north, dividing watershed for feeders of the Crooked and John Day rivers. The outer edge of the basin on the south and west is a gradual upthrust set-

8

ting the area off from similar valleys like Catlow and Summer, Abert and Silver lakes. On level stretches of the plateau, elevation reaches 4,100 to 5,000 feet.

Steens Mountain, towering more than 9,000 feet, throws out flanks on the eastern boundary for forty miles. That majestic topographical feature is bolstered by a broken ridge which cuts off Harney basin from tributaries of the Malheur River. Waters of the Malheur race to the Snake River. Its course and its tributaries marked the first entrance into Harney Valley by white men.

Malheur Lake receives the chief drainage of the basin, two branches of the Silvies River, starting as one from the Blue Mountains, and two divisions of the Donner and Blitzen River from the south, fed by tributaries born in Steens Mountain. Silver Creek, after a capricious course of fifty miles from the northwest, empties into Harney Lake. The area at the mouth is called Warm Springs Valley. Harney Valley, of 600 square miles, the largest area in production, lies north of the lakes. Its flat lands of fertility extend twenty-five miles east and west, fifteen to twenty miles north and south.

The central lakes of Harney basin stretch thirty miles from east to west. To red man, trapper, trader, soldier, immigrant and settler they have ever been intriguing — a barrier or an aid. The late Dr. Robert Carlton Clark of the University of Oregon, in "Harney Basin Exploration, 1826-60," penned a clarifying and accurate summary of the area:

The most westerly of these, Harney Lake, from which the basin takes its name, receives the overflow water from its connecting lakes. At some time in the past wind and waves built up a sand ridge, 10 feet or more in height, between Harney Lake and Mud Lake to the east, that cuts off the connection between the two. This ridge was broken by a narrow gap at a period of very high water in 1891. Mud Lake runs eastward for more than four miles to connect by means of a narrow channel, called The Narrows, with Malheur Lake, which runs somewhat north of east for a distance of 18 miles. The size of these lakes measured by the water within them varies with the wetness of the season. For several years immediately preceding, and during, 1931 they were almost dry. The bed of Malheur Lake at its lowest point is only about 15 feet below the average level of the surrounding land, and the bed of Harney Lake is at a level about 10 feet lower than that of Malheur. Thus even at high water levels these lakes are very shallow. Malheur at the high water level covers some 45,000 acres, while Harney Lake has an average area of about 30,000 acres. A characteristic feature of the latter lake, remarked upon by early travelers, is its very alkaline taste that makes the water undrinkable.

The first white men entered the Harney basin from the east early in 1826, as a result of the initial fur hunts on the southern tributaries of the Snake River, by an expedition that went forth from Fort Nez Perce (Walla Walla) in November, 1825. Antoine Sylvaille and five men, sent by Chief Trader Peter Skene Ogden of the Hudson's Bay Company to trap the Malheur and Owyhee rivers, discovered the river Ogden later named for Sylvaille. It is now called Silvies River.

They lost valuable horses to the hordes of Indians encountered. Handicapped, they halted exploration of the river to its outlet, but arrived safely at Fort Vancouver in late summer. The name Malheur, which in free translation means "unhappy," from *mal* (bad, or unfortunate) prefixed to *heur* (hour of time), was first given to the river of that designation presumably by the hapless French trappers when robbed of goods by Indians.

The fur-hunters saw little difference between these red men and those they had faced to the east and south. They called all of them Snakes, even as the term Snake (Shoshone) was applied to the tortuous river emptying into the Columbia. Ogden thought it "incredible the number of Indians in this quarter. We cannot go 10 yards without finding them. No Indian nation so numerous as these in all North America." They wandered afar, in their hunger and desires attaining considerable by theft — to them prowess, not crime.

On October 11, 1826, Ogden and thirty-five other men, after a horseback trip by way of the Columbia, Deschutes, and Crooked rivers and across the Blue Mountains, reached Silvies River. In searching for beaver they discovered the lakes known as Malheur, Mud and Harney. Food was scarce, they having to eat bear and a few of their beaver as two herds of antelope escaped unmarked.

Ogden's party explored and trapped the country around Klamath Lake until June, 1827. Again at the lakes of Harney basin, they caught 150 "prime" beaver in three weeks. By

mid-July they had left the Malheur River to pause at the Snake
River. Another fur-hunt by Ogden in 1827-28 was confined
to tributaries of the latter stream.

On a fifth expedition, however, in 1828-29, Ogden passed
through the Harney basin once more. It was on returning
from the headwaters of the Humboldt River. After following
the Silvies River in June, 1829, he struck out for waters of the
John Day.

The Snake River expedition of 1830-31 was commanded by
John Work, also a chief trader of the Hudson's Bay Company.
From a trek across northern Nevada to the source of Quinn
River, he faced northwestward. He crossed the parched bed
of Tum Tum Lake. Seemingly the guide Payette, with Ogden
three years previously, led Work's party around the southern
skirts of Steens Mountain to reach Harney Lake (then
called Sylvailles Lake) July 2, 1831. The water, high and dis-
tasteful, was ridden by many wild fowl. For the next six weeks
the group trapped and hunted up Silvies River. They could
boast thirty-six beavers, five black-tailed deer, two elk and
half a dozen antelope before they emerged into the John Day
Valley.

In command of the Snake River expedition of 1831-32 also,
Work searched widely. In June of 1832, he sent eight men
under the leadership of C. Plante to proceed up the Malheur
River, to the Silvies' headwaters. There they hunted before
taking the course of the Deschutes and the Columbia en route
to Fort Vancouver. Thus, half a dozen fur-hunting parties
had seen Harney basin by 1832.

Not long afterward the company's London map-maker, A.
Arrowsmith, was publishing the geographical findings of
Ogden and Work. The sketches which Ogden sent across the
Atlantic Ocean enabled Arrowsmith to picture quite lucidly
the Snake and its feeders on his map of 1833. Even Silvies
River, unnamed, was shown flowing into linked "Youxpell
Lakes," with no outlets. "Apparently the first name given to
the modern lakes of Malheur, Mud and Harney on a pub-
lished map," asserts Dr. R. C. Clark. He, also, observes:

So far as shown by any known record the Harney basin was not
again visited by the trappers of the Hudson's Bay Company. There is,

however, every reason to believe that these visits were continued at intervals in the years that followed 1832. The Snake River party was sent out each year until 1850, and must have visited in that time its usual trapping grounds.

Indeed, with the late appearance in print in 1948 of *The Autobiography of a Mountain Man* by Stephen Hall Meek, another venture came to light. This older brother of Joseph L. Meek died in Siskiyou County, California, in January, 1889. He had written of passing west of Great Salt Lake to Bear River and meeting Captain B. L. E. Bonneville. He said:

In the fall of 1834 I went with Bonneville and 22 men and trapped Snake river and all its tributaries to Walla Walla; then up John Day river, over to Lake Harney; then to Malheur, Owyhee and Powder rivers, and wintered on Snake river. In the spring of 1835 I started for the Willamette valley, and when I reached Walla Walla engaged to the Hudson Bay Co., staying until the spring of 1836 at Vancouver. . . .

The next known party of whites to see Harney basin did not appear until 1843, but cattle were acquired by the Hudson's Bay Company's posts east of the Cascade Range. Horses and horned cattle were seen at Fort Walla Walla and at posts in the Snake River valley after 1834. In 1845, immigrants stopping at Fort Hall on their way to Oregon's Willamette Valley traded off some cattle for flour eagerly apportioned by officers. It was McLoughlin's policy to lend cattle to the Methodist mission and the American settlers, to protect the company he represented, and to guard against older settlers taking advantage of newer settlers.

In the years after 1843, large herds of cattle were driven westward with the wagon trains. Orin Oliphant says: "The large movement into Oregon of American cattle in the forties was probably the most significant event of that decade for the future of the cattle industry in the Pacific Northwest."

The Harney country in that period, however, sustained only the few on the trail.

Chapter IV

EMIGRANT TRAILS

Oh, Indian chief
You have speared salmon in the river
Hunted the woodland caribou on stealthy feet
Did you not hear the alarm
Of ox-cart wheels?

—From "Lines,'" by Leah S. Brickett

THE OX-CART came not alone. There appeared, also, the soldier and his gun, later the miner and his mule. Meanwhile, the explorer penetrated Harney County's interior or skirted its surrounding kingdom.

In what was his chief trip as an explorer, in 1843-44 John C. Fremont aimed "to examine the broad region south of the Columbia River, lying between the Rocky Mountains and the Pacific Ocean." Late in 1843, his party of some two dozen men, including the intrepid Thomas Fitzpatrick and Kit Carson, faced southward from The Dalles, where Methodists had set up a mission on the Columbia in 1838. They followed the Deschutes River, sweat and ate mule deer upon the ground that Warm Springs Indians were to accept as a reservation. They saw the place where Bend was to rise, devoured ducks at Klamath Marsh, venturing on to the east and south. They named Summer and Abert lakes in Oregon, and Pyramid Lake in Nevada. Colonel John J. Abert was chief of the topographical corps at Washington, D. C., supposedly to whom honor was done by Fremont.

Pierson Barton Reading kept a journal of an overland trip from Westport on the Missouri River to Monterey, California, in 1843. At the age of twenty-five he had joined a small group of men who attached themselves to a large Oregon-bound company of immigrants as far as Fort Hall, Idaho. Reading, with twelve other men, each having a riding horse and a pack mule, went on to Fort Boise. In charge there they found Captain Francis Payette of the Hudson's Bay Company. It being the first of October, they decided to hasten to California by

13

leaving the Snake River at the fort and risking unmarked paths.

"Captain Payette," Reading wrote, "who has been west of the Mountains for 33 years, informs us he has traveled to some lakes on the course we shall take, but knows nothing of the country beyond." Payette was low on provisions but he shared what he could and warned of grave dangers. Reading remarked, "With the greatest of economy we have sufficient for about 15 days to eat but once a day and a scanty meal." They hoped to gain their destination "in 30 or 35 days," leaving the Snake on October 3 and camping on stone bluffs of Malheur River that night.

Each succeeding day they bore principally southwest, taking any advantage of streams or grass. On the sixth day, after having traveled 127 miles, they passed through "a beautiful valley 10 or 12 miles long and three miles wide, surrounded by mountains." Two small forks flowed into the main stream they followed. In another day's course of twenty-five miles they reached Silvies River, which Reading called Selvaille River. He described it as "10 to 15 yards wide. Sluggish and deep and empties into a lake a few miles from this." Here they lost one of their best rifles to an Indian.

Reading's entry for the next day, October 10, depicts arrival at Malheur and Harney lakes:

Early this morning a large number of Indians made their appearance and began to crowd into camp. Deemed it prudent to leave this place as soon as possible, as the character of this tribe is very bad, they having killed several white men in their attempt to trap this stream. An old Indian prophet, whom we took with us and who, so far, is an advantage to us, will act as our guide. After traveling a few hours, came in sight of two lakes lying about four miles distant from each other, one, the smaller, being fresh water which receives Selvaille River; the other being much larger, I should judge about 20 miles in circumference, is salt water. At the west end of this lake we found a village of Indians which we passed through, and camped about 5 o'clock on a creek passing through a marsh. After we had camped, the Indians began to be troublesome and we were forced to drive them away. Ten miles S., five miles, 5° S. of W.

Captain Payette had marked on their chart some nearby springs. Next day they found the water to be about seventy degrees Fahrenheit and pushed on for cool water. In view was a tree-sprinkled mountain and "a large red butte, . . . near which we pass . . . Near 12 o'clock struck a dry creek with water in holes."

The volcanic country grew more barren as they proceeded. They held their course southwesterly toward a high mountain as they found lowlands dry and sterile. The mountain proved dry, but they saw mountain sheep, the first game spied since seeing "the fowls on Lake Selvaille." The journal's entry for Sunday, October 15:

By daylight saddled our horses and packed mules. After traveling about five hours, came in view of a large lake situated in a low valley several hundred feet lower than our last camp. The appearance of this lake is very singular. The valley, for nearly a mile from the water, is covered with pure white salt, resembling snow. As you approach it, can easily detect the smell of salt, which we found clean and several inches deep. We were in hopes that this lake, when we first saw it, might prove to be fresh water, as we have been 30 hours without having seen one drop of water. The grass on the lake is poisonous. Traveled near the west end of the lake and to our great joy found some springs of excellent cold water where we camped, having traveled 14 miles southwest.

In fighting onward, facing colder weather and steeper, higher mountains, for several days the men partook of little solid food, sharing weak soup twice a day. A killed antelope gave "at least one good meal," and a buck deer fell later. Snow and rain further weakened both animals and men before they traveled on the 20th along a lake described as "about 40 miles long and 10 miles broad. Has its length N.E. S.W." At its southwest end the country became less mountainous. They rested "on a small creek which has its source a short distance from the lake."

Then they fought the ruggedness of northern California, viewing Indians, some of whom were "perfectly naked and wild as deer." They warded off attacks of hostiles. A number of the jaded horses and mules killed by Indians were butchered and eaten by the white group until game again was procured. It was November 7 before Reading and his fellows came within view of the forks of the Feather and Sacramento rivers.

It would be many years before any of these intrepid men could name correctly the features of Harney basin and other sections of the way over which they trod.

In the fall of 1845, 800 immigrants, giving ear to Stephen H. Meek, mountain man and guide, forsook the Oregon Trail at the crossing of the Malheur River. In following Meek's cut-off westward to reach the Willamette Valley more quickly, they defied the parched wastes with 200 wagons, oxen and 2,000 cattle in herd.

The train of 1845 had two rugged leaders, Captains T'Vault and John Hampton. Families included the Riggs, the Packwoods, Tetherow, Bagleys, Herrons, Wilcox, Parker, Warmeirs, Forrests and Statts—ancestors of later settlers east and west of the Cascades. Each day Jesse Harritt wrote of events in his diary.

In August's last week, they went twenty miles up the Malheur, then had to climb out of the canyon and arduously carve a road across the northward hills. On September 6 they came into Harney Valley, described by Harritt as "one of the most sublime places I ever saw. . . . the soil is rich and beautifully set with fine grass, intermingled with patches of sage." Seemingly, the party crossed the Silvies' eastern bank to set up a camp at the edge of Harney Lake. Indians got away with ten of their horses, and whooping cough claimed the life of an infant.

Although Harritt mentioned only the one death on the cut-off venture and wrote that grass was plentiful and watering places no more than twenty-five miles apart, there must have been reasons for grave fears. Meek and the Rev. Elijah White, blamed for leading a "wild goose chase," were sent northward to report the plight of the lost train. Rescue of the wanderers was effected as they gained the headwaters of the Crooked River, soon turned westward to the Deschutes, down which they journeyed to come out shouting on the Oregon Trail at The Dalles.

Only ten days had been spent in the Harney basin, the troubles multiplying after arrival at Harney Lake as searching eyes rested on Iron Mountain, like an inverted top on level sageland. Fears must have lessened as the undulating way swept past Wagontire Mountain and higher reaches. The flat, trackless way, with its interminable miles of dryness — yet the direct way out to the Cascade Range — conquered hope quickly. Haste seemed direly essential. When, reportedly, gravel rich with gold was discovered, enough to fill a blue-painted bucket, no one marked the spot.

Posterity was given the legend of the "Blue Bucket Mine," wealth often searched for but never rediscovered. The train of 1845 left no other permanent evidence in the Harney region save the ruts gouged by its ironbound wagon wheels.

These ruts were found eight years later by the next immigrants to penetrate Harney Valley. At The Dalles in May, 1850, companies of riflemen established Fort Dalles. From this important location the military could operate more easily north or south as well as command the road leading westward. The highest point of emigration over the Oregon Trail was attained in 1852, after passage of the donation land law. Definite numbers are not recorded.

Stout-hearted Elijah Elliott of the upper Willamette Valley had never followed the Meek cut-off, but he thought it a feasible route to the Middle Fork of the Willamette River in the Cascades. After traveling by way of The Dalles, he used persuasion in 1853 on immigrant groups numbering between 1,000 and 2,000. They went with him along the Meek trail of 1845, to lose it after reaching Harney basin's great reservoirs and marshes.

In devious, uncertain thrusts, various parties encountered tragedies in hunger, thirst, sickness and death for themselves and beasts. Yet a successful assemblage was effected on the northwest rim of the basin. The homeseekers struggled on to the headwaters of Crooked River, on to the green banks of the Deschutes at the Big Bend. Up into the mountains of white peaks they went, to stumble onto the glacial beginnings of the Willamette River, and to follow down the western slope.

Many were the tales to be told of the wagon cavalcade of 1853. Captain Tom Clark of Missouri led a train of ninety persons. They included his two brothers, Bob and Charles, and others who later would return to settle in Harney Valley; George C. Smyth with four sons, D. H., John, George A. and Prestley; James Watson, father of E. B., Loren and Finley Watson; and William Cummings, father of Chauncey Cummings.

From the west bank of the Snake River, Captain Clark sent his two brothers ahead. They went on with a pair of pack horses, to try and obtain timely help from settlers in the Willamette Valley. The captain's party reached Harney Valley at Little Rock Creek, now the Buchanan Ranch, went around to the south side of Malheur Lake, and crossed the Blitzen River at the spot to become known as the Sod House Ranch. Hardships blighted them as they continued westward to the Deschutes. They met no relief until they were halfway down the Middle Fork of the Willamette. Bob and Charles Clark, losing their way, had not reached the luring valley until late in the fall.

An enlightening account of a smaller group, the McClure Party, taking the cut-off is Walter H. McIntosh's *Allen and Rachel*. Those subscribing to the by-laws of the McClure Clan over the Oregon Trail, Oaktown Township, Knox County, Indiana, March 1, 1853, named Vincent S. McClure as captain and James F. McClure as lieutenant. The five-wagon train left Oaktown with oxen, horses and cows. They joined a larger train at St. Joseph, Missouri, under government guides, and left there in March, 1853. Captain McClure's group was a unit in the caravan of fifty ox-drawn wagons.

By way of Platte River and Fort Laramie, Wyoming, they arrived at the division of the road near Fort Hall. Some turned off toward California. The McClure party, accepting Joe Meek as guide, took the northern trail to Oregon, by way of Fort Boise. The sixteen men, women and children were joined west of Fort Hall by a single wagon of three young men from Missouri — Joel Kissner, Frank Owen and Christy Norman. In the last week of July all camped overnight with a five-man party going east, two ministers and three college laymen of the United Brethren Church. They held Sabbath services.

The McClure group and the trio of young men made a second crossing of the Snake River, at its confluence with the Malheur. "The moving stock at this date consisted of four wagons, three of McClure and the one wagon of the Missourians, five yoke of oxen, five horses, and a half dozen extra head of beef stock, two of the horses being the property of the guide, Mr. Meek." At the fork of the trail, to save hundreds of miles in travel, they chose to go westward along the Malheur River.

The trail now was a lonely one, the four wagons forming a square at night instead of the large circle. One night, some six Indians whooped with "Skiyi! Skiyi!" while encircling the party. The chief offered to trade ponies for a mother and infant son. He was persuaded to accept other gifts. The party recrossed the Malheur frequently, a woman being hurled into the water in one instance. Then the wagons crunched across level and dry grasslands, with poor water. At one camp cattle, after eating "some green food," died, leaving only two yoke of oxen able to go on pulling two wagons, and a few head of lean stock which had to be driven.

Summer waned with frosty nights, starry asters, golden poppies, and berry patches in the rocky brakes. People were chilled and discouraged, but fully trusted Joe Meek, their guide. He led them to a freely flowing spring of good water surrounded by rich grass. Here, as they camped, Meek pointed to the Three Sisters peaks — "Faith, Hope, and Charity." He told them to keep their eyes on the snow-clad mountains, to follow through the pass south of the Sisters. Then Meek left them, to go north to the Columbia.

"Uncle Vinty," the captain, called a council and it was agreed to send two single men, Andrew McClure and Frank Owens, on horses over the Cascades to notify authorities and to return with sorely needed food. The remainder, ten adults and half-a-dozen children, stayed in camp. They slaughtered the jaded stock, drying the meat for the final lap. They repaired equipment. Original thongs on wagon wheels still held tightly.

In resuming the journey after the first week of September, the people faced an overcast sky and misty rain. In camp that night, Uncle Vinty had to dig out stored paper, and he fired it with the powder-loaded, single-barreled shotgun. Sagebrush yielded the fuel. Next day, low and dripping clouds again were encountered, hiding the peaks. At noon the hopeful looked upon a fresh-cut track, thought to be of another party. By midafternoon they came to similar tracks again, and by nightfal the same thing recurred. Sadly, Captain McClure rec-

ognized their own traces, and, aside to the men, admitted they
were lost.

Without visible landmarks, for two weeks the fraying band
groped its way back and forth. The trail they fell back on was
their own, for it never got off the plain. The warm and moist
weather spoiled the meat, and food ran dangerously low. As
oxen weakened, loads were lightened. Nancy McClure's
feather bed went overboard, other women filling pillows.
Spare clothing, pieces of furniture and utensils were discarded. Brackish water from shallow pools caused mouth scurvy.
Tobacco and tea leaves were chewed to relieve it.

Then they rediscovered the spring from which they had
started. Clear, fresh water revived hopes, and they boiled a
thin stew from scraped bones, eaten with stale hardtack. Wild
elderberries were cooked in a tin coffeepot. They learned,
later, they should have given the oxen their heads, for their
smelling of fresh water and grass would have led them sooner
to the spring.

Two days after the fortnight of suffering, the sun shone
and wistful eyes gazed upon the Three Sisters once more. The
immigrants advanced slowly to the high range. Early in an
afternoon, a strange party weaved toward them. Rescuers, at
last, loosed two sacks of potatoes from pack animals. Everybody
roasted the vegetables in a dug-out hole, served with salt and
a bit of tallow by the two strangers. The pair had been sent
over the mountains from Eugene City to find them. They
had not seen the two scouts but had gauged arrival by old
letters.

After the two horsemen had set out, they soon joined three
other men, but all of these, too, got lost in the murky weather.
They ate a horse, crippled in an accident. By mid-October,
Owens and McClure followed a stream into the Willamette
Valley. They reached Eugene City as the month faded, at
about the same time as the main party arrived.

The linchpins had held to the end.

Harrowing as had been their experiences, the McClure
Clan knew they were more fortunate than others in the trek
of 1853. Long years after, the first settlers of Harney basin
saw only mute testimony of the blazed trail along which many
had perished. At the foot of a hill at the confluence of Spring

and Emigrant creeks, two graves were marked at foot and head with pieces of a wagon box. At the nearby campground, children found and played with rusty ox shoes and wagon tires.

Meanwhile, Harney basin was to wait until 1859, the year in which Oregon became a state, for another penetration by white men. This was to be by a detachment of the United States Army, exploring for possible road-building. Defying them were the marshlands with waving tules and the higher stretches of insatiable thirst.

Chapter V

EXPLORATION BY HARNEY'S TROOPS

In 1845 more than half of Oregon's white population of 2109 were males, and by 1850 nearly two-thirds of the white population of 13,087 were males. Taxes were not easily raised by levy. Males from 16 to 50 years of age had to work on roads in their districts for more than six days each year. Oregon Territory looked to patterns tried in other parts of the country, and its methods of construction, maintenance and supervision gave shape to needed ways of transportation. The county courts played their part. As taxes increased, the minimum days for road work required of able-bodied men lessened.

Early territorial roads, of course, were surveyed and constructed west of the Cascades and along the Columbia River. Ferry and bridge tolls increased as expansion went on, though authorization of a project by the Legislature sometimes got a road no farther than the plan on paper. Charters were granted for building of toll roads, the Barlow Road across the Cascades being outstanding.

Among roads approved were: a route from the Santiam River to Fort Boise, the charter granted to Thomas McKay in 1845; and a road between the Santiam and the Malheur regions, authorization for it being given in 1847 to William Hughes, William Hamilton and associates. Eastern Oregon, however, as a sparsely settled region, had to depend on federal appropriations for military routes.

Since the doors of the interior were pushed only slightly ajar, pioneers of Oregon Territory prayed for more caravans of covered wagons. And, in one swoop in 1854, they created Wasco County, an area of some 130,000 square miles—the full width of their future state and running from the summit of the Cascade Mountains to the crest of the Rockies.

About sixty different tribes and bands — 25,000 Indians — were diffused in the Oregon Country of 1846-1853. The red peoples, to make way for those who would create a productive kingdom, ceded land in exchange for reserves and fitting

22

aid. Most peaceable among Indians of central and eastern Oregon were those of the Wasco, John Day, Tygh, and Deschutes tribes. They went, in 1856, onto the Warm Springs Reservation west of the Deschutes River, forty-five to seventy-five miles south of their Columbia River fisheries.

In accord with the Walla Walla Council of 1855, the Cayuses, Umatillas and Wallawallas were to confine themselves to a reservation on the Umatilla River 120 miles east of The Dalles. The Umatilla Reservation, transected by the hard-worn emigrant road curving down from the Blue Mountains to meet the roaring Columbia, boasted no improvements until 1862. Superintendent Edward R. Geary was to report in 1860 that Indians not embraced in existing treaties numbered more than 12,600 in Washington Territory and more than 3,700 in Oregon. Warm Springs Indians, like whites, had to ward off attacks of Snakes for a decade after 1856.

Emigrants paid high respect to the third Fort Walla Walla in eastern Oregon country. In spite of treaty ratifications and Joel Palmer's fathering of reservations, aggrieved red men remembered how to wage war. At The Dalles, Colonel George Wright in August, 1856, issued orders emanating from Pacific Department Commander John E. Wool to let the Indians hold sway east of the Cascades. Immigrants were barred from settling until revocation of the order in 1858 by General William S. Harney, who in that year came to Fort Vancouver to command the Department of Oregon.

Harney had gained much rich experience in struggles with Indians in Florida, in Illinois and with the Sioux in the Platte country. At fifty-eight years of age, his intrepidity still matched his huge stature. He was forceful if need be, but promises made to red men he believed in keeping. Vision and understanding should establish less fearful conditions in eastern Oregon. First, a better, shorter road should connect Salt Lake City and The Dalles.

Harney ordered Captain Henry D. Wallen to lead a detachment in exploring a possible route up the John Day River, across to the headwaters of the Malheur and down that stream to the Snake. At this time, also, Indian hostilities in northeastern Washington Territory demanded attention. Troops established Harney Depot in Colville Valley in June, 1859.

Captain Wallen set out from The Dalles with his force on June 4, 1859. His nine officers and 184 enlisted men had 155 horses. With supplies for 319 persons for four months, carrying pontoon floats to cross streams, there were also 344 pack mules, 131 oxen to pull thirty wagons, and sixty head of beef cattle. The pontoons came in handy in crossing the Deschutes, as the party went on to Crooked River and up the stream's forks. Here, a division was effected, Lieutenant John S. Bonnycastle leading out a trail-blazing group back toward the Columbia.

With eighty-five dragoons and thirty-eight other men, Wallen soon crossed over the divide from Buck Creek to Silver Lake, calling it Whatumpa. He noted evidence of a fortified shelter. The captain, on July 7, looked upon "a large salt lake." This he named Harney Lake for his superior officer. Unruly horses provoked him to apply the name of Stampede Lake to Mud Lake. Pontoons came into use in turning to the north, enabling the party to cross branches of Silvies River, designated as Stillwater Slough. Odd indeed must have appeared the colossal embankment rising high above them, the narrow tableland running for miles across the valley's floor.

They bent northwestward, to climb the southern slope of the Blue Mountains, pushing before a descent toward Malheur River. The topographical engineer, Lieutenant Joseph Dixon, gazed rapturously on the stream-fed flat valley unfolded between Silvies River and the western skirts of the Blue Mountains — carpeted with "bunch grass, wild pea vines, and red clover, interspersed with fields of camas." Upon it fed "antelope, deer, elk, and several species of grouse, prairie chickens, ducks, geese."

Dixon, however, went on record against building a wagon road over the rocky and steep way from Harney Valley to the Malheur River. He recommended construction of a road from Harney Lake by way of the Owyhee River to shorten distance to Salt Lake City. No route was surveyed, although in this year Oregon mantled itself with statehood. The cloak gave covering mostly to rich black loam and red dirt west of the Cascade peaks.

In the next year, prospectors lured by findings of gold north of Harney basin invaded it in small parties hurrying from the southward. The Oregon Military Department speeded two surveying expeditions. A company of hard-riding dragoons under Captain Andrew J. Smith left Fort Dalles on May 12, 1860, to fashion a road between Lake Harney and the emigrant trail to California, as recommended by Dixon. On the last day of June, Smith's men encountered 150 hostile Indians two dozen miles northeast of Lake Harney. An hour and a half of fierce resistance convinced the captain he would need aid before pushing ahead.

Major Enoch Steen had left Fort Dalles on May 24 with another company of dragoons and twenty infantrymen to carve a wagon road linking Harney Lake with Eugene City. Over a route east of the Deschutes, by way of Crooked River, Steen's party marched 275 miles to Lake Harney. From there, with Dixon as topographical engineer again, they surveyed a direct line westward toward Diamond Peak. Lack of sufficient water despoiled hopes.

They surveyed another line, along Silver Creek to Buck Creek, westward across more of the Crooked River's feeders, marking off eighty-three miles to the Deschutes. Steen called Silver Creek "Indian Creek," quite aptly. On June 29, he received news of Smith's clash, and he resolved to forego his immediate task. He turned back at Lost Spring, twenty-five miles east of the Deschutes, but Dixon was sufficiently impressed to boast of this new route as a practicable one for wagons. The juniper country had good water and grass.

The Fourth of July saw the troops of Smith and Steen united on Silver Creek, about thirty miles north of Harney Lake, with the major in command. They had to forget road-building. From the base here, known as Camp Union, parties scouted and explored until September. Their undertakings in Harney basin were thorough. Silvies River they called Cricket River, the insects swarming over it. To the south, another group applied the name New River to the Donner und Blitzen, and their commanding officer was honored in the naming of Steens Mountain. Lieutenant Dixon, making comprehensive observations, corrected old maps, particularly the source of the Malheur River and the feature of lakes with no outlet. He gave attention, in his report, to the error in published maps of Wilkes and Fremont which traced the flow of

Malheur River into and out of the lake-chain of Malheur and Harney.

Striking is the statement by Dr. R. C. Clark:

Of the names given by Steen and Dixon to the streams, lakes and mountains of Harney basin, Harney Lake and Steens Mountain are the only two that have survived. Neither of these men seemed to know that the stream they called Cricket River already bore a name, Sylvailles, or Sylvies, that for some unknown reason was to survive the one they gave it. These four names, Silvies, Malheur, Harney, Steens, given to natural objects in Harney basin by 1860 seem to be the only ones to survive after that date. Malheur Lake came to be so designated upon the maps of about 1850 as a result of the erroneous belief that Malheur River headed in it. It drew its name from the river.

By 1860 Harney basin had enticed many adventurers in diverse roles, yet no white man was stepping in to claim any part of it for his permanent home. For another decade this region was to stir only with trampings of boots and beating of hoofs belonging to men who placated or fought off the resourceful peoples of tepee or wickiup.

Chapter VI

THE RUSH FOR GOLD

HAND IN HAND with southeastern Oregon's history is that of northern Nevada. By 1860, the Paiutes began to acquire increasing numbers of horses along with some cattle, many in payment for aiding white men. When Sarah Winnemucca was born near Humboldt Lake about 1844, her grandfather, Winnemucca I, was foremost chief of the Paiutes scattered throughout Nevada.

As a young man, he had worn one moccasin when greeting two trappers, first white men encountered. Moccasin, in Indian, was *mucca* and the trappers called him Onennemucca. It pleased the chief, but the name later was corrupted into Winnamuck and Winnemucca. Sagacious Winnemucca I, so called by Fremont, was rewarded kindly by the Pathmarker and ranchers in California for services rendered by him and his people.

After the old chief's death near Pyramid Lake about 1859, Sarah's father assumed the title of Chief Winnemucca. The next year Sarah and one of her sisters attended for a short time the Catholic mission school at San Jose, historic institution in the region of Port San Francisco. Back in Nevada, Sarah learned zealously from sympathetic whites and in turn taught her own people. Her Indian name was Thoc-me-to-ny "Shell-flower."

The Indian name for Chief Winnemucca II was Wo-bits-a-wah-kah, which meant that he was identified by the stick in his nose. This stick, about an inch and a half long, could be inserted through the thin part of the nostrils.

A decade after California had its gold rush of 1849-50, the Great Basin's robust sagebrush gave way to tawdry, bubbling boom centers. The short-lived Pony Express, carrying a letter for five dollars, started service between St. Joseph, Missouri, and San Francisco on April 3, 1860. Riders sped through Salt Lake City and Carson City, Nevada, where the California telegraph line ended. Then they crossed the Sierras, dashed through Fort Churchill, twenty miles from Virginia City, and upon reaching Sacramento transferred the mail to a speedy steamer. About 500,000 settlers were west of the Rockies. The Pony Express faded when, on October 24, 1861, east and west wires of the Pacific Telegraph Company met. Humboldt County soon was created in northern Nevada, with ore-rich Unionville as county seat until 1873.

To the large reservation of Pyramid and Muddy lakes in Nevada went the Paiutes in 1860, although numbers of them visited in Harney basin. Mining prospectors began to push northward through the arid bowl. The red man, with no lust for gold, may have been bewildered, but not the pressing frontiersman. Propelled by unflagging energy, the pioneer bore down on prospects, defying alkali flats or Indians alike. Fort Klamath rose near Klamath Lake.

Warm Springs Indians kept fighting off the Snakes. Chief Paulina had the dubious honor of being the most dreaded leader of half-naked and moccasined raiders. His tribal name, Tea-nam'ad (Buffalo Brush), was one to be whispered with mixed contempt and fear. Prior to 1861, companies of men rode over the Cascades to search for lost traces of gold in the desert. Sometimes they had their horses stolen by Indians and were forced to return afoot.

With discovery of gold in the Nez Perce Mountains in the spring of 1861, William Thompson, newspaperman, and other adventurers from the Willamette Valley joined the rush. In haste, by way of the John Day River, they consolidated with a large party returning from a search in Harney Valley. They went to Walla Walla to follow Nez Perce trails, to Lewiston and to Oro Fino city.

At the head of the west branch of the Malheur River in July, 1861, J. L. Adams, captain of a small party of prospectors, obtained paying dust and nuggets of gold. This was near the divide of the Malheur and Deschutes rivers where the Meek Emigrant Company of 1845 had started the legend of the Blue Bucket Mine.

The tale brought forth by Adams was too "tall," but it led to surprisingly good discoveries by fall. In an isolated gulch, Henry Griffin washed out fine color from a creek. In Griffin's Gulch, shortly, were staked out claims in the first big gold mining camp in eastern Oregon. Claims were drawn from numbered chips in a hat. By the spring of 1862, men laid out a town site on flat land at the junction of Blue Canyon and Freezeout Creek. The Powder River country welcomed the usual array of people who composed a wild and easy-riding boom.

Auburn, the center of this exceedingly rich region, drew hordes from Oro Fino, Walla Walla and elsewhere despite its low supply of water. By August, 1862, organized government and a code checked plundering among several thousand persons in Auburn. Lucier Garnier, a Frenchman, died on the gallows for poisoning his partner, but the saloons and dance halls, among 300 buildings, did an unchecked business. Ministers came to mine and preach, and Missionary Baptists built a log church in 1862, the first in the vicinity.

Baker County — including its present area and future counties of Union, Wallowa and Malheur — was created in 1862, as was Umatilla County. Auburn was the first county seat. A school, with properly conducted parties and balls, added to local pride. A peak of 6,000 population in Auburn was reached in 1863. And in that year Idaho Territory was organized, carved from territories of Dakota, Nebraska and Washington, including parts of old Oregon Territory. Lewiston was the first territorial capital. Within a twelvemonth, diggings in Idaho and other areas lured a surplus of citizens from Auburn. Houses were torn down.

Thwarted desires brought the Bannock Indians into headlong clashes with adversaries. They were further decimated when troops of Colonel Patrick E. Connor staggered them on a cold day in January of 1863. Two hundred Indians failed to survive a battle near the mouth of Battle Creek and Bear River, far above Salt Lake.

Meanwhile, events were shaping a close affinity of Harney basin with the John Day region. The road southward from The Dalles had been merely one on paper maps. In 1862 a rough road from the McKenzie River over the Cascade Mountains to what is now Crook County was initiated by Felix and Marion Scott. They had a large number of work oxen and cattle. Auburn was not the only spot to draw hard-fisted Argonauts. They eddied, also, close to 9000-foot Mount Logan, one of the highest peaks in the Blue Mountains.

On a gurgling stream in canyon walls, on famed Canyon Creek, discovery of gold in 1862 lured some 10,000 miners to narrow confines. Canyon City had its start toward an up-and-down life, figuratively and literally, a half mile south of the original camp at Whisky Flat. As in Auburn, the gold and its seekers vied for glory and pride. The first hotel, the City House, was opened in 1863 by George A. Bierson. The next year a frame building was erected for a hotel to supersede the City House. Its owner was a Frenchman named Fleurette (Fleurot).

Pack and saddle trains weaved over craggy and baked trails to the cauldron of Canyon City, on to the John Day, Burnt, Powder, and Owyhee rivers, into the granite troughs of Idaho. Old emigrant trails graduated into wagon and stage roads with stations pieced from rocks, logs and poles. Jonathan Keeney built a cabin of willow timbers, plastered with mud, at the favored crossing of the Malheur River in 1863-64. Ruby Ranch dared to begin its life, and a Scot-spirited McWilliams opened the Sheep Ranch of 1,100 acres in Jordan Valley in 1863. J. P. Merrill bought it in 1865, and the next year put up $2,000 worth of hay for the government.

Nevada entered the Union as a state in 1864, and in December of that year Idaho's territorial capital was removed from Lewiston to Boise. Shortly, Merrill listened to the ticking of telegraph messages sent through his station on the stage road from Silver City to Winnemucca, Nevada.

Mormon basin, in northern Malheur County, clawed by Chinamen, vied in mining glow with frothy Auburn. Freight by pack-saddle came to Canyon City over a desolate trail stretching northward 225 miles to The Dalles. Pony express gave swifter service in delivery of a letter for a dollar. Unwieldy Wasco County faded into a glorious memory. With President Lincoln's spirit dominating Oregon's Legislature, eastern Oregon had four counties. On October 14, 1864, Union and Grant counties stood forth. Grant County, carved from Wasco and Umatilla counties and having Canyon City as its county seat, contained all of future Harney County.

Although Grant County was named for the general who

brought victory to the Union cause, it had many citizens of Southern strain. At times their Democratic votes prevailed, and their influence is verified in such place names as Rebel Hill and Dixie. In the onrush to Canyon City were men whose tide swept them to fame beyond the jagged cleft echoing with its swishing creek and the hubbub of its miners.

Cincinnatus Hiner Miller—later the more popular Joaquin Miller — disappointed at the reception given his pro-Confederate editorials in a Eugene City newspaper, appeared in 1864. He arrived with his poetic wife, Minnie Theresa Dyer of Port Orford, an infant, a few head of cattle, a license to practice law, and some young apple trees lashed to the side of his horse. In frontier manner, the youthful lawyer built a cabin of four small rooms on the steep hillside above Canyon Creek, his home for the next four years. He set out the apple trees above his house, and nurtured the first orchard in that region.

At first, Miller formed a law partnership with Thomas E. Gray. The beginnings were slow, and Miller, being rather indifferent and too casual at times, kept occasional clients puzzled. Yet in due course the halting lawyer grew into one of keener tongue and perception. In less than a year he decided he could do better financially in single practice. He ran for county judge in 1866, winning on the Democratic ticket, and the judgeship paid him less than $100 a month. In December of that year, a Literary Society was organized, with lawyer T. C. Hyde as secretary. Miller headed the committee drafting its constitution and by-laws. At age twenty-five, Miller lent ear to the literary progress in California. Canyon City residents had slow thirst for higher arts, but they did dress fashionably on proper occasions.

Debates were held, Miller explained the law, and he recited with fervor. There were dramatic moments in the judgeship and at the bar, but Miller's zeal mounted as he delved into poetry of the world's renowned songsters. In his awkward chirography, he, by 1867, was well on the way to a new career so far as setting out on pages of his ledger the poems that were born in his heart and head.

Meanwhile, he partook of adventure in skirmishes with the hostile red men who endangered trail or settlement in this period.

Chapter VII

ROAD-BUILDING AND STRIFE

MILITARY UNITS organized in the state bore the brunt of smothering molestation in central and southeastern Oregon during the Civil War. They and a few regulars ranged over a wide area. An emigrant train of nearly 400 wagons was convoyed along the Oregon Trail westward from Fort Boise in 1863. In April, 1864, an expedition under Lieutenant J. A. Waymire, cooperating with a company of fifty-four volunteer cavalrymen of the Harney region under Cincinnatus Miller, fought stoutly against a force of Utah and Nevada Indians in Harney Valley.

The men, after undergoing hardships in the Steens Mountain region, by October looked forward to a rest near by, but Captain George B. Currey received orders from district headquarters stating fear of a secessionist outbreak on election day. Directed to report to Fort Dalles immediately, Currey marched his troops from the Malheur River's emigrant crossing to The Dalles in nine days. Yet nothing unusual arose to alarm the troops. At the same time, Major William V. Rinehart was in command of Union troops at Eugene City, forestalling untoward political offenses. This officer later was to become prominent in the business life of Canyon City and as agent for the Malheur Indian Reservation.

The volunteer cavalrymen had furnished their own horses, costing $125 to $250 each, and the allowance of forty cents a day for them (by congressional act of 1861) was ordered discontinued on June 20, 1864. This news, quite tardy, disappointed owners of wornout mounts, also discouraged over failure of the War Department to permit enlistment of friendly Indians as scouts. The enlistment period of the first six companies of the volunteer cavalry expired in the fall of 1864, and the men returned to civil pursuits.

A number of military camps established during the Civil War, along with those used as bases of supplies until unruly

32

Indians were checked in 1868, were of relative importance to Grant County's growth. These included:

Old Camp Watson and Camp Lincoln on headwaters of the John Day River.

Camp Logan, east of Canyon City and near Strawberry Butte.

Camp Lyon, near Sheaville, in the Jordan Valley, east of the Owyhee River; shortly renamed Camp Three Forks, partly in Oregon and partly in Idaho.

Camp Bidwell, in the northeastern corner of California, near the Nevada line.

Old Camp Alvord, near Andrews, on the east side of Steens Mountain, and in Alvord Valley.

Old Camp C. F. Smith, on White Horse Creek, north of Quinn River Mountain.

Camp Steele, at the entrance to Rattlesnake Creek Canyon. This was named for General F. Steele, Columbia Department commander in 1866. It became the post known as Fort Harney in 1867.

Camp Currey, about 45 miles west of Fort Harney, located at an all-year spring near the banks of Silver Creek.

Old Camp Warner, near Mt. Warner, east of Warner Lake, and Camp Warner, near Crook's Peak, west of Warner Lake.

Camp Wright, established at the eastern end of the long and narrow upthrust near Malheur Lake by Captain L. L. Williams of Company H, First Oregon Infantry, in August, 1865. Known as Wright's Point, the name honored General Wright who was lost in the sinking of the vessel *Brother Jonathan* before Crescent City, California, in the fall of 1865.

Camp Currey, named for Colonel George B. Currey, former officer in the First Oregon Volunteer Cavalry who became commander of the Columbia District upon the death of General Wright, often has been misspelled "Camp Curry." J. C. Cecil, whose present ranch home is on the site of the old camp, says his family removed foundation stones of about forty cabins, ten by twelve feet, probably built of hewn logs. Three graves were found back of the camp site and an excavation for storage had been dug in a hillside. In answer to a query concerning Camp Currey, Mr. Cecil received the following information from the Adjutant General's Office, War Department, at Washington, in April of 1930:

. . . Camp Curry was a temporary camp on Silver Creek, 40 miles north [sic] of Camp Harney, Oregon. It was established in August,

1865, and was abandoned in May, 1866. No formally declared reservation existed at this point. It was occupied on September 30, 1865, by Companies D and I, 4th California Infantry, Detachment of Company E, 1st Washington Territorial Infantry, and a Detachment of Company K, 1st Oregon Infantry. In November, 1865, the 2nd Battalion, 14th U. S. Infantry, was stationed at this post. Company K, 1st Oregon Infantry, was also at the post. In April, 1865, the 1st Oregon Cavalry was casually at the post.

It was commanded on September 30, 1865, by Captain L. S. Scott, Company D, 4th California Infantry, and on November 30, 1865, 1st Liety. [sic] Frank W. Perry, Brevet Major, Company E, 2nd Battalion, 14th U. S. Infantry, assumed command of the post and remained in command until the post was abandoned in May, 1866.

Of all the camps, after the sixties, only three — Forts Harney, Klamath and Bidwell — were to survive as garrisoned posts. Another, of permanent value, was Fort McDermitt on the northern edge of Nevada, a stronghold on the road to Winnemucca. Upon recommendation of Colonel Charles McDermit, in the late summer of 1865 while he was scouting in northeastern Nevada, several buildings were erected for a permanent post in the vicinity of Quinn River. McDermit (who spelled his name with one "t") soon was slain in warfare against the Paiutes.

Of a fight by First Oregon Infantrymen on a dry day of September, 1865, stories were told colorfully by "Long John" Craven, a native of Missouri who enlisted in Compay H. A portion of the troops under Captain Williams engaged a threshing force of Paiutes between Camp Wright and Harney Lake. Two soldiers, named Smith and Griffin, received wounds, the latter dying from his injury. Each side fought warily until evening Then the red men set fire to the tall grass, forcing Captain Williams and his men to confine themselves in occupation of a greasewood knoll hard by the site of the present house on the Island Ranch.

Meanwhile, Lieutenant Applegate, leading another group of the same command, was returning from Camp Currey. He and his men withstood an attack by the hostiles at the McGee Ranch. The leader of the warring braves was Chief Wahweveh, a brother of embittered Chief Paulina. Later, Wahweveh burned Camp Wright, and in due course he died in the hunting grounds of Steens Mountain.

A lone grave marked at Wright's Point proved to be that of a soldier called "Reddy" by his comrades. A reminiscence reveals: "While standing guard in February, 1866, while in camp on the Blitzen, he received a shot in his arm and another in his heart, . . . Mace McCoy, pack-master of the camp, and the first settler in Diamond, with Jack Mulkey, bore the dead soldier three days on pack mules to bury him at Camp Wright."

A flatboat of timber and lumber, framed and put together entirely with wooden pegs, it is said, was made under the direction of Captain Williams at or near Wright's Point. A crew of ten men sailed it in exploration of Malheur Lake. Indians set fire to the craft in 1866, ending its service hurriedly.

By 1865, Klamath and Modoc tribes, the Woll-pah-pe tribe of Snakes (Shoshone) and the Yahooskin band of Snakes were planning a new way of life on a huge reserve at Klamath Lake. Treaties were amended and ratified in 1866. Still, Oregon had 5,000 Indians wandering outside of defined boundaries. Some restless Paiutes of Nevada visited the lakes of Harney basin, but trouble sprang chiefly from a small band of Snakes. Regular troops, fresh from eastern battlefields, returned to Indian fighting.

Lieutenant Reuben Frank Bernard, a native of Tennessee and a veteran of Indian and Civil wars, was ready to initiate his campaigns in the Oregon country. In May of 1866, he led forty-five men of Company I, First United States Cavalry, out of Camp Watson to "pursue and punish" hostiles. His troops marched 630 miles in twenty-six days, the area including Crooked River, Silver Creek, Harney and Malheur lakes, and the Owyhee region. They routed the red men thrice, killing thirteen of them and taking nine horses, two mules and a sizable mixture of prisoners or guests. Camps were destroyed, as when Sergeant Thomas W. Connor and nineteen men scattered eighty warriors on Rattlesnake Creek, a tributary of the Owyhee River. Superiority in arms and equipment was telling.

Late in the same year, General George Crook assumed command of seasoned forces. Like General Harney, Crook could be determined and daring in his flailing, yet cautious and tactful. His word went far with yielding chiefs, for Crook took the field not merely to trample while severe changes affected the vital ways of peaceable Indians.

The old emigrant route of 1853, passing from near the high desert around the south side of Diamond Peak, was taken as a pattern for the Oregon Central Military Road, organized as a corporation by citizens in Lane County to shorten distance to Fort Boise. In 1864-65 and in 1867, surveying was done, along with some bridge and road construction. B. J. Pengra, chief engineer, and W. H. Odell, later Oregon's surveyor general, searched for the most practical pass.

The Oregon Central wagon route, with land grants, ran from Klamath country, across the sage plains and Steens Mountain to old Camps Alvord and C. F. Smith, then eastward to the Idaho line. Grants were made to the Willamette Valley and Cascade Mountain Wagon Road Company in 1864-66-67, to complete a road from Albany eastward to Idaho within five years. It twisted past Camps Currey and Harney and proved to be 448 miles long. Of this enterprise, James J. Donegan wrote:

By the Act of Congress of July 5th, 1866, there was granted to the State of Oregon to aid in the construction of a military wagon road from Albany, Oregon, to the Eastern boundary of the State three sections of public lands per mile for every mile of such road as the same should be constructed. The act provided for the type of road construction and authorized the State Legislature to dispose of the land as work progressed. By act of the Legislature all rights to the land were transferred by the State to the Willamette Valley and Cascade Mountain Wagon Road Company. . . .

Fulfillment of promises was another matter, and in later years there was a deal of litigation in the courts as to ownership.

By 1866 roads followed over the McKenzie and Santiam passes to present-day Crook County, named for the campaigner. Lieutenant John J. Coppinger rode out of Camp Three Forks on the Owyhee, ordered to view the Harney Valley with the aim of establishing a military post in that area. Properly, he produced a sketch map of the valley at that time, in 1866.

After one of Paulina's Snake assassins had treacherously slain Queapama, chief of Warm Springs and Wascos, some scores were settled. Paulina retaliated with a raid, April 25, 1867, on a John Day ranch. Then he attempted a night foray along The Dalles-Canyon City road. Howard Maupin, with four men, trailed the desperados, surprising them at an ox-feast in Paulina basin. Maupin killed Paulina with a Henry rifle given him by General Crook, and several other beef-stealers fell before deadly fire.

In 1867 the Central Pacific railroad slashed across the big reservation of Pyramid and Muddy lakes in Nevada, pushing east from Sacramento to join tracks of the Union Pacific in Utah. The railroad, in a friendly gesture to the Paiutes, put the name of Winnemucca on the construction depot at Frenchman's Ford, at the Humboldt River.

The Paiutes, however, lost some favorite fishing grounds. Again they roamed, reaching occasionally Malheur and Harney lakes, the Owyhee and southwestern Idaho. They bettered themselves by working for whites, and resented acridly Chinese intrusion. As mining and railroading developed, large numbers of Asiatics provoked a labor problem in the far West.

In eastern Oregon, the bold and supple warrior Egan leaped to a last fling. Born of Cayuse parents, victims of a massacre when he was a boy, he fell into the hands of a Paiute family. He accepted the name of Ehegante or Ezich'que-gah — "Blanket" — growing up to choose as a wife a sister of Shenkah, Paiute chieftain. Egan and a fiery group of Paiutes and Bannocks outrode forty Chinamen nearing the Silver City mines of Idaho. The Chinese, forced to surrender firearms, tried to flee hostile wrath. Only one Chinaman had a horse fast enough to outrace pursuers who dealt death to his fellows.

It was high time, swore the incoming whites, that Fort Boise be bolstered, and that Camp Steele be turned into an awesome fort on the western artery of Harney basin. The flimsy camp gave way to solid Fort Harney, established August 10, 1867. A two-day wagon ride south of Canyon City, timber was piled on the banks of Rattlesnake Creek, logs for sturdy buildings. A. H. Robie of Idaho milled the lumber and shingles in his small sawmill on the left fork of Coffee Pot Creek. J. J. Cozart, that year, hired E. C. Bulkley to plow forty

acres near the post, but powdery soil and killing frosts defeated the first farming effort in Harney basin.

Typical of ventures at that time was one of which Stephen
Meek tells, stressing his own prowess, in his *Autobiography*:

> . . . In the spring of 1867 I took a train of twenty-two wagons loaded
> with quartz machinery from Sacramento to South Boise, Idaho, and
> then went to the ranch of my brother, the well-known Joe Meek, near
> Portland, where I spent the winter. In 1868 I piloted a party of thirty
> men to Malheur river, where rumor had located the famous Blue
> Bucket diggings. This wild-goose chase being over, I engaged as wagon
> master for the government during the Bannock war, and soon became
> scout for Gen. Cook [Crook], finding in a few days the hiding place
> of the Indians, Sugar Loaf and Crater Hole which the troops had
> sought in vain all summer. The war being ended by the battle that
> took place there, I went to Silver City, Idaho, thence by stage to
> Winnemucca, and by rail to Sacramento. . . .

General Crook, in dogged manner and with considerable
tact, ended the forays of hostile groups. Many Indians surrendered on the site of the future Malheur Agency. In June,
1868, a peace treaty allayed much fear. The Bannocks agreed
to confine themselves to the Portneuf and Camas Prairie regions of Idaho. The Portneuf area became Fort Hall Reservation, but the food-yielding prairie of southern Idaho was
excluded from the survey, a stinging factor in the Bannock
uprising ten years hence. Chief Pokatello was a discerning
leader in the 1860's, to be succeeded by the more vengeful
Buffalo Horn.

Attorney C. B. McConnell has brought to light the numerous attempts to placate the red men when war ended. In a
preliminary agreement made at Fort Harney in December,
1868, certain leaders of the Snakes consented to take their
people upon a reservation to be selected for them. They were
not to be penalized or punished for acts done during the war.
Interesting was the article reading: "Complaints may be
made by the Chiefs or Head men of any offense committed by
whites, to the agents in charge of the Tribe or to any other
officer of the United States in the vicinity and in case wrong
has been done or crimes committed redress is guaranteed."

At a council held at Fort Harney in November, 1869, an
attempt was made to persuade the Paiutes or Snake Indians to

consent to go to the Klamath Reservation. This idea got cool reception, strong reluctance being voiced by the old and revered We-ah-we-wah, chief who loved his Harney country most dearly. Other chiefs taking part were Pon-ce, Ow-itz-e (Oits), Oche-ho (Ochoco), Chocktote, Teb-ah-ne, (Tst-ah-ne), and E-e-gan (Egan), who voiced his determination to stay with his people "and be at peace."

The Paiutes looked forward to proper adjustments. They held hereditary rights to large areas, including lakes of Harney basin. Forefathers of Peccoihee ("Water-belly") and Tonnat ("Head game driver"), as did they, gathered roots and bird eggs, and hunted waterfowl. General Crook, it was claimed, placed a military camp near by to control more easily the Indians at their source of food supply. They surrendered to him without relinquishing their claims and believed a hoped-for reservation would include Steens Mountain. For the time being, cohesiveness was lacking in various bands.

One such small group had just lost a notorious desperado, Big Foot, killed while attempting a holdup near Snake River. A veritable giant, he was half white, part Cherokee and part Negro. He had drifted to the Silver City-Boise stageroad region, taking an Indian wife. The small band with which he ran was evidently of Snake River Paiutes. Others closely related, he said, called themselves Fish Indians because they lived by fishing on the Malheur and Snake rivers. They did not readily associate with larger bands of Bannocks and Lake Paiutes.

The Paiute bands were led, principally, by Chiefs Winnemucca, Natchez ("Boy"), a son; Chee-ge-bah ("Leggins"), Ochoco (or Ochoho), Egan, and Oits, or Oytes ("Left-handed"), medicine man. Some Bannocks and Snakes of the Malheur-Snake area, under Eagle-eye, mingled with them. In agreement with soft-speaking but iron-spine Crook, warring bands dispersed, except for seasonal pilgrimages to luscious haunts.

Faithful bronze people followed Winnemucca and Natchez back to Nevada, to Fort McDermitt and vicinity. Some accompanied Egan and Eagle-eye toward Weisers and Bannocks of Idaho. Others moved along with Ochoco, through copice and forests, southward beyond the Klamath country.

Chapter VIII

KING GRASS BECKONS LIVE STOCK

THE YEAR OF 1868, with peace settlements, induced a feeling of security, and made possible home-making pursuits.

Beyond the western edge of Harney basin a new peeled-log school glistened on Mill Creek — the first in central Oregon, of the country reaching from The Dalles south to Klamath Lake. Barney Prine paced off a chunk of land, and staples went on the shelves of his store as Prineville was founded.

Settlers were taking to the bosom of the fertile and timber-dotted Ochoco Valley, no longer the camping grounds of placid Chief Ochoco and his band of Paiutes. Ochoco was backtracking to the burial land of his fathers, in the shadow of soldiers' sheds at Camp Bidwell, a coyote's run over the Nevada line in northern California. Like people at Canyon City and Fort Harney, early settlers of Ochoco Valley got their mail from The Dalles. On horseback, lonesome Mr. Walker carried letters and papers regularly to and from Canyon City and the military postoffice.

North of the Malheur River, William Moffit isolated himself on the first ranch of upper Willow Creek. L. B. Rinehart turned out, to gaze at the Washoe ferry on the Snake, the first band of cattle to range that far south in Baker County.

Idaho assumed its present shape in 1868 when Wyoming became a territory. Mining towns roared ahead or slipped back. The postoffice at Auburn was discontinued and in June, 1868, the county seat was removed to Baker City. With this crushing blow, the town fell apart and its decadence was marked as Chinese cleaned up the last of gleaming dust. Near Eldorado, which bloomed as a lively camp in 1865, Malheur City was to rise in 1870.

Erosion of gold-bearing rocks makes placer gold. Where erosion is greatest, there is little left of the veins for the lode miner to extract. Gold mining in eastern Oregon was carried on mainly in Grant and Baker counties. Three-fourths of the lode gold in Oregon has been produced there, one of the many mines yielding more than a million dollars.

A branch of the United States mint was completed at a cost of $110,000 at The Dalles in 1868. It never, however, turned out any coins. In the Argonaut era of the sixties, when millions of dollars in pouches of buckskin were being carried to the important river town, Congress was prevailed upon to establish a mint closer than San Francisco. Easy profits from the diggings ceased by the time the building was finished. The idle plant, taken over by the Diamond Milling Company in 1889, now stands as a monument to the era of rushes for gold and the heyday of river boats.

Stagecoaches increased as, in brightly painted bodies with flowers and scenes and curlicues, they achieved popluarity in the flush mining days of the 1850s, '60s and '70s. At a cost of "a dollar a pound," a Concord weighed 2400 pounds, manufactured by Abbott, Downing & Co., of Concord, New Hampshire. Sturdily built, it never failed until completely worn out. Pony express riders with light saddles and shoes, in a 24-hour day of relays, conquered 250 miles. The stagecoaches, with six-horse teams, wheeled 100 miles or more a day, in well-spaced changes. The cargo rested in the forward and rear boots, the driver on a high box seat handling multiple reins.

As the coach halted, the driver usually signaled to the station tender with a breezy "Yip-yip!" It described relief and triumph, though the horses might be in a lather.

Better for buckarooing were cold-blooded, calm ponies. Hot-blooded horses became ill-tempered and excitable, not good to cut out, round up and drive cattle. And already drivers of sheep and cattle in eastern Oregon grew in number.

The red man, though born to the soil, though partaking of its bounty, had little inclination to vitalize it into a fully productive kingdom. King grass, sustainer of needful beef, sheep and horses, was the ally of the miner, the military, the stageman and settler who came from beyond the horizon. Procurement of beef for Indians on or off reservations and imports to the Sandwich (Hawaiian) Islands bolstered economic prosperity.

Herds owned by Indians east of the Cascade Mountains

grew fat on lush pasturage. The white men, when they came for gold, saw the local advantages for cattle-raising, and by the early sixties, in the Owyhee country and elsewhere, stockmen took to the far-flung ranges. Cattle now were driven from the valleys of western Oregon to supply bustling communities not only of eastern Oregon but also of British folks north of Puget Sound. Herds came into eastern Oregon from Nevada and California. Cattle drivers from Texas to Idaho Territory ranged from the Snake River into Jordan Valley and beyond. The white sage and tall rye grass fed them well in winter.

Two events transpiring in California in 1864 gave impetus to drives northward. California suffered from a devastating drought, and its Legislature enacted a "herd" or "no fence" law. This law made "owners of trespassing cattle liable for damages whether the lands trespassed on were fenced or un- fenced." Applied at first to a few counties, this ruling grew speedily in scope.

In 1864, also, Oregon's Legislature enacted a law saying:

All cattle . . . and other stock driven into this state for pasture or to a market from other states or territories, or driven through this state to a market in any other state or territory, shall be assessed as personal property is assessed in this state, in any county where tran- sient stock may be found; . . .

Taxes in any one year, however, were collected on such transient stock only in one county in Oregon. This law, it seems, was to meet no alteration in the Oregon Code of 1887 or in the revision of that code published in 1892. Taxes on migratory live stock protected cattlemen and aided in equal- izing competition between resident and nonresident owners of herds.

Routes of drives from California varied, the one used most leading from Red Bluff by way of Goose Lake to Boise basin. After 1865, cattle and allied products increased in movement from Oregon to California, testifying to alteration of eco- nomic conditions. Portland's *Morning Oregonian* in June, 1869, remarked on the necessity of bringing cattle "from be- yond the Cascade Mountains to supply the market of Port- land. . . . cattle are yet abundant in some of the eastern counties and in the Yakima Valley in Washington Territory.

The consumption of cattle, at Portland, is now from two hundred to two hundred and fifty head a month."

By 1870, the red meat of eastern Oregon's range cattle was moving down the Columbia River, heralding a great and lasting movement to a nearby and ready market. Another outlet was provided when a golden spike was driven at Promontory Point, Utah, on May 10, 1869, completing the first transcontinental railroad by the Union Pacific and Central Pacific tracks.

Many settlers were attracted to the rich valleys of Quinn River and Paradise, north of Winnemucca. The town became a busy trading place for ranchers and also for mining businesses and their developments. Southeastern Oregon was at its doorstep.

Dan Wheeler, of near Reno, drove cattle from Oregon to Nevada as early as 1867. He saw chances for sheep-raising and imported the Shropshire and French Merino, highly improving sheep stock. Sheep had come into Nevada as early as 1865. Wheeler, with other Humboldt and Elko sheepmen, was able to boast of 185,486 sheep in Nevada by 1874.

The heyday of the great sheep trails spanned two decades. There were three main periods: 1865 to 1880, when breeding sheep comprised the bulk of the drives; 1880 to 1885, a period of transition to wethers (sterile rams) ; and 1885 to 1901, when wethers became the great majority.

As early as 1862, California sheep (derived from Mexican-Spanish ewes) were driven to mining camps of Idaho, Montana and, doubtless, Oregon, to provide mutton. In 1866 Major G. G. Kimball trailed a large band from Idaho eastward to the Missouri River. In various drives, sheepmen learned that lambs and ewes had to eat grasses of fine quality. Yearling ewes were less particular, and wethers could thrive on coarser growth and mere browsing.

Early drives of sheep into southwestern Montana were chiefly from Oregon, the Jesuit fathers trailing 300 Oregon sheep over the Mullan Road to a mission below Helena, in 1867. In 1869, John F. Bishop and Richard Reynolds bought 1,500 sheep at $2.50 per head near The Dalles and headed for Montana with them. They went by way of the Deschutes River, through the Blue Mountains, to Canyon City, along the Malheur to the Snake, to Boise, over Bannock Pass, to Medicine Lodge and the Beaverhead River. They paid a ferry fee of $50 at the Snake. At other streams they used rafts or felled logs upon which to cross.

With what they could bring through of 10,000 longhorns from Texas in 1869, Jack Renihan, former Confederate Army captain, and his wife Josephine pushed across Nevada, forded the Owyhee, and gained the valley of the Snake. Con Shea and Tom Bugbee did likewise. And still other herds came to the range. J. R. Keith, familiar with the scene, reminisces:

The first of the Texas herds established headquarters on the Snake, afterward moving back to Cow Creek in Oregon. They ranged from the Bruneau to the Owyhee river. They were the Con Shea cattle, the old Ox-yoke brand. . .

Jack Turner of Bruneau was also one of the early cattle owners of Idaho, also Mr. J. E. Hawes of Bruneau. . . . Gradually the herds crossed the Snake and the hills around Boise and the Camas Prairie country became stocked. For many years the Texas strain showed in the Idaho herds. They were high shouldered, low thin hipped, and all one color, only for their tremendous horns they would have passed for Jerseys. They were very wild; even after being crossed for several generations with the beef breeds they retained much elusive cunning and were hard to corral, and as for loading them on a ferry boat it couldn't be done. Whenever it became necessary to cross Snake or Boise rivers they were rounded up at a strategic point and pushed into the stream. . . .

Coincident with appearance of longhorns in Oregon came the first permanent settler of the future Harney County. In 1869, John S. Devine appeared in the White Horse country with cattle that were a nucleus of the huge herds he assembled.

It was in such a virile period, also, that Grant County welcomed the publisher of its first newspaper.

Chapter IX

CANYON CITY AND ITS FIRST NEWSPAPER

PERHAPS NO KEENER PERCEPTION of life in old Grant County and Canyon City is to be gained than in the story of its first news organ. R. H. J. Comer was responsible for this.

Though not quite sure, Comer thought his migration to Canyon City in the fall of 1868 was justified. He considered it entirely justified after finishing the trip from The Dalles, carefully lifting off pack animals a job press and sacks of lead. The lead was news body and ad type. The road was The Dalles Military Highway, over whose rutty and rock-clogged bed it took a freight caravan six weeks to make a round trip.

The route twisted southward sixty more miles to reach Fort Harney. That post was a year old in 1868's frost-time. A battalion of cavalrymen, after swishing rides for General Crook, blinked at peace and pruned themselves as garrison soldiers, treading ones. Rattlesnake Creek was properly named. Any treading done around the post or on the steep road leading upward to the rimrock and high plateau had to be done cautiously.

Each of the four counties of eastern Oregon had huge size and pride as the decade neared its end, each with a newspaper to lean upon. Or, more aptly, the papers leaned upon them. Not until 1874 would another county — Lake — be born of the many-ribbed Wasco.

Doubtless persuasive merchants "sold" Comer on the field when he assembled his box-size printery in a roomy building. All of Grant County was his meat, and it was a large steak. Some folks, down near the Nevada line, had to travel more than 200 miles to reach the county seat of Canyon City. Many of the Argonauts had scurried on to richer fields, but still the town flourished.

Crops were raised, round-about, even though the first planting of grain near Fort Harney had been blasted by ill weather. Blue-clad soldiers, with big yellow chevrons on their sleeves, visited the town quite often. And they had to haul supplies through from The Dalles. Live-stock business buds opened wider.

Woefully short of sorts in his type-case built of dry-goods boxes, Comer issued the first paper in Grant County in October. He named it *The City Journal*. A three-column folio, the page size was 10¾ by 7½ inches. Philosophically inured to handicaps, he admitted he'd be happy as printer-editor if he could gain a good mining claim and some support from readers and businessmen.

The journalist, in practicality, looked up and down hills rearing back from gurgling Canyon Creek. He saw tunnels, tailings, ditches, flumes. He saw homes perched on ridges and, in between or behind each, small outbuildings ventilated by cut-out half-moons, stars and diamonds. The business district, with false fronts on just about every edifice, appeared substantial. Mining was not yet dead thereabouts; neither was its Chinatown. If there was some ribaldry, there also was a deal of subsistence.

Comer cultivated friendships, but he had to ponder on the next issue of his paper. He adjusted himself to a claim on Dixie Creek and worked it for pay. November and election were coming up, but neither Democrats nor Republicans aroused his editorial gunning. Many folks, including Judge Cincinnatus Miller, had sympathized with the South. Some recalled days under General Price and on the fringes of Missouri. Stone or picket fences only separated them from robust, fiery Unionists.

General Grant was elected President of the United States, while the editor elected himself to favor among the local citizenry. As the weather grew colder, he stuck closer to town, gaining some job work and advertising for his next edition. He observed astutely his neighbors, happily reconciled to a tight little world of their own choosing. Credit and honest promises went hand-in-hand. Satisfaction smiled from board walks, dung-ringed hitching posts and churned-up streets.

At last the year gave out. By the light of candles and a kerosene lamp, Comer hunched over his type, to fill in two vacant columns of his four pages. Now and then he sipped from a glass, squinted as the type clicked in the stick. Doubtless he had no companion save the indispensable mouse-chasing cat.

In holiday mood, he printed, edited and published again. He dated his sheet No. 2 of Volume I, January 1, 1869. Thankful for help of several collaborators, then probably under quilts, he thrust the masthead on page two:

Sev. Eral, ... Editors

Below this line, in a faithful editorial, shone the nimble wit and bubbling gratitude of the man who composed in his head and stuck the type by hand:

New Year's Eve! Another pearl, the Persians say, has dropped from the horn of Time into the ocean of Eternity. Another wrinkle on the horn of time, say we; and at the thought of horn we seize the 'our glass and turn it up till we see the sugar in the bottom.

'Tis the hour for reflection — with a spoon in it. Let us contemplate the situation. Two hundred miles from a college, steamboat or a circus. But then we are also remote from the perils of the plague, earthquakes and the Grecian bend. If we have had some marriages we have also had some divorces, so that a bachelor's chances are the same. If we have had some deaths, there has also been a demand for soothing syrup and peppermint, and if there is a coldness between this city and the Dalles, how can we help it at this season of the year!

The horn of plenty is poured upon us, the editor is lovely, and all's well! All the year our jail has been tenantless, and no man has been tried in the high court for crime. There is not a Borbon amongst us and temperance is the rule. There is not a pauper in the county, and our paper is going up to par. Lawyers are retiring in disgust at the prevailing peace, and doctors complain of a state of health. And we know more now than we did before November. Wonderful how fast we learn! We know who will be the next President, and we know better which side of California to bet on now. Again we look at the sugar in the 'our glass, and say, be thankful!

Memory rushes past the old year and turns down the corridors of time. We see plains, sage-brush and alkali. Beyond, a lonely and white-haired man, standing, like a mile-stone, on the road to eternity. Beyond him still, a buxom lass, with a face as red as a web-foot apple, a waterfall, sweet pug nose, and ankle like a — oh krickey! we must quit or give up the ghost. And still beyond, school, birch, mud pies, mumble peg and stolen apples; while far back, dim in the distance, measles, mumps, catmint tea and paragoric are blended in indistinctness, while sitting on our mother's knee, and merry memory to go farther. Again we shake the sugar!

Let us be thankful. Let us be just. Let us not put wiggletails in our milk nor dog's claws in our sausage; let us tell the truth when we can't help it, and not drink dog gnats in our lager, so that when the hand that writes this is still and the eyes that read this are glazed and looking up at the grass roots on yonder hill, we may have our Happy New Year in the Better Land, where all together we will smile on the troubles of to-day, as we do now over those of the days ere gold had an attraction and birch had lost its terrors.

The cock from his lofty roost calls midnight and 1868 is but a date in history. The merchant will write '68 for a time, when in a study; and ye miner will so date his epistles to his Florence Matilda, and she will read and wonder on what day New Year's comes at Canyon.

Welcome New Year. Very tenderly do we greet you, as a new born babe that comes to us an immigrant across the great plains of eternity. Very tenderly do we greet you, and ask that you give us hope in our hearts, love on our lips, sugar in our — coffee, and spondulicks in our stockings! Selah!

The name of Comer did not yet appear in print. At the top of column one, page one, was bait for the curious:

THE CITY JOURNAL
Published Occasionally
By the Typographical Society, for the
Proprietors.
Terms — Cash or any equivalent.

On pages one and three were printed in full an article and clauses under the heading:

MINING LAWS OF JOHN DAY DISTRICT
Adopted by the Miners, at Canyon
City, on Wednesday, Dec. 31, 1862.

Signed by George L. Woodman, Recorder, they defined a creek claim, a bank claim, a tunnel or shaft claim, a surface claim, rights to same, working of them, and other details.

A few news items were squeezed in while two-thirds of page three and all of page four displayed an ad for George B. Fearing & Co., "Wholesale and Retail Dealers in General Merchandise and Commission Merchants, Canyon City and Camp Watson, Grant Co., Ogn." Members of the firm were Fearing, J. J. Cozart and C. N. Thornbury. Cozart sustained the crop failure near Fort Harney.

SARAH WINNEMUCCA

GENERAL WILLIAM
SELBY HARNEY

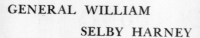

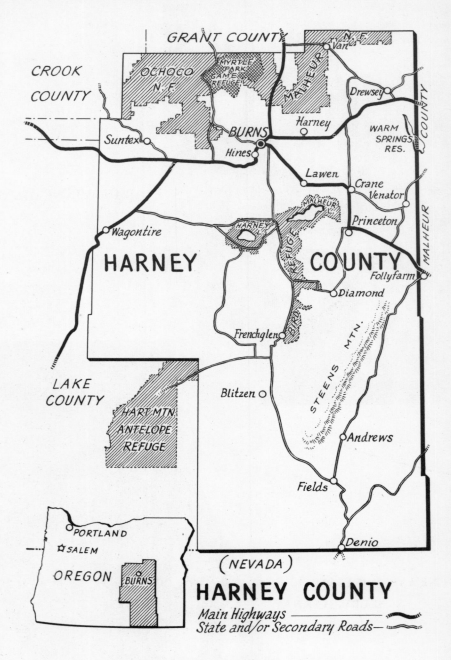

SKETCH MAP OF HARNEY COUNTY

AS OF TODAY ..

FORT HARNEY, 1872

PAIUTE INDIANS
AS OF TODAY

KIGER GORGE IN STEENS MOUNTAIN

Upper Left—PETER FRENCH

Lower Left—JOHN DEVINE
(on left)

Upper Right—
WILLIAM HANLEY

Lower Right—
WILLIAM (BILL) BROWN

MRS. WILLIAM HANLEY

GEORGE McGOWAN

First Postmaster of Burns

JULIAN BYRD

Pioneer Publisher at Burns

PIONEER SCHOOL GROUP PHOTOGRAPHED AT EGAN
IN 1882

Taught by J. W. Nevius, standing center behind back row

GROUP OF EARLY SETTLERS

Back Row, left to right: Tom Vickers, Mart Brenton, John Witzel,
Joaquin (Chino) Berdugo, Prim Ortego, Bill King.

Front Row, left to right: W. D. "Doc" Kiger, Stilly Riddle, Rye Smith
and wife, George Miller.

FIRST PICTURE OF BURNS, 1884

TOM VICKERS' EARLY DAY FREIGHTING OUTFIT

The ad listed almost everything essential: groceries, hardware, implements (Web-Foot walking and gang plows), liquors and saddlery to ladies' goods. It offered "highest prices for Gold Dust, Bullion, Legal Tenders, and all Government and Local Securities." Produce from farmers was "taken in exchange at the highest market prices."

The third issue came off the clanking job disc three and a half months later, April 17, terming itself "A Paper for the Miner, Farmer, Mechanic and Professional Man." All of the fourth page, and some of the third, carried ads, among them the California Brewery (Stahl & Voght), maker of high quality beer.

A few of the news bits pictured optimism:

Mr. Comer, our printer, is prospecting on Dixie Creek. Hope he will strike it rich. "Blue clay and the bed rock pitching." No man is more deserving, and if he don't find it, industry and perseverance are not at fault.

Miners pass through our town almost daily, for Willow Creek and Burnt River.

. . . the placer mines of Canon Creek, which gave life and vitality to this City, are not now what they once were; but the hills and quartz veins that supplied this creek with its millions of gold, are, in a manner, untouched, . . . Of the gold bearing quartz in this county, the ledges are innumerable. Some have been imperfectly developed, most of which are rich. When we say rich we mean to say that they will work from $20 to $300 per ton. . . .

An article told of a Sabbath school, under the superintendency of L. B. Trowbridge, Esq., and entertainment to be given in the Court House by this group. The Rev. W. H. Goddard urged observance of the Sabbath as a day of rest and worship.

Came the fourth printing of the *Journal,* June 28, and at last all could read the benignant "Our Say" by "H. H. J. Comer, Printer," as announced on the masthead: "Local news being of such a nature that everybody, or any other man, knows other person's business, except their own, we shall publish only such as suits our purpose."

Society news? Well, men were men in those red-flannel days, and women were adept at conveying their own news.

Pertinent briefs told of a meeting of the "Methodist persuasion" at the Court House and services at the Catholic

Church. In time, Methodists and Episcopalians had churches, too. If their preachers were busy elsewhere, members climbed flights of steps on a rocky hillside to worship with the Catholics.

By-laws of "The Settlers' Mutual Aid Association of Grant County, Oregon," a farmers' group, were printed, along with names of its members.

A page was given to arguing against acceptance of the monopoly of The Dalles Military Road Company, deploring that "every person who now sets foot on the road is taxed." Protest was made "against giving over 600,000 acres of land for nothing," thus causing farmers to leave the country because of fear they would be plowing the land of the monopoly. The road was said to be some 330 miles long, never finished in decent manner, some of it hardly discernible as a road. It grooved along two miles east of Canyon City, and often was clogged with slides from rains and melting snows. A bridgeless hazard at the South Fork of the John Day claimed lives of resolute persons trying to cross ugly swellings.

A better array of ads passed into Comer's sheet. Summarization of a few identifies Canyon City's pioneer builders:

C. H. Miller, Attorney, etc. Will practice in all the courts except the County Court. Office in old Court House.

W. V. Rinehart. Dealer in groceries, wines, liquors, clothing and general merchandise. . . . San Francisco Store, corner of Main and Washington streets.

Canon City Bath House. Baths, hot, cold and shower. . . . One room especially for ladies. . . . A. Ferguson.

Canon City Meat Market, corner of Canon and Main streets. . . . Fresh meats, . . . delivered to customers, at their houses, free of charge. Philip Metchan.

Blacksmithing. . . . Henry Cole.

California Store, Washington street. . . . Sels & Stemme. Wholesale & Retail dealers in groceries, hardware, clothing, farming and mining implements, wines, liquors, tobacco, cigars and general merchandise.

Wagon Work, Door, Sash and all sorts of Carpentering work done. A good assortment of well-seasoned lumber on hand. Overholt & Pellett.

International Hotel, on the European Plan, opposite the Post Office. . . . George Besen.

Livery Stable . . . to let horses and buggies, and saddle horses; also to feed and take care of horses carefully. Hay and grain for sale. Wood & Church.

Lawyer Miller, elected to a four-year county judgeship in 1866, now was making strides in poetry that led to the outer world where, as Joaquin Miller, he would be titled Poet of the Sierras. With the fires of turmoil and regrets leaping against upheaval of literary expression, the bard of the mining town neglected marital responsibilities. His first publications were two tiny books of poems. As the mature man later polished off his creations, his output had the distinct value of color and the stamp of his background — a true voice of the frontier.

Saturday was an especially busy day at Ferguson's Bath House. Tubs elsewhere were few. The establishment also became haircutting headquarters. A tonsorial artist was Ferguson, for many years attentive to "ladies' hair dressing and all kinds of false hair work done in the latest styles."

A strong man in stature and in civic affairs was Phil Metschan. At fourteen years of age, he had left his native Germany, bidding farewell to a family of high culture virtually rendered penniless because of involvement in the Revolution of 1848. Strapping Phil sold a flood-ruined bakery in Portland to seek fortune in Canyon City in 1863.

After seasons of meat-selling, he engaged in the mercantile business. A sturdy Republican, he was elected treasurer, judge and clerk of Grant County, becoming state treasurer at Salem in 1890. Eight years later he went to Portland with his family of nine.

William V. Rinehart, upon his discharge from the Union Army as a major, had opened a general store at Jefferson, Oregon. After getting the San Francisco Store under way in Canyon City, he took in David G. Overholt as a partner. The firm later became Rinehart, Overholt and John Muldrick. The Rinehart family lived on Rebel Hill for a number of years. The Union veteran and Judge Miller, familiarly known as "Nat," got together often, agreeably saturated in classical and contemporary literature.

Francis Clemens Sels, of the California Store, was in the party which discovered gold at Canyon Creek in 1862. In time, he operated the City Brewery. Affectionately called "Uncle" by all townsmen, his photo reveals the dressing-up of the day. He posed in evening clothes with heavy lapels, square cut, crinkly trim, U-shaped vest, tri-cornered tie with big middle knot, ends tucked under starched white shirt collar. Sels had bushy hair around his ears, shady eyebrows, crow's feet radiating from twinkling eyes, close-cropped mustache and circular goatee.

Overholt was a solid man and a solid merchant, his family increasing the magnetism of the marketing center. Mary E. Overholt, a daughter, was to marry D. I. Asbury after he, as editor, steered the *Grant County News* from 1886 to 1898.

Other venturesome residents of early Canyon City included W. S. Southworth, sawmill- and lumber- man, and G. I. Hazeltine, photographer.

Printer Comer shared the times that were lacerating as well as soothing. In the fifth issue of his *Journal,* two weeks after publication of the fourth, he stuck this poignant item:

Poor Lo has been in this neighborhood again, and driven off eleven head of horses. They took them to Elk Creek and pawned them for $35. The Indian Agent at Umatilla had better keep his Siwashes at home, or some of them may have to take a Galena pill administered by Henry Repeater.

Further delving reveals that the red man was not the only thief against whom a repeating rifle must be kept ready to discharge a dose of lead. Some rustlers of paler color also came a-sneaking.

Comer's fifth and succeeding issues in 1869 continued to record genetic steps, as in comparison of a news item and an ad:

Mr. John R. Roy, long the popular P. M. of this city, has been superceded by Major W. V. Rinehart, and the Post Office removed to the San Francisco store.

The Dalles Express and Stage. John R. Roy, Agent.

Three more lawyers were inserting ads: W. B. Laswell, B. Whitten and G. Reynolds. F. C. Horsley, M. D., announced an office at his drug store and private hospital.

Comer, with eyes roaming beyond Chinatown on the rugged end of the "city" as well as over neatly trimmed lawns, told that "the country generally is as dry as an ash heap."

Some grocery items, jobbing rates for cash, were listed: Coffee, Java, per pound, thirty-four cents; tea, Japan, in paper, seventy-five cents at $1.00; nails, per keg, $11.00; eggs, per dozen, fifty cents; flour, Pioneer, per 100 pounds, $4.50 to $5.00; flour, Standard, per 100 pounds, $8.00 to $8.50; kerosene, $1.12 to $1.25.

The recorded life of Canyon City in 1869 proved exceedingly valuable, for in 1870 came a consuming conflagration. Property destruction amounted to $250,000, and 150 persons were left homeless. Eight years later the county seat claimed a population of 800 persons.

In the early seventies the paper's name was altered. It became the Canyon City *Express,* then the *Grant County Express.* The frontier journalists tried hard to keep the voice of the frontier from falling too low.

Among those who improved traveling between Canyon City and Harney basin was C. M. Lockwood. In the decade of 1863-1873 he overcame numerous obstacles in building the road that was the forerunner of a highway for increasing commerce.

Chapter X

HARNEY BASIN YIELDS TO SETTLEMENT

ON WHITE HORSE CREEK, with its source close to the Nevada-Oregon boundary, lay the abandoned military camp C. F. Smith. The location was ideal for an expanding stockman. Information about it reached John S. Devine of Marysville, California, a native of Virginia, thirty years old and of rugged stature and visage. Experienced in stock-raising, he saw the far-reaching possibilities. W. B. Todhunter of Sacramento, handling a large-scale butchering business, was equally visionary. The partnership of Devine & Todhunter was spurred into action.

With 2,500 or 3,000 head of cattle, half a dozen vaqueros, a cook and a supply wagon, Devine took over the sprawling camp in the late summer of 1869. He made it his permanent headquarters His boss cowman was Juan Redon, serving loyally for twenty-five years and sharing the early days with Horace Layton. Other helpers, as with many under cattle barons to come, were of Spanish-Mexican origin.

Devine dressed like a Spanish don, with wide-brimmed black hat, tight trousers, and a bolero jacket. He rode a white horse, fitted with silver-mounted trappings. He was the first of the aristocratic cattlemen who brought a type of range fancifulness that was limited on the north by the Blue Mountains and the Columbia River. Spanish names imbedded themselves in the occupation.

Usually, the vaqueros wore rosideros, aprons of buckskin fitting closely like pants when tied around the leg with buckskin thongs. Vying in splendor were bright-colored shirts and kerchiefs, and the silver-mounted hackamores, bridles, riatas and mecartes. In or out of a single-cinch saddle, the carefree men prided themselves in expert handling of finely trained horses and in being exponents of hospitality. Races were held at the Oregon State Fair in Salem in 1870, and in that year Oregon Thoroughbreds got a start in splendid grassland at Fossil.

54

Between the grasslands of White Horse, Willow and Trout creeks and the eastern escarpment of Steens Mountain lay Alvord desert, ten miles long and ten miles wide. Once a lake bed, it had become a flat, smooth and baked stretch. The crusted alkali supported no living thing. To the west grew June and bunch grasses, and juniper trees.

Most of the plateaus have a rainfall of less than ten inches a year. Only at Steens Mountain is there more than twenty inches yearly. There is a deal of surface water, but some streams are in deep canyons. Mahogany grew in Steens and Blue mountains, a few fir trees in Fir canyon of Steens, quaking aspens in the hills, alders and willows along creeks. Plentiful in the Steens region were badgers, beaver, skunks, foxes, and large muletail deer. Antelope ran on benchlands while long-eared rabbits carved a patchwork of trails through sagebrush.

Besides more than 200 different species of birds frequenting the area of Malheur Lake, the country had wildlife in abundance. It included sage hens, black and bald eagles, cat and buckaroo owls, hawks, magpies, rattlesnakes, and the raven, a scavenger which picked eyes out of sheep. Kangaroo rats, some as small as a tiny mouse, others as large as a chipmunk or pine squirrel, packed grass seed into cheek pouches. The sage thrasher sang with silver tongue, and the small Brewer's sparrow expressed nervous concern over its nest in the gray-green shrubs.

Free range was enthroned. In the frontier history of America, fields not enclosed became common pasture land. As late as 1890 the United States Supreme Court declared that from a custom of 100 years had grown an "implied license" that the country's public lands should "be free to the people who seek to use them where they are left open and unenclosed, and no act of government forbids this use." Restraining laws, however, grew apace with settlement.

Devine came to build a kingdom for his live stock. Home-seeking settlers did not come to Harney basin until 1871. Years before their arrival, Abner Robbins traded among the Indians. From Fort Harney's beginning, many civilians became employed there. Among the first were A. T. Clark, a sutler, and Adam Adrien, an enlisted man and butcher for the camp. Widely known in the sixties and seventies was Frank McBean of Canyon City, sharp-tongued stage driver, miner and land promoter.

At Fort Harney, April 10, 1868, soldiers and hired civilians beamed congratulations upon Martin A. Lucas, who was stationed there. On that day his wife gave birth to a daughter, Jennie, the first white child born in what is now Harney County. Jennie grew up to become the wife of Walter Fields of Canyon City.

Oregon had its first governor from eastern Oregon. He was George L. Wood, a lawyer and Republican of Wasco County, serving as the state's chief executive from 1866 to 1870.

William Clark, a merchant of Canyon City, went to the Oregon Legislature in 1868. As a member, he obtained an appropriation for the opening of a wagon road from the John Day Valley to the new railroad at Winnemucca, Nevada. The route, after passing Warm Springs, led over the Blue Mountains and Summit and Crane prairies to Otis Valley. It followed down Otis Creek to a ford on the Malheur's middle fork, near the present town of Drewsey, south to cross the Malheur River, mounting a spur of Steens Mountain to gain Barren Valley. Along the base of the mountain, it wound past Juniper and Mann lakes to Alvord where it turned south, reaching the Nevada line by way of Sand Gap and White Horse.

The road, of poor construction, was not well traveled. In its long distance it had virtually no proper station. It did, however, draw enough attention to the country to aid settlement.

The Willamette Valley and Cascade Mountain Wagon Road still was a poor sort of highway. Nortwithstanding, says James J. Donegan,

The entire course of the road . . . was certified to have been completed in the manner required by the act, by four certificates of the Governor of Oregon, the first bearing the date of April 11th, 1868, and the last of June 24th, 1871. . . . In 1871 the Wagon Road Company sold its interest in the land to H. K. W. Clark, and on September 1, 1871, Clark conveyed the road land to David Cahn in trust for the grantor and T. Egerton Hogg and Alexander Weill. . . . On June 18th, 1874, Congress passed an act recognizing the transfer to the

Wagon Road Company and authorized the issuance of patents to the land. . . .

Major E. S. Otis, for whom Otis Creek was named, was in command at Fort Harney in 1870 when Mace McCoy came there from Walla Walla. McCoy intended to take a preemption or homestead claim on what is called McCoy Creek, but he dropped this idea. He, with several others, took advantage of the Act of March 12, 1860, whereby they could buy swamp land cheaply from the State of Oregon. They purchased a few claims in the lower or western portion of Diamond Valley, northwest of Steens Mountain.

A. H. Robie, the sawmiller, brought a herd of cattle from Idaho the next year. Their diamond-shaped brand became responsible for naming of Diamond Valley. In its southeastern portion, free from tule and flag, Robie erected a house at the base of a bluff. He soon acquired the lands of the group headed by McCoy.

Claims on Alvord Creek, near old Camp Alvord, were taken up in 1871 by James Abbott and H. Whiteside. At about the same time Philip Mann settled on land in the vicinity of Mann Lake.

While expanding their holdings, Devine and Todhunter had secured help from the government in having some surveying done. They bought huge tracts of swamp land from the State of Oregon at $1.25 an acre. Only ten per cent was paid to gain possession. Still, unclaimed land unfurled on all sides.

An English drover, John Catlow, lured by mining riches of Idaho, and by 1872 having prospered in the Silver City district, desired to return to his old business. He turned westward to the unplowed fields along Trout Creek, south of Abbott and Whiteside. There he located as a homesteader, shortly to secure title to an additional section of natural meadow adjoining his claim.

Though all those locations were enticing, the best of the country lay north and west of Steens Mountain, from the upper waters of the Blitzen to the marshes of Malheur Lake. In addition to others, "Hen" Owen was busily peddling Oregon swamp lands for small down payments. The opportunity of establishing a cattle baronage on the Blitzen stood forth and Peter French, in his early twenties, seized it.

French was born near Red Bluff, California, on the ranch of his father, a native Virginian. Also from Virginia was a good friend, Dr. Hugh J. Glenn, who had gained large holdings in the Sacramento Valley and operated what was said to be the largest wheat ranch in the United States. Peter, at maturity, weighed only 135 pounds, with a height of five feet five inches, but his muscles were firm. Unlimited energy and determination flashed from gray eyes set in a large and well-shaped head.

Dr. Glenn quickly took cognizance of the youth who, after years of untiring interest in horses and cattle, displayed zeal and ambition to carve his own realm. Together, they met the challenge. In the spring of 1872, Peter set off northward from Surprise Valley with about 1,200 head of young cattle, some twenty horses, cook and supply wagons, and half a dozen vaqueros and ranch hands.

Summer's sun had eaten deeply into the snow atop Steens Mountain when his journey ended. He established the headquarters of what was to become famous as the "P" ranch on the upper Blitzen River, in the heart of Harney County. It was twenty miles from the stream's source. Sixteen miles above, on Steen's summit, lay Fish Lake, sky-blue water edged by quaking aspens. At first, French brought in supplies by way of Surprise Valley. Soon he was reclaiming marshy land and adding it to the dry ranges as his herds multiplied.

Into the Harney basin in 1872 and 1873 came a number of its earliest settlers with horses and cattle. The Jezreel Venator family moved up from Goose Lake, located between branches of the Silvies on "The Island," near Wright's Point. Thomas Prather chose a place on the creek still bearing his name. James Sheppard appeared with a few cattle.

The sizable George A. Smyth family from the Willamette Valley picked a spot at Warm Springs, destined to become the site of a mammoth sawmill. Smyth and his wife were accompanied by three unmarried sons, George A., D. H. and Presley, and by son John and his wife. Stilly Riddle, a son-in-law, camped with them, while another son-in-law, John S.

Miller, took up a claim a mile northwest, at a spring continuing to carry his name.

Joe Cooksey, who married a daughter of Venators', settled close to Wright's Point, on the west branch of the Silvies.

John Chapman and James Weaver arrived, taking up claims at "the Sod House," near the mouth of the Blitzen, and at Weaver Spring, a few miles west of Wright's Point. Andy and Hank Chapman selected a place on the Island, since called Chapman Slough. John Bohn had camped on Poison Creek, and Marion Scott in Catlow Valley, a puzzling place name, for John Catlow remained at Trout Creek.

The Krumbo family gave its name to the creek south of McCoy Creek. Mace McCoy, after selling out to Robie, returned to Walla Walla in 1873. After his departure, came George McKay, of Indian blood and whose name was confused with McCoy. The Cummings, with some sheep, found sustaining pasture. P. M. Curry, aided by William, turned horses and cattle out on the Silvies not far from the future city of Burns.

It was Frank McLeod, however, who was first to reside on the present site of Harney's county seat. He came from California with 250 head of cattle, turning them loose in the summer of 1873 on the west side of Silvies River. On the point of the hill just within the limits of today's Burns, he built a home which he occupied with his family for a few years.

At this time, also, Maurice Fitzgerald, scout in the Modoc War, appeared with the soldiery at Fort Harney. As a sergeant major he served in rigorous duties. In due course, he became a leading participant in the growth of Grant and Harney counties.

On September 19, 1873, John Smyth and his wife welcomed an infant daughter into their frontier abode, and named her Margaret Louise. It was a notable event, for "Maggie," as she became intimately known through long years, was the first white child born of settlers in Harney County range land not associated with the military. The weather was so pleasant until Thanksgiving Day that, at the hot spring, the mother often rocked baby and crude cradle out of doors.

Then snow fell continuously for three days, covering the native grass and sagebrush to a depth of three feet. The

Smyths and Riddles had reason to be afraid of losing their small bunch of live stock. Young Riddle, upon Robie's advice, rode his horse southward to select a safer location. He found virtually no snow at the lakes and only a little of it in a valley of good range between Diamond Ranch and the hem of Steens Mountain. Upon his return in a few days, the families moved out with all they had.

In Happy Valley they started life anew. Two creeks — Riddle and Smyth — still designate the places of their permanent settlement. The country yielded much in sustenance.

All the earliest home-builders in the Harney region had other reasons than the nation-sweeping panic to remember the year of 1873. The smaller possession was precious. Neighbors, widely separated, proved of high value in mutual assistance. A long trip to market or minister or doctor or midwife demanded unusual exertion and caution.

Now the challenge was accepted more readily by others.

Impressive became the memories of Alphena Venator who was about seven years old when his parents, Jezreel and Eliza, located near Wright's Point. Jezreel, who served in the Mexican War and was at the capture of Chapultepec in 1847, married Eliza Miller at Fort Dearborn. They crossed the plains to Harrisburg, Oregon, in 1851-52 and to them eight children were born. Of the early settlement in the Harney basin, Alphena recalls:

Joe Cooksey came to Harney Valley as a neighbor on the west branch of Silvies River in 1872. He married my sister Mary. Rye and John Smyths actually came to the warm springs in 1871, settling in Happy Valley in 1872. We Venators at first had 300 head of cattle; Cooksey, 200; Smyths, 300 to 400 head, brought from Rogue River. The sand reef at the Narrows then was 15 to 20 feet high. There were sod buildings at Alvord in early '70s where John Weaver stayed a year after settlement, building the Sod House where the Game Refuge headquarters now is.

Joe Cooksey sold out to Todhunter and Devine in 1877. In the fall of 1877 my parents sold out to Todhunter and Devine, taking their note for almost the entire amount that was due. We moved back to our holdings south of now what is Lakeview and bought the Moon ranch and some other holdings and added to what we had. . . . I well remember when Jake Ish and Henry Owens were filing claims on the Island Ranch and adjacent country. Later on when the settlers were contesting the swamp lands in their proof Ish and H. Owens had sworn they rode from Camp Harney to the Venator Ranch in a boat. They did, but it was on a wagon. In 1884 I located on Deadman Creek on the south fork of the Malheur River, buying out Ed Kiger. I engaged in the cattle business which I have followed most of my life. Later on I acquired large holdings north of Malheur Lake and was joined by my brother Ira. . . .

John Catlow was tall and of broad frame, a big and rough Scotchman. . . . He ran about 4000 head of cattle in the early days. Catlow supported Dave and Bill Shirk who used the dollar mark for their brand. Shirks outstripped Catlow, then on the west side of Steens Mountain and named Catlow Valley (where Catlow did not live but had run his cattle there). Dave and Bill married sisters (from the Crow family) and later split up, the property being divided, and French-Glenn ranch later acquired the cattle and property of Shirks, before Bill Hanley took hold.

Anderson Valley was named for Doc Anderson, who took up a homestead and desert claim (about 800 acres in all). Anderson's title later was contested by John Mahan. Doc waylaid Mahan and beat him up badly with an old needle gun. Later, after much litigation, Jim Mahan, brother of John, acquired most of Anderson's property, losing a full section, and P. & S. Co. bought the remaining 160 acres from Doc. Doc, earlier, had bought 200 head of spaded heifers, but ran them for several years anyway, making up for the loss by building up the herd otherwise. Doc lived there and died some time after his losses. He retained his home place — always was a bachelor.

Much dispute has been waged over the origin of the "P" brand first used on Pete French's cattle. Mart Brenton, pioneer and buckaroo for French, says the "P" was used in a branding iron by a pack man or old trapper and was picked up by French when he came in and bought a few head of cattle from him. He continued to use the P brand, it later giving way to the FG brand under Lusk's administratorship.

Perhaps the oldest water right recorded in the Harney region was taken on July 11, 1874. Berry Nichols claimed the water of Nichols Creek situated at the northwest end of Juniper Lake.

Chapter XI

ASSURANCE — ORGANIZATION OF
SCHOOL DISTRICT

THE SMALL STOCKMEN, even as the larger ones like Devine and French, enjoyed advantages of the virgin country. They chose the valleys rich in hay and water. For cattle, the locations were disease-free, and large calf-drops with fine chance of survival increased herds rapidly.

For the hundreds of Indians who still roamed in the region, an immense area called the Great Paiute Reservation had been sanctioned in the fall of 1872. It extended eastward from the Silvies River to feeders of the north fork of the Malheur.

Soldiers had improved their road between Fort Harney and Camp Currey, built along the foothills to escape marshland.

Space outside the Paiute Reservation's boundaries was claimed by a goodly number of newcomers in 1874. Thomas Whiting, that winter, kept his stock near McLeod's place. The next year he moved two miles north, on the Silvies. His family's first shelter was a cabin of aspen poles and dried mud. Soon Whiting floated logs down-river from Emigrant Creek for a better home. Peter and John Bohn became close neighbors.

W. D. (Doc) Kiger arrived in Diamond Valley in the spring of 1874, giving his name to another creek, and he settled there with three brothers. Walter Riddle came then, as did R. E. Reed, Thomas Howard, G. W. (Doc) Anderson and Jimmy Gentry. The last named came from Linkville (Klamath Falls) to Fort Harney, staying there as an employe for several years before moving to Barren Valley.

Anderson carried a few trips the post's mail, which included that of settlers. Then he selected a claim in a little nook of Steens Mountain, Anderson Valley, building a one-room, frame shack beside a clear spring. Past it wound the high road from Fort Harney, fifty miles north, to Fort McDermitt, Nevada. It was twenty-five miles over the rugged mountain to Juniper Ranch on the south, and other houses were many miles distant.

62

More than a few weary travelers sought a night's lodging and care, Maurice Fitzgerald later wrote, and they "would have to partake of such fare as Doc furnished. This had to be cooked in the one pot he possessed and was anything but appetizing. Turnip tops was often the sole occupant of the pot and that, with a chunk of his frying pan bread, constituted the menu." A native of Kentucky, lanky in frame and story-telling. Doc, however, became recognized as a genial and generous host.

At the Sod House at this time was Peter Stenger with cattle driven from Douglas County. In 1875 he and his family start-ed a long residence on Poison Creek. A year or so later, Peter welcomed his brothers John and Ed, who engaged in raising of stock.

"Land-pacing" grew faster in Harney basin and on its fringes by 1875. Amos W. Riley, a storekeeper of Santa Rosa, California, paired up in the cattle-raising industry with James A. Hardin, who had interests in California and Nevada. They established the Double-O (OO) Ranch west of Harney Lake, with Tennessee Murphy in charge. When Murphy became foreman for Devine and Todhunter, Isaac (Ike) Foster car-ried on the business. Ike set up headquarters at Warm Springs Ranch, near the northwest corner of Harney Lake.

At abandoned Camp Currey, with Buck Mountain in the background, Logue Cecil picked a likely spot for his cattle and a home. A spring gushed out of a hill in all seasons, and fertile soil extended along Silver Creek. Within two years, Logue was to be joined by his brother Carl.

Dan Wheeler, a bachelor, located beside another spring on Sage Hen Creek. As the only justice of the peace in Harney basin for many years, he adjusted not a few ticklish problems. Tom Potter set up quarters at the foot of Wright's Point ridge, edged by a tule marsh. From the vicinity of Spokane came J. W. Scott to take contracts for delivering cordwood and hay for the garrison of Fort Harney. His stay lasted until the post's abandonment.

In the early or mid-seventies a few others settled tempo-rarily or permanently. Among them were Nick Oliver, near the future town of Egan, and a Simmons family in Prather Creek Canyon. William Barton and his family located first at what is called Barton Lake. Later, fearing overflows, they moved a few miles up the valley to build a house on the east side of Riddle Creek.

A. W. Howser set up a home near Silvies River and Poison Creek. Charles Rann transferred his cattle from John Day Valley to Silvies Valley. Crane Creek acquired its first settler as Frank Burns started building up fine herds of cattle along its banks.

Robert J. Baker took up a homestead on Silver Creek, four miles southeast of old Camp Currey, in May, 1876. To some sheep he added cattle, and procured more land. His wife died at Fort Harney in the winter after the Bannock War of 1878, leaving four children, the oldest twelve years of age. Unable to attend to his ranch during hostilities, the father was with volunteers at the Battle of Silver Creek.

Robert Baker's two brothers, Nick and Douglas, also took homesteads in 1876. The three brothers remained to spend the rest of their lives in Harney County.

It was in 1876 that John Devine appeared in Canyon City for the first time, to answer a somewhat tardy summons. Late in 1874 a tramp had secured work at the White Horse Ranch where few seekers of employment were turned down. He did chores for a month, during which time a stray horse with an unfamiliar brand was put in a corral. It was the custom that such animals become the property of the rancher if no owner appeared in lenient season.

The odd-chores man, wishing to resume travel, received his just wages. He had kept his eye on the stray horse and, at a propitious moment, caught it and rode away at a fast clip. Of the events which followed, Maurice Fitzgerald related:

When Devine learned what the fellow had done he swore he couldn't get away with anything like that. So, mounting his horse he started out on the trail of the horse thief. He caught up with him at the ranch of John Catlow on Trout Creek, thirty miles from White Horse. He commanded the tramp to mount the stolen animal and come back with him to the ranch from which he had taken him. The fellow obeyed reluctantly; but when about half way back he stopped and said he wouldn't go any farther. (He probably thought he might be lynched when he got there.) So, getting off his horse and picking up some large stones he told Devine to go right on home, or he'd knock him off the horse. (He evidently didn't think

Devine was armed.) Devine told him to put down those rocks or he'd plug him. He called Devine a hard name and then he dropped in his tracks.

There was nothing done about that homicide for two years thereafter. Then the authorities at Canyon City began to realize that some judicial steps should be taken to comply with the law in such cases. It was then decided to notify Devine to come to the County Seat to give account of his actions in taking the life of his fellow man. He did so, two years after it happened. It took a good four days to get to Canyon City. I remember meeting him in his buggy a few miles from that town as I was on my way back to Camp Harney. He asked me a few questions regarding the distance to Canyon, as this was his first visit to the County Seat. That was the first time I ever saw John Devine, but we became very good friends in after years.

His explanation satisfied the authorities and nothing further was done regarding the homicide of the unknown horse thief.

At this time a husky youth from southern Oregon, Charley Jones, came to ride as a vaquero under Joe Cooksey on the Island Ranch. Devine recognized ability when he saw it. When, later, Cooksey's position was vacated, Jones accepted promotion to a managership which, under Devine, covered many years.

In 1877, Harney Valley stockmen greeted another newcomer, John Hanley. He had two younger brothers, William and Edward, to arrive later. Their father, onetime Mississippi flatboatman, owned a large ranch near Jacksonville, Oregon, specializing in fine mules. It was cattle, however, in which the boys were immediately interested. John remained in the basin two or three years before returning to Jacksonville.

Though hardships were many, the pioneers frowned on any recession in the education of their children. In the vicinity of future Burns, by the meandering waters of the Silvies, the first school meeting of Silvies River District was held early in 1875. Minutes of this and subsequent meetings down to March 5, 1888, were kept in a well-preserved journal. The first two ruled pages read faithfully:

Minutes of organizing Silvies River District, Grant Co., Oregon.
School meeting met according to notice of February 10th, 1875. Posted according to law in three different places in the proposed District Persuant to order. W. F. McLeod was called to the chair and on motion of P. M. Curry William Jennings was elected secretary. On motion of P. M. Curry the Chairman appointed a com-

mittee of three to select boundaries for the School District. The following gentlemen were appointed by the chairman: P. Bohn, James Sheppard, P. M. Curry. The report of said committee was as follows: Running from Wrights Point N. E. to Camp Harney and including said Camp. Thence to the north Boundary of P. M. Curry Ranch on Silvies River, then South to Sage Hen Spring, then southeast to Wrights Point. By motion of John Bohn the above report was adopted and said lines established for said School District. Next business in order being the election of directors, Ballots stood as follows: W. F. McLeod 7, J. S. Miller 3, P. M. Curry 5, Peter Bohn 4, Thos. Whiting 2, Thos. Prater 1. W. F. McLeod receiving the highest No. of votes was duly [sic] elected for the term of three years. P. M. Curry receiving the next highest No. was elected for the term of one year. The next business in order was the election of School Clerk. Votes as follows: Thomas Whiting 5, William Jennings 2, J. L. Noe 3. Thos Whiting receiving the highest No. of votes was duly elected. The trustees then elected were sworn in to office and the meeting adjourned.

W. F. McLeod,
Chairman

Wm. Jennings Sect.
This 10th day of February, A. D. 1875.

The yearly report of this School District, No. 13, discloses a total of twenty-five legal voters, seventeen male scholars, fourteen female scholars. A term of one quarter was taught by Sarah Latham, who received $100 from subscription. Only in the fall or spring could the students attend, because of scattered homes and weather-fouled roads.

In July, 1875, J. S. Miller succeeded Curry, resigned, as director, and J. L. Noe became clerk. In 1876, Thomas Whiting became director, and Curry and Daniel Wheeler successive clerks. Financial assistance came from the county treasurer that year as more stockmen and families took up the land.

Silvies River School advanced slowly in a residence. A. W. Howser was elected a director in 1877, and Miss S. Howard received $150 in "U. S. coin" for teaching one term in November. Although new settlers came in 1878 into various sections of what is Harney County, District Thirteen had only twenty-seven legal voters and thirty-six students in March of that year. D. B. Rinehart was superintendent of schools for Grant County, succeeded by J. W. Mack.

Optimistic, assured parents envisioned the first schoolhouse for Harney Valley, at the western edge of the Great Paiute Reservation.

Chapter XII

INITIATIVE OF HOME-BUILDERS

MERCHANTMEN FROM BOSTON who sailed around Cape Horn, fur-traders, soldiers, missionaries, schoolteachers, mountain men with the long rifle, pioneers with oxen and horses and wooden plows had all contributed to making Oregon a state by 1859. For a score of years thereafter eastern Oregon went through the initial stages necessary to its building of an inland empire. Nowhere did the pioneer face more grim beginnings than in the Harney country.

By ingenuity and perseverance a pattern was carved for succeeding generations. Wood is scarce in Harney and Steens areas. Willow, mahogany, juniper and quaking aspen were used to build corrals and fences and gates, also cribs, barns and shelters. Willow poles were erected between sets of vertical posts. Juniper trunks, set up in V fashion, became cribs for hay. Steep walls of a rimrock or bluff could furnish one to three sides of a corral. Tall poles with timber across the top made its gateway. Juniper posts well set for fencing outlived the builder. Peter French erected long barriers of rocks on slopes.

The early folks built huts and houses of sod, rocks, poles and hay. They moistened sod with water and laid it bricklike, the hot sun completing the baking process. They had small, deep windows and timbered doors. Juniper poles often served as rafters, and a layer of willows covered with sod made a weather-tight roof. Sometimes vertical planks sufficed for siding. Many sheds were constructed of field rock. Others had vertical poles with interlaced willows for sides, roofs of sod and hay matted together in layers, and a plain doorway between upright poles in one corner. Slim, tall poles usually supported porch or veranda roofs on the houses and, later, on the stores.

Only in sheltered and fertile valleys, or by hillsides where water and pasturage were abundant could ranchers be found trying to fulfill their destiny. Within a few years, some replaced original abodes with houses of logs, of lumber and shingles procured from Robie's mill or from near Canyon City. Maurice Fitzgerald tells how John Catlow of Trout Creek, in 1876, enclosed a whole section of natural meadow:

> . . . He wanted that 640 acres fenced as quickly as possible. So he rode over to the Diamond Ranch to see Mr. Robey about getting lumber from his mill, near Camp Harney, for that purpose. Satisfactory terms were agreed upon.
>
> Robey had an ox-team for hauling logs to his mill, and having a large supply of sawed lumber on hand, he loaded all that his eight span of oxen could haul and started it out for Trout Creek, some 160 miles away on a very poor road.
>
> I remember very distinctly seeing that ox-team plodding along by Camp Harney, two men geeing and hawing as the creaking wagons moved slowly along. One would think that they would never reach their destination, but they did. Two or three trips were sufficient. . . .

Isolated ranch homes were stage stations, the trail was rough and often uprotected, and the fare was none too low. As much as $35.00 a day was earned by a driver who could fill his vehicle to capacity with passengers and luggage.

As on all frontiers, wives were not to be had for the mere seeking — or asking. Femininity came at a high premium. Girls did not seem to have the chance to grow up in the same pace with their sisters of the more populous centers. When a girl of the ranch or mining area reached her early teens she became a prospective bride, with many suitors. More than a few times women who came in by stage for a visit with relatives or friends received offers of marriage in brief time. And, quite often, a proposal was accepted promptly, the first step in a lengthy career of home-building.

Sooner or later, most settlers saw Rinehart's ferry at the crossing of the lower Malheur River or the ferry at the mouth of the Boise River owned by Peter L. Keeney. Captain "Pete," in the 1870's, had a landing and residence near the site of Old Fort Boise. The county seat of Canyon City, however, was the principal magnet.

In the *Grant County Express* of Saturday, October 21, 1876, evolving into the *Grant County Times*, Editor H. R. Gale informed readers of his paper that, because of ill health, he was about to seek "a more congenial climate." The same issue of his four-page weekly revealed glimpses of the trading center:

Fine four-horse coaches and number one teams are now used between here and the Dalles.

Dalles and Canyon City Stage Line, E. Shultz, Proprietor; regular trips, twice a week; leaving The Dalles and Canyon City Mondays and Thursdays, arriving at each place on Wednesdays and Saturdays.

Stage Line to Baker City from Canyon City; leave Canyon City and Baker City every Monday and Thursday; Greer & Kellogg, Proprietors.

Peter Kuhl advertised his local blacksmith shop for making and repairing of plows, and for horseshoeing. He handled buggies and wagons, took in hay and grain in exchange for work, and advertised further:

FEED STABLE

In connection with the Shop I have a commodious

FEED STABLE

Horses boarded by the day or week, at reasonable prices.

Also, Wood & Church proclaimed a livery stable, feed stable and corral. J. W. Allen had a harness shop.

Ferguson's Hair--Cutting Headquarters on Washington Street, opposite the City Brewery, kept up with the times, as did A. Hupprich, "Fashionable Boot and Shoe Maker." Biesen & Nicholas invited guests to "Our Hotel and Restaurant." John Woolsey stressed a billiard table in his saloon for entertainment. Other advertisements included:

Eureka Meat Market, Neil McNulty, Proprietor.
Henry R. Sels, General Merchandise.
Max Metschan, Stoves and Tin Ware.
J. W. Howard, M.D., Physician and Surgeon.
F. C. Horlsey, M. D.
N. H. Boley, Dentist, opposite Golden Eagle Hotel.

Listed were four attorneys-at-law: Charles W. Parrish, George B. Currey, M. L. Olmstead and W. B. Lasswell.

Out-of-town ads merited close attention of the sick, the pleasure-bent, the student, or just the shopper:

HO! FOR SODA!
                    Jas. C. Fitzgerald
would announce to the public
                    And mankind in general, that the Famous
                    Soda Spring, in Bear Valley, is the place
                    to visit, for health or pleasure. Good
                    accommodations for visitors.

Warm Springs Hotel, Thos. Howe, Prop. These springs are situated at the head of John Day Valley, 25 miles above Canyon City. . . . Invalids find them a sure cure for all infirmities. . . . A Pleasant Summer Resort.

Railroad House, Baker City . . . first hotel ever started in Baker City.

Flagoellet's Hotel, Prairie City; meals and rooms.

Jules LeBret's Variety Store, Prairie City; also keeps A Livery and Feed Stable.

Baker City Academy, Mr. Wm. Harrison, Principal, assisted by Miss Kate Hunsaker, Preceptress, and Miss Belle Hulsey, Teacher of Music. . . .

Strawberry Valley Flouring Mills, located in Strawberry Valley, in upper John Day Valley, Grant County.

Widely separated, the settlers used their homes at rare intervals for entertainments, such as quilting bees, house-raisings and dances. The family altar was their church. Ofttimes women and children accompanied men on hunting trips. The abundant game was ever a needful source of replenishment for the family larder, and the hides, furs and feathers were utilized in various ways.

Poindexter & Clark, general merchandisers at the Stone Corner in Canyon City, advertised "a large supply of Carbine Musket Cartridges" in the fall of 1876. Although some volunteers had procured good arms in fighting Indians, settlers' guns did not keep pace with improved weapons of the army. Muzzle-loaders still were bruising many shoulders, and the roar of their discharge could be heard far across hills and plains. Some of the Oregon militia equipped themselves with the needle gun, a kind of breech-loading rifle which had been developed in 1836. A peculiarity of this old-timer was the firing pin which passed through the charge for detonating. The Prussians had used it in 1870.

Among the many models of carbines and also longer rifles brought into use were the Springfield, Winchester, Spencer, Sharps and Henry. And a Colt revolver met with deep admiration as an accessory, along with the keen-edged hunting knife.

Strict economy in the household or for essentials of the ranch had to be maintained by those who relied on their live stock. Beef fell, in 1873, to three to six cents a pound from butchers' carts in The Dalles. In Corvallis, the price slid from a listing of five to six cents a pound. In overproduction, a beneficial rise in price did not commence until 1880.

To help solve the problem, good markets for preserved beef had to be found when live markets fell abroad. Steps for preserving meat had been taken in Salem by 1869. Packing of meat had to attain a greater pace. Canning of salmon was not enough. Thomas Cross, who had been a pioneer in meat-packing at Salem, tried unsuccessfully to establish a plant at The Dalles in 1875. The fish canneries on the lower Columbia took over the new beef business for canning. Their maximum output was reached in 1876, declining as export trade for fresh beef brightened again. Toward the railroads in Nevada, for shipment to San Francisco or to the East in 1876, were driven at least 36,000 head of cattle from eastern Oregon and eastern Washington.

By 1875, Henry Villard, a better financier than Ben Holladay, gained control of the Oregon Central railroads as well as the Oregon Steam Navigation Company and railroads at portages. It proved to be a big step east and south.

Movement of sheep into eastern Oregon increased strongly in the seventies, and cattle would not graze on land used by sheep. By 1872, Oregon's *Willamette Farmer,* already an adult publication, sounded off for a herd law in the Willamette Valley. Controversies over herd laws rumbled year after year in eastern Oregon, arguments waxing hottest between farmers and cattlemen. They resulted in few drastic changes. Fence laws of various nature were applied by counties, but Oregon's Legislature, like that of Idaho, says Oliphant, seemed averse to "authorizing the electors of any county to vote on the question of adopting a herd law in rela-

tion to cattle." In Washington Territory, however, a herd law
grew sharp teeth.

This researcher also remarks:

No records of stockmen's associations and no private papers and
account books of cattlemen have been collected by historical societies
in the Oregon Country. It is doubtful whether any such records ever
existed. Organizations of cattlemen in the Pacific Northwest, with
perhaps one exception, seem to have had only local significance, and
the business methods of individual cattlemen in that region were, so
available evidence indicates, rather haphazard.

Regulations of the cattle industry were strikingly similar
in Oregon, Idaho or Washington, recognizing special needs
of particular areas. Laws protecting animals on unfenced pasturage had vital provisions for owners. An officer in each
county kept a registry of marks and brands, and recording was
mandatory from early days. Laws against thievery and other
malconduct were enacted, and restrictions were placed upon
designated ranges; books were kept on slaughtering; laws were
amended to protect ownership of estrays. Advertising often
was required in newspapers. Stock districts were organized by
the seventies, with regulations as to overproduction, diseases,
range improvement, and other factors.

Many enemies faced the eastern Oregon cattlemen — predatory animals, poisonous weeds, alkali dust, rattlesnakes, diseases, fire and drought — but the rustler was the meanest. No
viler man than the cattle or horse thief under God's heaven,
averred the honest stockman. Pretentiously, the posing law-
abiding fellow would violently protest against illegal ways of
vigilantes.

Unclean, the rustler practiced devious methods of crooked-
ness. He hurriedly picked up estrays to sell to butchers; he altered brands or markings; he laid claim to imperfectly branded stock; he pulled unweaned calves from cows. The rustler
"played Indian" by inciting alarm and then driving off stock,
or he would put a road brand on cattle not purchased properly for driving.

Laws there were, but also much expanse and an industry
ever demanding initiative. Trials were held, some men acquit-
ted, and there were lynchings. "The newspapers," it is de-

clared, "ranted and threatened dire vengeance on the evil-doers, but the nuisance of cattle-stealing was not wholly abated in the Pacific Northwest by the beginning of the decade of the nineties."

Most destructive enemy of the cattleman was Winter, a surprising and untamed foe in some years. Yet, even as they prayed or cursed for a Chinook, too many stockmen failed to provide properly against ravages of ice, wind and snow. Winter losses appalled or damaged some men irreparably. Blame rested on those who did not guard against freezing of water supply, lack of feed and shelter, as well as blades of grass turned into needles of ice.

In the Harney country, though, there were blessings to off-set the adversities. The new land and the free life held forth bright promises. Merry days outweighed the dark. Through-out the "driving" seasons, hills and lowlands echoed with the beat of hoofs, the bawling of bewildered strays, the barking of dogs, and the halloo of chaps-wearing herders as the beef trudged to market. Preferably, the wide trails led to the stock-yards at Winnemucca, Nevada. Sheep men usually carried their wool for selling to The Dalles.

They were a hardy lot, these open-range settlers and hill-exploring miners of old Grant County. Deprived of many ad-vantages, they wittingly or unwittingly carved out a new em-pire. If pasturage for their increasing herds did not suffice, they reached out for more, buying it outright or gaining it by intimidation. Some were benevolent and some were not. Yet quite a number who were considered weakest proved them-selves to be the strongest. They enlarged their homesteads slowly but legally, awaiting the day when law and order would bring them an unstained fruitfulness.

Engagingly, Arnold J. Toynbee, great English historical scholar, has compared the nomadic stock-breeder with him who follows the path of agriculture. Ever mindful of the sea-son, the nomad of the challenging steppe changed his pastur-age. Cattlemen and sheepmen of Oregon's high desert virtu-ally lived off the grasses because the grasses built up the flesh of their animals.

Chapter XIII

RECLAMATION AND CATTLE INDUSTRY

FOUR-TENTHS OF THE CONTINENTAL ACREAGE of the United States, excluding Alaska, is classed as arid, arbitrarily applied to regions having less than twenty inches average yearly rainfall. Grazing, forest and desert lands fall in this range average.

Prehistoric traces of irrigation are found in North America. The Mormon founders of Utah who, in the summer of 1847, were forced to put water on their fields before they could plow, actually gave irrigation its first start as applied to territory belonging to the United States. Rights for appropriation of water on land came along with water rights for mining. Congress, by the Act of July 26, 1866, asserts Professor John T. Ganoe, "recognized priority of rights that had already accrued and rights recognized by local customs and decisions of courts." State aid boosted irrigation.

Two main systems of irrigation law, Ganoe says, developed in the United States: "the California System," relying on "the common law of riparian rights with regard to land that was privately owned," and the "Colorado System," application of the doctrine of appropriation to private lands. The latter claimed right for an appropriation in the state's sovereign power, "not as a pre-existing property right in and from the United States." As actual experience progressed in the 1870's particularly in Utah, California and Colorado, the question became more involved.

By 1875 individuals were allowed to buy land (640 acres at $1.25 per acre) if they would reclaim it within two years. Neither surveying nor residence on the land was required. By Congressional Act of 1877, desert lands were defined for reclamation in three states, California, Oregon and Nevada, and in eight territories. It was the government's "first policy toward the reclamation of arid lands." Prior appropriation decided rights to water.

The Desert Lands Act of 1877 defined desert lands as those without timber or minerals which could not produce agri-
74

cultural crops without irrigation. The law still is in force, supplemented by the Carey Act in 1894 and the Newlands Reclamation Act of 1902. Modification of land laws, because of a boom in irrigation in the late eighties, met the old problem of reclamation.

Such steps affected the course taken by the first cattle barons in the Harney country and by later ones. Henry Miller, a young German immigrant, got his start in a meat shop in San Francisco in 1850. After taking over the holding of Henry Hildreth, 7,500 head of cattle and the Double-H brand in San Joaquin Valley, he formed a loose partnership with Charles Lux in 1858. The firm became known as Miller & Lux, with Miller in the dominating role. "Then," declared biographer Edward F. Treadwell, "began a veritable orgy of land and cattle buying which continued without abatement for thirty years."

Miller bought land not to sell, but to produce, and he made it pay. He bought out those who gained titles by entry and he bought land script used by the government at the time, 160 acres of script being worth about 180 dollars. For $1.25 an acre he obtained land later valued at several hundred dollars, along with swamp land, homesteads, preemptions and school land. Cattle bearing the Double-H brand invaded ranges far and wide. By irrigation, dredging and other means, he made sure the land and cattle were going to pay large dividends. No other man had a greater system of canals, and he hired the most brilliant legal talent to protect his water rights.

Many years were to pass before Miller pushed his cattle domain through Nevada into Oregon, but his power and methods had influence from the beginning. Among pioneers of the seventies, Devine and French as chief reclaimers of the wilderness gambled with fate while possessing rare vision and ability to create a huge business from land raw and wild. Himself a pioneer attorney of Harney County, John W. Biggs observed keenly:

. . . At this time this was all Government, State or specially allotted land. The State owned all of the swamp and school lands, several road companies held large grants, a great part was an Indian reservation, but none was occupied by white people. It was the custom for several years thereafter for anyone to squat and call the land around, upon which he could settle, his own, and began to use it as his property. A short time thereafter outside persons began to purchase the State lands, and this caused these earliest settlers to take notice; and in self defense to try to acquire a legal claim to the lands which they had held up to that time, by right of possession only. As the laws at that time did not allow anyone who was largely interested in livestock to acquire sufficient lands to feed and care for a great number of stock, it became a custom among the early settlers to acquire a part of their lands through subterfuge, and also another part through a liberal construction, at the very least, of the law.

After once acquiring what they supposed was a title to their lands, whether the acquiring had been strictly legal or otherwise, they naturally were inclined to fight for it thereafter.

In the initial stages, a cattleman could equip his large ranch for a few thousand dollars. Labor costs were low, and little money was expended as cattle drifted from summer to winter ranges. Though corrals were built at convenient spots for branding cattle at roundups, too few enclosures for hay to feed in winter were built. The largest herds prevailed in southeastern Oregon and in southern Idaho. Outside of roundup time, a dozen cowboys could care for a herd of 8,000 cattle. They received, apart from board and lodging, $35.00 to $40.00 a month.

Rightful increase of a herd was secured to an owner by brand and marks, the brand burned into the hide, an ear of the calf notched or pointed. The most important roundup occurred in springtime when young calves kept close to their mothers. Voluntary co-operation generally prevailed. The other roundup of the year was in late summer or in early autumn, when calves missed in the spring were branded and the beef cattle were gathered in for market. However, spring roundups were necessary when cattle buyers from the East contracted animals during the winter, and delivery had to be made by summer-long drives. The road brand of the buyer then was used.

Calves that escaped the branding-iron at roundups were called "slick-ears" or "mavericks." In absence of law or of district agreement, custom decreed that slick-ears belonged to "the person who could get his brand on them." This was a profitable sideline for callused cattlemen. The next step was rustling, or plain thievery and alteration of brands. Cattle clubs and district associations of stockmen, with improvement of herds, did good service in the seventies and eighties.

The buckaroos soon began to acquire the best type of calm and intelligent ponies for herding and driving. They replaced those of fractious or high-strung nature. As many of the mustangs — half-wild, small and hardy horses — were turned loose on ranges, their numbers increased. Prosperous ranchers smiled upon the "Thoroughbreds," race or running, horse, an original British product of a century of importations and selective breeding. The trotter and pacer, a standard-bred product of America, was developed for harness and racing.

Devine and French, aspiring for the best, bided their time as they increased and improved their holdings. Each enjoyed being the friendly host as well as an ambitious overseer. Each believed in courtesy and rewarding of loyalty. Big-framed Devine, however, was more of a jovial proprietor, a good mixer. French, short and audacious, was polite in an aloof fashion, and as he gained the power of a prince he dressed like one.

Both men, of necessity, maintained busy and expanding headquarters, bases of supplies at their isolated homes. The roomy houses were warmed with large fireplaces which, like the cooking stoves, devoured hard-to-get wood. Poplars and other trees were planted for shade and windbreaks. Logs and lumber for building cookhouses, bunkhouses and barns had to be hauled over soft dirt roads from the Blue Mountains.

French established a store at his "P" Ranch. Essentials were kept in stock or procured for the many hands working under him. A driver was almost constantly on the road to and from Nevada or California, his wagons bringing renewed lists of items. Though not always sufficiently cautious or well-disciplined in business acumen, Pete French kept an account book at his headquarters which he designated "Steins Mountain." The one for 1876-1879 is a long and narrow ledger with ruled columns, and virtually all entries are in ink. On the first page of this bookkeeping journal, in 1876, the owner writes in his indubitable fashion as to his assets:

I began Apr 17 as follows
Cash on hand to

H. J. Glenn	owes me	4000.00
C. T. Burges	" "	250.00
A. Greenleaf	" "	200.00
Joe Bates	" "	25.00
M. B. French	" "	200.00
Barney Radz	" "	15.00
Jno Vance	" "	40.00
J. Devine	" "	125.00
S. Mann	" "	20.00
W. Henley	" "	2.50

In 1877, French and Glenn purchased from Robie the land and cattle of Diamond Ranch on McCoy Creek, about sixteen miles southeast of the main headquarters of "P" Ranch. About the same time, also, they bought the interests of Robie, Frank McBean and others in thousands of acres of marsh on the Blitzen River and Diamond Swamp.

French's journal is a mine of information concerning names of men, cost of goods and equipment, handling of notes, buying and selling of cattle, and other sundry records. Frequent entries refer to "Old Yank," once identified as Old Yank Langly, indeed a prodigious chewer of tobacco — "17 plugs at $4.25." Many names of early-day settlers appear. Of course credit entries for benefit of Glenn, the ranch's promoter, are numerous, such as of May 29, 1877:

H. G. Glenn Cr.
By check 4330.00

The method in the following was repeated with various parties: "Bought promissory note of Thos. Walls payable to John Curry $456 due Nov. 20th," and ticking of a check mark denotes payment of the same.

Again: "Gave P. Bohn my note payable on or before 1 of March 1878 for 4400.00," with entry duly checked. Or, "Ed Kiger Dr. to 1 Saddle 37.50 Paid." Or, "Bought of A. Strouf 18 head of Steers, gave check for $300.00 and 1 horse valued at 50.00."

Now and then appear detailed expenses incurred in trips to Canyon City, to Winnemucca or Reno or elsewhere, along with tax and recording bills. In December, 1877, the Christmas spirit as well as business dealing is in evidence: "Sent my sister 400.00. Gave Farmer National Bank Note for fifteen thousand dollars pay 11 of April with interest at 1¼ per cent. Rec cash $8000. Bal. to be sent to Win[nemucca] on 6th of Jan." Also: "Gave Cattle due bill on mule teams 750.00."

Three- or four-year-old steers were the kind most acceptable in the open market for slaughter. The price is shown at various times:

Jan. 28, 1878	(Sold Miller & Lux (340 Steers at $34.65 (148 cows at 25.00

On February 12, 1878, is this: "Sold Lux 77 at 6½ cts, weight 511, 178 head . . . at 7c, weight 602 lbs., 286 head at $23 [each], 20 head at $23." This item follows on February 14: "Paid Todhunter 281 dollars on check of $1781.00 on Glenn." Enlightening is this glimpse at the San Francisco beef market in March, 1878: "Sold to C. F. Wagner 551 Steers 21489.00."

Then up pops Old Yank again as debtor (checked as paid):

To cash on acc	100.00
To 5 lbs Tobac	5.00

There were accounts with Robie's sawmill, with the military at Fort Harney, and money paid to Indians for clearing land. Gold, silver and note received totted attention.

Separate pages of the journal were given over to "Time Book" for the hands on the main ranch as distinguished from men on "Diamond Rancho." Some began work at $20 a month, while others got as much as $50 a month.

For years, Prim Tebo Ortego, a full-blooded Mexican, was French's chief buckaroo, and he gained special favor, being permitted to have a small herd of his own. Tebo, after selling his cattle in Winnemucca, would blow in most of the profit and come back to start over with French. Tebo lost much by gambling, but averred he "made 'em work for it."

By the summer of 1878, it is claimed, French's firm owned

more than 20,000 head of cattle and a large number of horses. Devine and Todhunter were gaining steadily. In that year, Catlow secured Dave Shirk as manager of his property. A brother, Bill Shirk, held forth in Catlow Valley, and John H. Witzel rode the range hard by the Blitzen's marshes.

Others appeared in the dawning of renewed hostilities with red men. Unable to legally lease Indian grazing lands, cattlemen were wont to trespass thereon.

Chapter XIV

DAYS OF FORT HARNEY

By LOCATING FORT HARNEY on the banks of Rattlesnake
Creek where it eased out of its high-walled, rock-shelved canyon, the military appreciated many advantages. It was sheltered from northern blasts in winter and was accessible by the
high road from Canyon City, dipping steeply off the eastern
ridge. A wagon trail, dusty in summer and, in winter, muddy
or frozen or choked with snow, skirted or climbed sage-cov-
ered hills to the east or west. The huge expanse of marshy hay-
lands, along with floors and tables of rabbit and sage brush,
unfurled southward, eastward and westward across Harney
basin.

Virgin pine covered the mountains to the north, and it was
handily milled by Robie, first on Coffeepot Creek, then on
Cow Creek. Soil along Rattlesnake Creek had fertility for
vegetables and grain. Where it flared from the canyon jaws
into a full day of sunlight, it yielded tall and luscious grass on
unconfined meadowland. Rattlesnakes, large and small, had
to be avoided in the hay yards or on twisting trails, but few
settlements in the new country were free of them.

The post's importance increased with settlement. The
Camp Harney postoffice, established August 10, 1874, was the
first postoffice in the area later to become Harney County.
William T. Stevens, storekeeper, was appointed its first postmaster. The postoffice took in or gave out mail to people
when they did not ride to Prineville or to communities of the
lower Malheur. The post gave employment to civilians and,
among other things, it purchased horses, oxen and cattle from
settlers. On January 28, 1876, the Fort Harney Military Reserve of 640 acres was created.

That year, on Saturday, October 21, H. R. Gale's *Grant
County Express* in Canyon City published an advertisement
for the civilian store adjoining the post:

81

SNIDER & STEVENS
Dealers In
Dry Goods, Clothing,
Boots & Shoes,
Hardware, Crockery, Gro-
ceries, Liquors,
and Suttlers' Goods
of Every Description
CAMP HARNEY
Grant County, Oregon

Frank McBean used the same issue of the paper to attract attention to another vital business:

ATTENTION
Harney & Canyon City
Mail and Passenger Line
F. W. McBean   Proprietor
I would announce to the traveling
public that a PASSENGER COACH
will leave Camp Harney and Canyon
City on
Wednesday of Each Week,
Arriving at the same places on
Thursday of Each Week.
Military Express matter and other Ex-
press matter arrives Saturday evenings
from both ways, and goes out on Sunday
morning.
Good   accommodation   for   passengers
along the route.

W. S. Southworth was moving his sawmill from east of Canyon City to the "Harney Road." Times were changing.

Frank Whiting, at seven years of age, was at Fort Harney in 1878 when his sister, the future Mrs. E. W. Luckey, was born in one of the barracks. His memory of the camp contributed to enrichment of this book.

Off the Agency road on the south led a wide, smooth dirt street that split Fort Harney into halves. Northward, on the left, the target range lay flat and to the right the stream purred over a pebbly bottom. Hard on the left was the bulky cavalry stable with its corrals, back of it the squat guardhouse or jail. These were of stout logs and poles.

Above them, at the edge of the street, were four rectangular barracks for the soldiers. A long drill ground lay between them and a dozen quarters for officers below the broken rimrock on the west. Built of rough lumber and painted or whitewashed unsparingly, their roofs sloping gently, the barracks and quarters gleamed. A weighty building of logs fortified with a square enclosure of tall, thick posts headed the drill ground. It was dwarfed on the north by the huge log commissary. Beyond, and below the hill-cove cemetery, showed the short roofs of a frame store and saloon erected by civilians.

On the east side of the street rested the camp's facilities, divided by the road leading uphill to Canyon City. To the east of the stream and on the south of the dividing road were the slaughterhouse, blacksmith shop and the bakery. Several log pens, shoulder high, squatted between the lower street and creek. Opposite the barracks, along the thoroughfare, stood the combined kitchens and mess halls of log construction. Each, in the rear, had a small bath house. Then, elbowing the street, was a large log building housing the quartermaster's supplies.

A long pumping pole slanted at a well east of the creek. Above, at the northern limits, a reservoir straddled the banks. Trout raced or lurked in pools and riffles shielded by willows.

The blacksmith shop always was busy. Minnie, six-year-old daughter of freighter Bill Bonham, spent a few months of 1877 at Fort Harney. She marveled at the craftsmanship of her uncle, barrel-chested and iron-muscled Carlos Wells Bonham, the smithy. The ring of the anvil, flying sparks from the roaring forge, a red-hot horseshoe singeing a hoof or causing hissing steam to rise from bubbling water in a huge wooden tub, the fashioning of a wagon tire, or other labor, all held her entranced. From the low porch of the blocky jail she stared at a civilian prisoner wearing an Oregon boot. The heavy iron boot encased a leg halfway up, its chain fastened to a post.

Of Irish-French stock, Bill Bonham was a tall man, weighing 230 pounds. His feet almost dragged the ground when he rode a small mule or horse. Nobody outdid him at freighting. Jimmie, an adopted Apache youth, was an apt pupil, he later handling one of three outfits — 10-team, six-team and four-team.

At an isolated post like Fort Harney, soldiers and their wives met and overcame many obstacles. A four-year resident on Rattlesnake Creek, Mrs. Eugenie M. Bacon, in 1930 was granted an honorary degree of Doctor of Letters by James Millikin University, Decatur, Illinois, for many years of public service. She was the widow of Lieutenant George R. Bacon, who died in 1911. Their only son died at the age of eight.

Graduate of West Point in 1869, Lieutenant Bacon served with Troop K, First U. S. Cavalry, at Angel and Alcatraz islands in San Francisco harbor and at Fort Grant, Arizona, before arrival at Camp Halleck, Nevada. From there he went into the Modoc War in the Lava Beds, 1872-1873. On a leave of absence, he married his sweetheart, Eugenie, in Tuscola, Illinois, in March of 1874. Of their trip to Oregon's frontier, Mrs. Bacon wrote:

. . . I was at that time 20 years of age and my husband aged 28. We were sent to Cavalry barracks at St. Louis that summer to await the assembling of recruits for western posts.

There were then only two transcontinental railroads, the Central and Union Pacific, and only one train per day each way.

The meeting of these trains was an event of interest and to a young woman, such as I, of thrilling interest.

After leaving the recruits along the way, my husband and I spent a few days at the headquarters of our regiment, Benecia Barracks, California, in the home of the Commanding Officer, General Gillam, and his wife, where we met all of the Army people stationed there.

We sailed from San Francisco on a three days' ocean trip to Portland, Oregon. Then up the Columbia River by boat and train and portage around the Dalles and rapids to Fort Walla Walla where we were fitted out with an ambulance and escort of soldiers for an eleven-day trip across the Blue Mountains to our post, Camp Harney, in Oregon, Col. Elwell S. Otis in command.

Fort Harney was garrisoned by two companies of the 21st U. S. Infantry, and Troop K, 1st U. S. Cavalry, 1st Lieut. Chas. C. Cresson in Command of Troop, as Captain Chas. E. Bendire was on leave of absence and whom we had met at the Cavalry barracks at St. Louis.

Brevet Major Cresson had gone to Fort Harney from the Modoc War. His little son was then eighteen months old before his father had seen him. . . .

I was at Camp Harney four years. Colonel Otis was replaced by

Colonel John Green and our Captain Bendire came to relieve Lieut. Cresson who went on leave.

At one time Captain Bendire was in command, and as he was a bachelor it fell to me to do some of the honors.

At one time General O. O. Howard and his daughter, Grace, came to inspect the fort, and dined with us.

Howard, who had lost his right arm at Fair Oaks, Virginia, recovered quickly. In subsequent major engagements he fought as tenaciously as he clung to his faith in divine guidance. As a student and teacher of the Bible, he became known as "the Havelock of the Army." He, said Mrs. Bacon, conducted "the only Protestant service held in the fort during my four years of sojourn there."

"When I went to Camp Harney some of the wives had been there seven years. A bride with modern clothes was a curiosity," she said. Mrs. Bacon had other memories:

I never had a new garment during the four years I spent there, and made over my wedding clothes myself, my husband turning the hand sewing machine which we bought in Portland, paying $30 in Gold for it.

There was absolutely no comparison in the privations of those frontier posts and the larger garrisons such as Fort Clark, Texas, as I found out on a visit to San Antonio with my little son to try to restore his health.

At Harney when General Custer's command of 253 men met death on June 25, 1876, Mrs. Bacon said "the terrible battle of the Little Big Horn almost broke my heart. I wrote to Mrs. Custer and had a dear letter from her." When Lieutenant Bacon rode with his troop in the Nez Perce War of 1877, Eugenie waved farewell to friends on Rattlesnake Creek and returned to Illinois.

Captain Bendire, while stationed at Fort Harney in 1876-77, kept a diary which has yielded rich information of wildlife in the Harney and Malheur regions. He commanded Troop K in the Bannock War of 1878, and his scientific observations benefited the Smithsonian Institution. In the summer of 1880 he led an expedition for a topographical survey of specimens, chiefly mineral, over a large area of the inland Northwest.

Major Green, several years after the campaign of 1878, became a leading citizen of Boise City. Cresson's son followed in the soldier footsteps of his father, for a long army career.

Life of the regular army man at Fort Harney by 1878 had its allurement and its vicissitudes. On February 7 of that year a set of log and frame quarters for officers burned to the ground. In the teeth of wintry blows, they utilized tents until barracks were rebuilt. Wall tents prevailed, but conical shelter of cotton duck could hardly be more snugly drawn. Furniture and conveniences were scarce.

Each company retained a strength of thirty to fifty men, infantrymen mounted when necessary. On the Columbia, at that time, the army paid an average of $121.54 for a cavalry or artillery horse, and $145 for a mule. Twelve oxen, for hauling supplies, cost $960. Six-mule wagons, made in Pennsylvania, cost $99.25 each; high-wheeled ambulances from the same manufacturer, $169.90 each. Two-horse wagons and others of light weight, obtained at Leavenworth, Kansas, cost $92.50 each. The sum of $67.49 was paid for harness sets for a six-mule team, and $57.84 for four-mule ambulance harness. Usually, the horse or mule bore a "U.S." brand on the hip.

S. Rinehart contracted to transport supplies from Winnemucca, Nevada, to Fort Harney — 252 miles — for four and a quarter cents (coin) per pound. George Gundlach brought supplies from The Dalles for about the same rate. Military mail was conveyed weekly between Canyon City and Harney by Frank McBean for $108 a month.

Portland and other points west of the Cascade Mountains had good telegraphic connections with southern towns, but the hook-up to the east was disconcerting. The newly built Nevada and Northern telegraph line extended from Winnemucca to Walla Walla, whence it connected with Portland lines. It ran by way of Camp McDermitt, Silver City and Boise City. Portland got its first telephone exchange in 1878. Pendleton was not to acquire an exchange until 1889, and Baker waited until 1898, when Canyon City was connected with Richland, by way of Baker.

The army and settlers of Harney basin had to rely on couriers to bear dispatches. These and others, when riding horseback, made good use of saddlebags fastened behind the cantle of the saddle. Canteens, or holster bags, often were secured to the saddle's horn.

Much of the soldier's clothing came from California mills. His shoes were made by convict labor at the military prison at Fort Leavenworth. Boots, a prideful matter, required upper leather of the best oak-tanned from slaughter-hides, with soles of "best oak-tanned from 'straight' Texas hides, or from South American (commonly called 'Spanish') dry hides." The use of split leather was forbidden. Sewed well and with double soles made secure by brass screws, the boot was a serviceable one.

The shirt problem, meeting weather changes, long had been a tantalizing one. Colonel J. W. Redington, scout who in peacetime enjoyed Chief Egan as a hunting and camping companion, bemoaned "those dirty-gray army shirts made of saddle-blanket stuff." Prevalent had been the shirt of dark-blue wool flannel or Canton flannel, cursed on hot days.

The soldiers, averse to tight and itchy shirt collars, rebelled — in their fashion. There came a statement from the quarter-master chief: "The troops have been in the habit of cutting off the collars of their shirts. Inquiry having shown that this habit was general, shirts are made without collars." A new shirt, therefore, was adopted in January, 1878. It was collarless, loose, with shoulder-yoke and collar band, made of gray flannel.

The brass-buttoned coats or blouses were of dark blue, but the trousers sky-blue. A wide stripe — the color denoting the branch of arms — ran vertically up the outside seam of each trouser leg. The cavalryman's color was yellow, the artilleryman's red, the infantryman's white. The infantry later changed the color of the pompons, hat decorations, to a light blue. On the front of his accordion-like cap the cavalryman wore crossed sabers, and the infantryman, crossed rifles.

Saddles and harness, of durable quality leather, were costly items. The soldiers found them plainly standardized, but did not envy the cowboy's fancy ornaments. The lighter the saddle or harness the easier it could be lifted or carried.

The Springfield rifle, made in the United States armory at Springfield, Massachusetts, was the adopted model in service from 1868, with Model 1873 carried in the Nez Perce and

Bannock campaigns. A breech-loader, it had metallic cartridges. Models of 1873 were made in regulation rifle, carbine and cadet sizes. Cartridges for the rifle and shorter carbine varied for some time. The revolver, Gatling gun and howitzer were other weapons. The sabre had ceased to be of practical use.

The soldiers at Fort Harney, as elsewhere, came from all walks of life. They assumed guardianship of the last frontier's line. They simply obeyed instructions to the best of their ability — and asked their questions after the dust of the trail had settled and the smoke of battle had long since ascended.

There were many who, settling down in the new country, became permanent builders.

Chapter XV

ESTABLISHMENT OF MALHEUR INDIAN RESERVATION

EARLY INDIAN POLICY had allowed politicians to select Indian agents. Capable and honest men were hard to obtain for isolated agencies. Too many agents labored for personal gain, and contractors provided inferior goods at prices for best quality—Indians and taxpayers being the losers. Reform was needed.

In March, 1869, President U. S. Grant withdrew appointments of civil agents and placed army officers in charge, but these served only until July of the next year. In 1869, by authority of Congress, Grant named a board of Indian commissioners. Comprised of philanthropic men who served without compensation, the board supervised jointly with the Secretary of the Interior appropriations made for the Indian service.

To provide education, culture and religion for the red men, missionary boards were asked to name the agents. The latter were to appoint employes of Christian character. Salaries for agents, doctors, teachers, millers, blacksmiths, farmers, and others ranged from $600 to $1500 annually. Education was the chief objective after 1871, when the treaty-making period ended. Revised Statutes, March 3, 1871, declared "that hereafter no Indian nation or tribe within the territory of the United States shall be *acknowledged or recognized* as an independent nation, tribe, or power, *with whom the United States may contract* by treaty."

The Indians were neither aliens nor citizens, but wards. Before its dissolution in 1874, the original Board of Commissioners was to note how land patented in fee simple to red men brought responsibility in stock-raising and farming. Unfortunately, not until 1924, 100 years after formation of the Bureau of Indian Affairs, did there come actual organization of the division of health in the Office of Indian Affairs.

Felix Reville Brunot of Pittsburgh, Pennsylvania, became president of Grant's Board of Indian Commissioners. He, accompanied by the board's secretary, Thomas K. Cree of Pittsburgh, visited distant reservations. In 1871, on a 75-mile trip from Yakima to Warm Springs Agency, part of it roadless, they spent a night at a cabin. Their horses cared for, they were given a basin by their hostess, to wash their hands. "When," wrote the philanthropist Brunot, "they had both used it, she took it again, and dressed a chicken in it. Then she made biscuits in it; in a moment it was on the stove full of boiling milk. It is not surprising that even with their indulgent courtesy the guests found their appetites subdued." The woman, in this isolated spot, had no other pans.

Again, two dozen miles from any dwelling, on a treeless stretch, the tongue of the men's wagon broke. Steep hills ahead forbade use of a rope. The day was saved when, in a gulch, they salvaged wood from a forsaken sled.

Brunot, devout and conscientious, studied thoroughly the Indian situation in Oregon where remedies lagged. He recognized the worth of proper placement of homeless Indians of the Harney and Malheur regions. In eastern Oregon, the divisions by church for the four Indian reservations were: Malheur, Christian Missionary; Klamath and Warm Springs, Methodist; Umatilla, Catholic.

On September 12, 1872, an executive order set apart the Malheur Indian Reservation for "all the roving and straggling bands in Eastern and Southeastern Oregon, which can be induced to settle there." About 800 in number, they eked a sustenance among settlements and at Forts Harney, Klamath, Bidwell in northeastern California, and McDermitt. The Paiute bands were led, principally, by Chiefs Winnemucca, Natchez, Egan, Leggins, Ochoco and Oits. Some Bannocks and Snakes under Eagle-eye mingled with them.

The reserve, roughly, was the region drained by three forks of the Malheur River; South, Middle and North. An area of about 2285 square miles, or 1,778,560 acres, it contained 12,000 acres considered tillable. The agency was to be located south of Castle Rock, on the eastern limits. A wagon road, twisting about 60 miles through what is now Drewsey and past headwaters of Pine Creek, was to connect it with Fort Harney near Silvies River, which marked the western boundary.

T. B. Odeneal, Oregon superintendent, gave heed to new policies, training for rights of citizenship withheld until 1887. After submitting, November 20, 1872, an estimate of $47,500 to establish and care for Indians on Malheur Reservation the first year, Odeneal awaited appropriations by Congress. Timber for buildings and fences had to be hauled 10 to 30 miles from the Blue Mountains to the agency site. A portable steam sawmill at a purchasing price of $3500 was expected to save more than its cost.

Samuel Ball Parrish was appointed special commissary in charge, February 5, 1873. His brother, Charles W., was a prominent attorney of Canyon City in that period. Sam, the son of the Rev. Josiah L. Parrish by his first wife, was an Oregon pioneer of 1840, having come from New York by way of Cape Horn on the missionary ship *Lausanne*. The father, a leader in Methodism and at the forefront of the state educational movements, became a trustee of Willamette University at Salem.

With Odeneal approving, Sam Parrish selected the site for agency building in May, 1873. It was 18 miles from the mouth of the north fork of the Malheur River, on the west bank. The best hay and grain lands lay on the east side, threaded by Warm Creek and two feeders, Egan and Mule creeks. Two hot springs on Warm Creek near the Agency long had been used for bathing by Indians.

Most of the Indians had wintered at Fort Harney, they had only wigwams for shelter, and in good season went out to fish and hunt. Parrish moved with them to the building site August 2, and, upon receiving the first load of lumber from the Blue Mountains eight days later, started construction.

He reported, February 7, 1874, that he was ready to leave the Agency, after having superintended construction and outlining a program for 513 wards. He had received no compensation, and his employes had not been paid since the preceding June. In spite of inclement weather, five buildings had been erected. Money was lacking to buy windows, paint, and finishing material. Parrish, forced to economize, postponed purchase of flour.

Shortly, Agent H. Linville came to take charge. Friction arose between him and Oits who, as medicine man, made it disagreeable for many. Old Winnemucca and some others left. Linville found Oits so refractory he wrote Major Otis, commanding at Fort Harney, on March 7, asking that 20 soldiers be sent to arrest the disturber and confine him at the post, thus forestalling an outbreak. Parrish had won the respect of the bronzed people by handling Oits firmly, but Linville emphasized the fear instilled among Paiutes by medicine men's preachings.

A rigorous winter forbade sending of troops on the run. Snow was two feet deep around the isolated post and more than twice that depth near by. Pack mules were worn out carrying mail, and civilian packers charged high rates. Team mules, if used, would balk or wallow in the snow.

Lieutenant Charles C. Cresson arrived at the Agency on April 5, with a detachment of Company K, First Cavalry. He observed conduct of affairs and issuing of rations by a Mr. Hatch, commissary. His report charged skimping of rations, flour and beef being of poor quality and sometimes withheld unnecessarily. Blame for withholding a surplus was directed at the commissary rather than at the agent because of the latter's inexperience in handling Indians and their subsistence.

Several Paiute leaders, including Jerry Long (Ang-é zah— "Riding down hill with hair standing on end"), interpreter, and some employes defended Linville and vilified Oits. But the agent's anxiety over Indian troubles resulted in his being replaced. Parrish was recommended to succeed him, higher officials agreeing with Major Otis that disorder seemed inevitable because of the Indians, expressed preference for the former commissary.

Meanwhile, Dr. L. L. Rowland, prominent in educational circles of Oregon, was aiding the Malheur peoples. Possessor of a medical degree, he rendered significant service as a missionary to Oregon's Indians by indorsement of the General Christian Missionary Association.

Appropriations for Malheur Reservation lagged. The total of outstanding debts contracted by Parrish up to January 12, 1874, was $12,549.52. Payment on a beef contract came to $8,200.59. W. V. Rinehart was listed in purchase of flour. Debts contracted by Linville prior to July 1 totaled $6,904.73.

A wagon cost $227.27, and C. W. Moore was paid $250 for carrying mail.

Parrish took the reins as agent August 1. He issued food to no more than 521 Indians in the summer. Many groups tried to obtain rations at military posts, and enjoyed fishing and hunting.

There still was space for the nomad. From Klamath Lake to Malheur Agency in the fall of 1874, a traveler took 10 days to cover 350 miles. His route lay through Camps Warner and Harney, and he found no good water or settlement except near Goose Lake. The Malheur's North Fork surprised him in that, "although the stream is small yet the salmon runs to this distant point from the sea."

General Oliver Otis Howard, who had been sixth ranking general in the Union Army and had served as commissioner of the Freedmen's Bureau, came to command the Military Department of the Columbia in 1874. In the fall of that year he visited Malheur Reservation. Of this meeting with Chief Egan, Oits and other Indian leaders, he wrote:

I noticed how superior Egan was to the others. He had on an ordinary farmer's suit of light linen duck with a leather belt around his waist, a sheath holding a sheath-knife by his side. He wore a straw hat that he removed when he spoke to me. He had all the features of a full-blooded Indian, but wore no braid or ornament. His hair, parted in the middle, was cut short at the neck. His pleasant face and resonant voice were mainly used . . . in praising Major Sam Parrish. . . .

When Jerry Long, cousin of Sarah Winnemucca, left for San Francisco to seek treatment for eye trouble, Parrish sent for Sarah in May, 1875, to serve as interpreter. Since 1868 she had done commendable work in that capacity at Fort McDermitt, beseeching General John M. Schofield at San Francisco as well as military and civil officials in Nevada and Oregon. While at the Nevada post she had married a dashing white officer, Lieutenant Bartlett, and they became permanently separated when he was transferred to the East.

At the time Parrish offered employment to Sarah, she was visiting her father at Fort Harney. Her mother and a sister had died; the chief obtained another wife after a dark period of mourning. Among his children was a daughter named Sihuwita-tse-ah, meaning "One little girl." She had a sister known to early whites as Daisy, wife of Joe Slavin, whose Indian name, Ee-be-natches, is translated "White paint boy."

Sarah's brothers included Lee, approaching marriageable age and companion of his father; Tom, with a family of his own at Pyramid Lake, and Natchez, who headed a band that chose the vicinity of Winnemucca for "campoody" sites. In 1874 friction arose between Natchez and his agent in Nevada, the subchief being accused of brewing trouble among Indians on the Humboldt. Arrested, he was taken to Fort Alcatraz, San Francisco Bay. Natchez, aided by Sarah, charged that his tribe and government were wronged, and support came to him in California and from some Nevada papers. "He was made much of," says a Nevada historian, "loaded with gifts, and sent home rejoicing."

Natchez and Lee were tall, fine-looking men, a contrast to their father. Of short stature, sometimes wearing an oversize army uniform, Chief Winnemucca nevertheless was proud of his position as a Caesar. He liked to get around. The Central Pacific railroad gave free rides to the Paiutes, and the chief delighted in viewing the realm of Nevada from the front of an engine. At other times he would push a skinny horse to a full day's limit. Sometimes he would borrow money from white citizens and head for Reno. There, assembled with other Indians below the wooden bridge over the Truckee River, he risked the "loan" in games of chance at their "Monte Carlo."

Thirty warm summers in Nevada had not erased the comeliness of Sarah. Of middle size, her pronounced Indian features were accented by large brown eyes. These eyes could either flash fire or sympathy as occasion demanded. Her outward bearing was usually one of calmness, shielding a firmness and determination seldom met. As a teen-age girl she had washed clothes to pay for books to study. She never faltered in pursuit of education, and her language was rich in native eloquence. This, coupled with dramatic action, placed her in the van with discerning leaders of her race.

When possible, Sarah chose to dress in the prevailing fashions of the white women. When necessary, she carried a knife for self-protection. She resolved to point out to her people advantages in the white man's mode of living—mainly to overcome ignorance and poverty. Yet she never was averse to expressing her pride in the fact she was of Indian ancestry. Her idea of education for her race was one of practicality.

Irked or inflamed by criticism of red or white, she displayed unswerving loyalty to her people and immediate family.

Chapter XVI

LIFE ON THE RESERVATION

AT MALHEUR AGENCY, Sarah Winnemucca was listed on the payroll as Sarah Bartlett, her legal name. She received $40 a month, paying $15 for board, and lived in a plainly furnished room next to the doctor's office. Her energy and knowledge aided in carrying out needful programs.

Plans were made for building a schoolhouse, but sustenance required first attention in 1875. Step by step, about 75 young men learned to farm by demonstrations. They planted corn, potatoes, turnips, squash and onions. In an effort to teach the benefits of individual ownership, Agent Parrish that summer had all cultivable land near the Agency surveyed and divided into 40-acre tracts. Help was given on the Agency's farm of 100 acres, planted to grain and vegetables. The fine grain had to be cut green for hay because it could not be turned into flour.

Indians worked on a dam, cut rails and built fences. They constructed a ditch about two miles long and 10 feet in width to supply water for irrigation, shops, and a hoped-for grist mill. Parrish believed wards should have enough flour from their own crops if the mill could be procured. The Indians received little in pay other than subsistence and annuity goods. That year they tilled 120 acres and owned 200 horses.

Illness seldom invaded the wigwams, only shelter of the Indians so far, and they still preferred native doctors. After harvest, came a pleasing issue of shoes and clothing, colorful shawls, calico and flannel, unbleached muslin, handkerchiefs, blankets, and mirrors.

Recipients expressed happiness—virtually all except Oits, who threatened Parrish's life. The agent, however, converted an enemy into a friend. For a period, Oits even withdrew support of forbidden transactions with renegade Columbia bands who held reservation life in disdain. To Paiutes the Columbias offered horses for blankets, furs and buckskins, returning to northerly trade routes to barter with white traders. Some Cayuses, nearer to the Nez Perces in relation-

96

ship than in exemplary conduct, were adept at exchanging.

Although Parrish expected to care for 800 Indians at the year's end, friction with settlers had developed. In July, 1875, the Wallowa country was thrown open to white men. Chief Joseph of the Nez Perces received the shocking news from Lapwai that he was to take his people to the reservation in Idaho near Lewiston. Like a Polish corridor, the Malheur Reserve became a barrier between the northern and southern sections of massive Grant County. Large herds of cattle had to be driven to the Central Pacific in Nevada for shipment. Thousands of horses grazed on ranges. Consequently, streams and pasturage increased in value.

On April 26, Parrish had urged the Office of Indian Affairs that surveyors then running lines of the Malheur Reserve be permitted to include "tributaries" of the North Fork and fix the eastern boundry along the mountain range about six miles east of the Agency. It would avoid future conflict with settlers, closest of whom were 20 miles distant. Agent Linville had fenced in 70 acres, cultivated for the most part, east of the north fork. Indians were digging the ditch there. Too, Egan laid strong claim to his farm along Warm Creek, free of ice the year around.

Proximity of The Dalles Military Wagon Road and the Cascade Mountain Military Road presented a problem as to extent of land grants authorized. On May 13, H. R. Clum, acting commissioner of Indian Affairs, believing that limits of granted lands would not "reach or cover the improvements in question," recommended to the Secretary of the Interior that a request be made of the President for an order to enlarge the area wherein sale to or settlement by the whites would be forbidden. In suggesting the new limits, he excepted "such lands within said boundaries as have passed or may pass to said Wagon Roads; . . ."

An executive order two days later which altered the eastern boundary was followed by a survey which elicited protests from citizens of Willow Creek Valley. They contended that portions of public lands which were improved or being settled by whites were included. Remedial suggestions came from Parrish and the surveyors, leading to correction.

Meanwhile, citizens petitioned for modification of the

reservation's western boundary, to exclude Silvies River Valley and Harney Lake basin. But the Indians still claimed heredi-tary rights. Parrish and Major John Green, commanding Fort Harney, fought successfully for retention of defined limits as they stood after correction of the eastern boundary by presi-dential decree January 28, 1876.

In April, 1876, Parrish reported progress of the Agency school, with the wife of Charles Parrish as teacher and Sarah (Winnemucca) Bartlett as assistant. Sarah gave up the position of interpreter to the returned Jerry Long and, with Annie Parrish, opened school the first of May. She could talk fluently with both Bannocks and Paiutes, overcoming many difficulties, and had a useful knowledge of Spanish. The three-month term of school had an attendance of 40, costing the govern-ment $400.

The boys learned how to farm and the girls acquired ability to cut out, sew, and fit their clothes. The girls also made shirts and dresses for the blind women, of whom there were many. Proper cutting of cloth and rescuing it from bartering prevented waste. About 50 Indians dressed some-what like the whites.

The school system provided for studies in the morning, boys aiding their elders at tasks in the afternoon. A second irrigation ditch was built east of the North Fork. Sagebrush was uprooted on 90 acres which were plowed and harrowed. Another open field below the Agency was enclosed on three sides with a board fence. The reservation had six service employes. Ten deaths and 15 births among the Indians were reported.

The Malheur agent, for the fiscal year ending June 30, had estimated his needs as totaling $83,483, including building and farm requirements. Annual appropriations, notwithstand-ing, decreased. Complaints from critics increased. Charges that Parrish overpaid his employes, that he provided excess food and clothing for Indians under his charge, and that his system of farming for self-sustenance was uneconomical, stirred officials.

W. V. Rinehart, then residing in Los Angeles, was appointed to replace Parrish, who commended him to the wards as a worthy successor. The newcomer took charge July 1. As agent, his postoffice address was Eldorado, and the nearest telegraph office was at Baker City. When the Parrish families departed, Frank Johnson became schoolteacher and his brother, W. W. (Broady) Johnson, was employed as blacksmith.

Rinehart found the lot of the Indians much improved. They had good dress and lodges, with reed matting. Hay and vegetables were plentiful, but a grist mill still a dream. The stock had only low sheds, and employes' quarters were insufficient. Carpenter and blacksmith shops served well. Some Indians did only enough work to get part-rations. Most of them were personally honest, though many liked to gamble and barter with the northern Indians for procurement of horses.

To bring about economy and stability, Rinehart endeavored to apportion supplies only in return for proper amount of labor. This served to keep work-avoiding people at disliked tasks. Pursuance of the regulation and conduct of farming provoked disagreements. Injured pride and an empty hand led to a high degree of puzzlement. Chief Egan and some of his fellows carried their grievances over to the military. Sarah Winnemucca aided them, against Rinehart's wishes to work out a solution among themselves.

The complaints were forwarded from Fort Harney to General Howard's headquarters. The agent discharged Sarah for disobedience to orders, she admitting insurbordination. With what money she had saved, she left her cookstove behind and rode sidesaddle through Fort Harney and Canyon City to John Day Valley. There she did housework on a ranch, selling her mild little bay horse to the Robert E. Damon family of Mt. Vernon, neighbors of William Bonham, imperial driver of 10-horse-mule freighters. Then Sarah earned enough cash to buy a team and wagon, and supposedly to procure a divorce from Lieutenant Bartlett.

In December, 1876, General Howard authorized Major Green to investigate and report on conditions. He also requested informal reports from Rinehart, who complied willingly. Major General Irvin McDowell, commanding the Pacific Military Division, at San Francisco, upon receiving Howard's reports, indorsed the inquiry. Reluctantly, he advised his superiors to forward the information to the Department of the Interior, hoping it would "overlook the matter of form and sanction the course taken in this instance, as nothing is to be done but gain information at the earliest moment."

Without mills to produce lumber and flour, Rinehart found individual farming retarded. He deplored weak support from Congress as an injustice to the wards. Appropriations that totaled $40,000 annually for 1874 and 1875 fell to $25,000 in 1876 and to $20,000 in 1877. Issues of beef and flour cost $13,646 and $6,000 went for employes' salaries in the last year. School ran eight months. Crickets plagued the crops. As a bounty for "cricket scalps" the Indians received an issue of sugar.

Uncertain Chief Winnemucca envisaged independent living in Duck Valley, northern Nevada, where in 1877 a reservation was established for the Western Shoshones. Yet crickets also held sway there.

Counted on June 30, that year, as belonging to Malheur Reservation were 759 Indians. Heads of families, excluding chiefs, numbered 116. Tribal bands, under four chiefs, with the number of family heads, were: Snake (Egan) 31, Paiute (Oits) 25, (Tan-wah-da) 39, (Winnemucca) 21. As head of families, Po-top-tu-ah had the greatest number, 16. Egan's immediate family consisted of 12—five men, five women, and two girls.

At this time the Pacific Northwest frontier developed tense forebodings. Warned in May to leave Wallowa, within a month Joseph had led his people to Idaho, only to rally under War Chief Looking Glass for a memorable struggle. The long trek from White Bird Canyon to northern Montana kept General Howard and his troops afield the rest of the year. Chief Buffalo Horn of the Bannocks led a group of his scouts in Howard's forces for a time, but the Nez Perce campaign aggravated discord of malcontent red and white men.

William M. Turner was appointed by the Department of the Interior as special agent to assist in placing straggling Indians on Malheur Reserve. Ten thousand dollars was appropriated for the purpose. Turner first went with Egan as guide as far east as Boise Valley. Eagle-eye, with a band of Paiutes and Bannocks, Winnemucca and Leggins promised to return.

In Bear Valley and on the reservation's western boundary, Columbias were advised to go northward or seek residence with the Paiutes. Up to January 5, 1878, Turner had brought to Malheur Agency 37 of Winnemucca's followers and 70 Shoshones under Eagle-eye. Rinehart said that 200 of his wards still were adrift.

Chapter XVII

OUTBREAK OF THE BANNOCK WAR, 1878

In November, 1877, an Indian, Tambiago, became enraged at the arrest of a brother who had participated in the wounding of two teamsters as they drove past Fort Hall Agency, Ross Fork, Idaho. Tambiago sought revenge by slaying Alex Rhoden, a young cattle-driver who had not seemingly been involved in the previous shooting. The Indian slayer was duly arrested, tried and sentenced to hang. Although the execution of Tambiago, at the territorial prison in Boise City, did not take place until June 28, 1878, a spirit of hostility among the Bannocks was not allayed.

About 1,500 Indians resided on the Fort Hall Reservation. The Shoshones, who remained peaceful, numbered 900. The Bannocks composed the remainder, of whom 150 were termed "warriors." Generally, they were fairly tall. Buffalo Horn, their leading scout and in his early thirties, was comparatively small. How he and many Bannock scouts rode with troops in trailing the Nez Perce in 1877 is described by Chester Anders Fee:

. . . As the cavalcade approached, the Indians were seen in full regalia on pinto horses decorated as brightly as their riders with skins, fur, feathers and buckskin. Instead of war bonnets, the braves wore on their heads oddly colored horses' tails, trimmed to fit, porcupine skin ornaments, the hair standing erect like a ruff.

In the winter of 1878 troops from Fort Douglas, Utah, were brought to Fort Hall to aid in calming the malcontents. The Bannocks resented imposed restrictions, their discontent smouldering They tried to persuade Western Shoshones of Duck Valley to become their allies, but most of them preferred peace. Other red men on the Klamath, Warm Springs and Umatilla reservations in eastern Oregon were neutral. Fragmentary and roving bands displayed more eagerness for warring.

At the end of May, 1878, Bannocks were stirring trouble

among the Paiutes who then were fishing on the Malheur
River. Fish traps on the main Malheur, some distance above
Westfall's ranch, often yielded large quantities of fish for hosts
and visitors.

Egan and Oits, with Indians of their bands and some Bannocks, invited Sarah Winnemucca to join their parley in a
council-tent at the fishing grounds. They spent two nights
and a day in warm debate over past and present problems.
Egan showed a willingness to join the daughter of aging
Winnemucca in .efforts at peaceful settlement, despite expressed ill feeling toward the Malheur agent. Oits argued for
use of force, recalling days of freedom and plenty on ancient
trails. Bannock John, who had come from Idaho, recited the
plight of imprisoned red men at Fort Hall.

Sarah put in writing the complaints. Egan explained his
inability to read or "what to think," arguing that Sarah be
sent to talk with the Great Father in Washington. The group
obtained her consent to intercede for them if they would
contribute to her expenses. Egan, passing from one Indian to
another, collected a total of twenty-nine dollars and a quarter.

When the council broke up on June 7, Sarah promised to
depart immediately for Elko, Nevada, where she might
consult with influential citizens and officials. On the next
morning, she headed her team toward Silver City, Idaho. A
Mr. Morton and his child, wishing to go to Malheur City,
agreed to pay her a fare of $50.00. Half of this he handed to
her at the start of the trip.

Hoofing of the team and rotation of the wagon wheels in
the pulverized ash of the trail churned billows of dust. It
puzzled the party that the weather-beaten houses along the
road were vacated.

Three days later, as the trio neared Fort Lyon at the eastern
Oregon boundary, a settler met on the road gave the first
information that had been received about the Bannocks
actually being at war. He advised their proceeding at once to
a nearby place popularly known as the Stone House.

Quickly, the team drew to the Stone House. Groups of
volunteer scouts and families of settlers displayed excitement
as they lent ear to one another. News of the death of Buffalo
Horn near the mining village of South Mountain, Idaho,

circulated. George McCutcheon, stage driver, had been killed by Indians and his stage burned between Dry Creek Station and the Owyhee River crossing. Captain Reuben F. Bernard soon was to arrive with troops.

The powder of war became ignited when on May 30 three white herders of Big Camas Prairie, southern Idaho, were attacked suddenly by Indians posing as traders. The trio, two of them wounded, escaped and soon met freighters who aided them. For a long time Bannock leaders had been warning white men to remove cattle and hogs from the camas ground which had been promised the red men in the treaty of 1868. Ostensibly, Buffalo Horn looked upon the new outbreak as convenient for a challenge, for he quickly led the malcontents into plundering. They had camped a month in the lava beds between Big Camas Prairie and the Snake River.

Desire for revolt had been stirred among bands of Indians numbering 1,500 to 2,000. They had an abundance of horses, but lacked adequate preparation and organization. The 700 or 800 warriors had a poor supply of arms and ammunition. The Indians of Malheur Reservation possessed 700 horses, while the Agency had only nine horses, two mules, and 113 head of cattle.

Agent Rinehart reported that the aggregate number of Indians belonging to Malheur Reservation at the time of the Bannock outbreak was 846. Present for one of the last issues of rations, on a Saturday, as usual, were 196 men, 224 women, 156 boys, and 128 girls. Absentees numbered 142.

On June 1, 370 Malheur Indians sought and procured rations at Malheur Reservation, but 46 Bannocks accompanying them were denied. Chief Egan, after making a plea that the visitors be fed, divided his rations with them. The next day runners brought word that the Bannocks had started on the warpath in Idaho. The Malheur Indians fully deserted their reservation the first week of June. Within a short time, most of them had reached the Steens Mountain vicinity, some held there against their wishes.

Of the crisis at the Agency, Mrs. Johnson, wife of the blacksmith there, recalls:

"Old Chief Winnemucca and three other Chiefs had their big talks in my kitchen, as they didn't want the other Indians to hear them. Chief Winnemucca tried to get them not to go on the war path, but couldn't do anything with them. Five days after they went home, they came after their rations, as usual. Egan and all his warriors rode up in front of our house, got off their ponies and shook hands with me. They said they were going hunting and would be back to gather their vegetables. They went twenty miles from there, where they met the Bannocks and had their war dance. The Interpreter sent to Harney for the soldiers. All the women and children packed and we all left for John Day. Some men remained a few days.

Troops of the First United States Cavalry left Fort Boise the night of May 30 to quell the uprising. The 45-year-old Captain Bernard, three years younger than General Howard and with a record of 98 fights, led them. Hurriedly joining him was Orlando (Rube) Robbins of Idaho, leader of citizen scouts throughout the campaign. The hostiles, moving fast, had a fagger's start.

Within a few days after the outbreak, Howard sent orders from Vancouver starting other troop movements. Infantrymen and artillerymen from Forts Vancouver, Canby, Stevens and Townsend went up the Columbia River by boat to Umatilla Landing, to march or ride in wagons on the stage roads. Later, reinforcements from the Departments of Arizona and California (including Nevada) followed the same routes after arrival by ship from San Francisco. Some troops trudged across country from Nevada and Utah.

At Fort Harney were Companies A and K, First Cavalry, commanded by Captains Thomas McGregor and Charles Bendire, respectively, and Company K, Twenty-first Infantry, under Captain George M. Downey. In obedience to Howard's orders of June 3, these units left only a skeletal force at the post as they marched eastward. Afield, infantry and artillery companies seldom mustered more than 20 men, while a company of cavalry averaged about 40 men.

First word of the Bannock insurrection came to Fort Harney June 3, carried from Fort Boise by a one-legged expert horseman. A few days later "Jim" Crowley, stockman of Barren Valley, after warning settlers in the Steens Mountain country, brought Harney troops news of the Bannock-Paiute war alliance. As settlers flocked to the post for protection the post commander made efforts to send a message to General Howard, to be telegraphed from Malheur City.

Most of the 110 miles to Malheur City lay through the forbidding Malheur Reservation, reluctantly vacated by employes. An Indian youth named Savage who worked at the post store agreed to carry the message, but he was fatally injured when thrown from a fractious horse at the start. Sergeant Maurice Fitzgerald, Troop K, First Cavalry, was prevailed upon to be the courier, he having to mount Fandango, a half-broken horse picked for endurance.

Howard arrived at Walla Walla on June 9. There he consulted Colonel Frank Wheaton and, three days later, took personal field command at Fort Boise. Lack of maps added to confusion once the soldiers encountered dim and rugged trails. This situation was deplored by General McDowell, commander of the Military Division of the Pacific.

In advancing westward to join the Paiutes and other malcontents, the Bannocks had raided King Hill Station and Glenns Ferry before crossing the Snake on a ferryboat. On their way into the Bruneau Valley they had killed three white men while trying to keep well ahead of pursuing soldiers.

With 26 mounted and armed volunteers, Captain J. B. Harper rode out from Silver City on June 8 toward Battle Creek. Seven miles from South Mountain, near the eastern boundary of Oregon, they headed into a force of 60 Bannocks led by Buffalo Horn. Hard by the Juniper Mountains, red men and white men faced spontaneous action. Well concealed by rocks and trees, their women and children diverted from the field of possible encounter, the defiant warriors awaited the approach of the enemy.

Bullets and war cries hurled a challenge at Harper's men as they neared. The riding volunteers made sentinel-like targets, but they clung tightly to their mounts to stave off a stampede. Harper gave the command to charge. As the horses leaped into the crossfire of the red men, the whites responded with jerking of triggers.

Volunteers O. H. Purdy and Charles Steuder tumbled from their saddles. Mortally wounded, their hands let slip the reins. Three of their companions fell of injuries at the same time. The loose horses reared and plunged among the other animals.

Yells of the Indians increased in volume while firing from rifles crackled incessantly. The volunteers leaped to the ground to gain better shooting advantage from the wooded and rocky area. But the enemy was too strongly ensconced. Harper ordered a withdrawal and remounting.

Skillfully Buffalo Horn jabbed his horse into a leap toward the retreating whites. His fellow warriors rallied to the assault that might have spelled doom to their foe. A volunteer, however, wheeled and fired at the Bannock leader. Buffalo Horn plunged from the back of his pony. The Indians encircled his body, giving the enemy the chance to escape.

Buffalo Horn soon bled to death from his ugly wound. The Bannocks, warily fearful of being overtaken by the cavalry, hurriedly hid the body of their leader in a ravine. Then, leaving no evidence of this or other loss, they hastily fled.

Colonel F. J. Parker, frontier scout and courier, later wrote from Malheur Crossing how the news of the event was received in the camps of the hostiles. Scalps of the whites were brought in dangling from poles. But they offered little solace. Buffalo Horn's followers lamented fervidly. The warriors, swearing vengeance, urged haste, toward Steens Mountain. They would persuade Paiute War Chief Egan to lead them in a solid front.

Egan, in middle life, became active war chief against his intent. He was cautious while being courageous. He allowed intercessors and friendly white men to escape harm.

Meanwhile, Captain Bernard's Troop G and Robbins' scouts had followed the hostiles to Bruneau Valley, then galloped across sageland toward Jordan Valley. Bernard paused at the Stone House, hastening to interview Sarah. To this man of heavy black beard and soldierly perspicacity, she gave all the information she had gained. She also offered her services to the military for the war's duration.

Bernard promised to telegraph General Howard, then at Fort Boise, as soon as he reached Sheep Ranch. The cavalryman rode on. The wire stretching southward to Nevada had been cut, but a message could be flashed to Boise.

Sarah remained at the Stone House overnight. She greeted, next morning, a quartet of Indians and a white man whom she recognized as friends. They were conveying a message from the commander of Fort McDermitt to the leader of the cavalry in the field. She decided to conduct them to Captain Bernard at once.

Regretfully, Sarah had to part with her team and wagon. She gave a negative reply to Morton when he wished her to accompany him to Silver City and marry him for his daughter's sake. In an overskirt, clinging to a sidesaddle, the Paiute woman joined the four red men in a 30-mile ride, on horseback.

In the evening, they dismounted among the stubble-bearded soldiers who had cheered Bernard as he turned somersaults to prove his athletic fitness. The Indians gave the captain the dispatch and said they had heard that Natchez, like his father, Chief Winnemucca, had placed his life in jeopardy to escape from the hostilities. They would go with Sarah to help all Paiutes who wished to flee from the Bannocks.

Bernard wired Howard that Sarah was in his camp, willing to aid her people. Soldiers fed and cared for the Indian runners and their ponies. Sarah spent the night in a room at the hotel.

In the reply received from the department commander in the morning, he suggested a reward of $500 for Sarah if she succeeded in diverting her kinfolk from the way of war. She and two of the braves, John and George, soon got onto freshly saddled ponies to speed westward to their people. Bernard handed Sarah a hastily scribbled note. It read:

> To all good citizens in the country:—Sarah Winnemucca, with two of her people, goes with a dispatch to her father. If her horses should give out, help her all you can and oblige.
>
>   Captain Bernard.

The chief's daughter displayed her letter to a group of white scouts resting at the crossing of the Owyhee River. They offered a change of horses, and she accepted. Beyond the winding Owyhee, the Paiutes shortly struck the trail of the warring Bannocks.

The trio rode on thirstily until darkness forced a halt. They ate hard bread. The two braves agreed to take turns through the night in watching and sleeping. Sarah slept with her head on her saddle.

The travelers, up with the sun, galloped across Barren Valley. No house rose in view as they neared the ranch of G. B. Crowley. Faint whisps of smoke floated upward from ashes, circled by tracks of Bannocks. A few chickens pecked in the desolate barnyard.

The party then followed the trail that bent toward Steens Mountain, Sarah surmising that her own people were trying to reach Fort McDermitt. At noon, John shot a mountain sheep as it plunged down a steep bench. The animal was skinned and the fresh meat taken along.

About five miles from Juniper Lake, the Paiutes espied two Indians running along a crest. Sarah waved her handkerchief to attract them. When they descended, Sarah recognized one as her brother Lee, who had become the husband of Mattie, small orphaned niece of Chief Egan. Quickly, they were in an embrace.

Lee Winnemucca excitedly told how the Bannock war groups had met his father and his band, had disarmed them and forced them to surrender some horses and blankets. The Paiutes had pitched camp with the Bannocks, and the latter had posted scouts. If Sarah was to effect contact with her father, Lee advised, she would have to unbraid her hair, replace her hat and dress with a blanket, and daub her face with paint.

Hastily, Sarah accomplished the transformation. John and George, after stripping to the waist and smearing paint, concealed their guns and the fresh mutton. On hands and knees, all reached the summit. They looked down upon a spectacle unknown to Steens Mountain since.

More than 300 lodges were pitched below, and a hundred more warriors than there were lodges threshed busily in the trough of Little Valley. Many were riding or catching excited horses, Others, slaughtering beef, wielded knives in dexterous slashing. Blue-gray smoke fluttered from open ears of tepees and, here and there, billowed upward with a pink or rosy tinge where fires in pits or trenches consumed wood as meat was roasted or dried.

The sun sinking fast, Sarah and her party left their near-exhausted horses behind the crest and slid downward. Lee, in a spurt, darted into his father's shelter, then reappeared.

Sarah entered the lodge, to throw herself into the arms of her parent. Of a full circle of people she asked that they go to the lodges of relatives and hurriedly make ready to follow her and Chief Winnemucca to join approaching troops. The majority of their lodges being at one end of the encampment made easier their escape in darkness.

After Chief Winnemucca and his people, by prearrangement, had assembled with horses at Juniper Lake, Sarah advised immediate departure. Hour after hour the Paiutes pushed eastward through the inky night.

At daylight the weary column reached Summit Springs. There the seventy-odd persons rested. Chief Winnemucca wakened Sarah when a Paiute courier brought warning the Bannocks were thinking of overtaking Winnemucca's people.

Sarah, with Mattie, decided to ride on and notify the cavalry of her people's whereabouts. It was June 15 when Sarah ended a ride of 220 miles since leaving the cavalry's campground.

General Howard and officers of his field staff had arrived at Sheep Ranch the previous day. They included Lieutenant C. E. S. Wood, of the Twenty-first Infantry, who acted as aide-de-camp and adjutant general of troops in the field. Howard turned over rescue of Winnemucca and his band to Robbins' scouts. In due course these Paiutes joined Natchez and his followers at Fort McDermitt. Robbins more quickly rejoined Bernard's command. Sarah and Mattie remained with Howard's marching column of troops.

On June 16, at Sheep Ranch, Howard announced his first major campaign plan. He assigned lines of advance to three principal columns with means of communication and supply. By June 18 military units of the Department of the Columbia got into full stride. Howard had 852 men under his command.

First to pursue the enemy, by shortest route, was Captain Bernard with four companies of cavalry, designated as the left column. His Troop G, accompanied by Robbins and his 20 scouts, joined Troops A, F and L of the First Cavalry near the Owyhee crossing.

The center column, under Colonel Cuvier Grover of the First Cavalry, consisting of three cavalry companies commanded by Major George B. Sanford, along with Company F of the Second Infantry, was to march from Boise City by way of Keeney's Ferry.

The remaining right column served as immediate reinforcement for Bernard. Although Major Joseph Stewart of the Fourth Artillery held command of the force, General Howard made arrangements to accompany it with his personal staff. In the group were five companies of the Twenty-first Infantry in addition to two of the artillery, their ways soon to diverge. The advance was to Rinehart's Crossing of the Malheur River to Malheur Reservation.

Meanwhile, scouts of the hostiles had learned of the proximity of marching troops. The warriors turned to veteran Egan, who well knew their weakness against heavily armed and fast-moving troops.

Greatest safety lay in flight, far to the west across Harney Valley. The white soldiers might not pursue so readily into a country where few white settlers ventured. Too, thought Egan, if the Bannocks and Paiutes were forced to fight, they would let the mighty mountains to the north be their protector.

Hastily, the Indians broke down their camps at Steens Mountain. Food, horses and implements of battle they had to have, and the unscrupulous gained by wanton destruction.

The main body of Bannocks and Paiutes passed north of Happy Valley, to cross the Blitzen River at Rock Ford and twist by Weed Lake. It skirted the south shore of Harney Lake and, on its western side, proceeded north to Silver Creek. Pillaging and scouting parties spent wrath in forays. After burning the home of Crowley and his son James, they set afire the unguarded home of G. W. Anderson, in Anderson Valley. Then red men rode into Happy Valley.

The white fugitives at Fort Harney grew restless as days passed without reliable reports of warring Indians. Some began to think the "scare" had been overplayed. "Doc" Kiger had joined Happy Valley neighbors, the Smyths, when they fled to Fort Harney. Then, Doc recalled:

Went to the barracks and . . . they was all gone but 13 soldiers. So they issued us guns, carbines to protect the family, said, "You men will have to protect the families now." So we went out and tried them guns, didn't like the looks of them. It was an old linen cartridge with a lead bullet or slug, one of these old carbines, you know.

You would have to pull up and put in your cartridge, pull up this lever and that would cut the cartridge and then the powder would run out on a pan there and a thing you pulled way back and whis-s-s-s boom she went. Well, we shot at marks and I couldn't hit any. . . . We said we couldn's hit the damned cavalry barn down there. You have got better guns and we want them. He [the man in charge] says, "Yes, we have got better guns." He issued us Springfield rifles with a long copper cartridge, 50 caliber. We took them out and we could shoot pretty good. . . . John Smyth — that is Rye's brother, not his father —and a man by the name of Sam Miller — we kept hearing from over there [toward Happy Valley], men coming in, nobody had seen any Indians. We thought we had better just go back there and get the best of things out of the houses and bring in our horses, back to camp; so we started back. . . .

After riding all night, Doc and his brother accompanied John Smyth and his father, George Smyth, to their homes in Happy Valley. Then Doc accompanied his brother to Diamond Valley. There they met French and a number of his men. None had seen any Indians, and Doc spent the second night at his brother's place.

John Smyth went to the home of his father at fall of darkness. They planned to go back to the fort the next day. Armed well with rifles and ammunition, the Smyths bolted and barred the doors.

At daybreak, from two upstairs windows, they saw a group of Indians piling sagebrush, hay and wood against the house. The ranchers hastily went into action at each window, their gunfire forcing warriors to seek shelter. Soon, however, hostiles succeeded in applying a torch to a huge pile of brush which, in turn, set the dwelling aflame. Rapidly spreading fire and smoke compelled the defenders to seek the ground floor, so thought surviving neighbors. Father and son made a desperate stand at the doorway, but the burning home became a funeral pyre.

On the morning the Smyths met death and the hostiles continued depredations, Doc Kiger was about to go to Happy Valley again. Sylvester Smyth, with a span of horses hitched to the running gear of a wagon, drove up, looking for a "safe location."

They drove on and overtook Sam Miller as they wound up the bluff road leading over to Happy Valley. Miller had seen no Indians, so they proceeded to a wide double-gate which

POKER GAME AT EGAN SALOON, 1882

PETER FRENCH (extreme right) AND BUCKAROOS

Left to right: Bert French, brother of Peter; Charles Wheeler; Jim Brannon; Jack Cooper; Phil Burnhardy; Charles Ward; Kid Hudson; Bill Dyer; Mart Brenton; Abe Hostetter; Johnny Fisher; Boland Fine.

FIRST OFFICIALS OF HARNEY COUNTY, 1889

Back Row, left to right: W. E. Albertson, Assessor; Wm. Miller, Deputy Clerk; Wm. Grace, Clerk; L. B. Baker, School Superintendent; A. A. Cowing, Sheriff.

Front Row, left to right: Thos. H. Roberts, Treasurer; Thos. Shields, Judge; T. B. James, Commissioner; Lytle Howard, Commissioner.

TOWN OF HARNEY IN ITS HEYDAY,

FOURTH OF JULY, 1890

BRANDING

CATTLE BRANDS ON
DOOR OF BLACKSMITH SHOP

CHUCK WAGON

MART BRENTON'S RED FRONT LIVERY STABLE

VOEGTLY BUILDING
IN THE FREIGHT TEAM DAYS

DREWSEY ABOUT 1900

BURNS IN EARLY 1900s

TYPICAL HOMESTEAD CABIN IN HARNEY COUNTY
BEFORE 1900

FAMOUS P RANCH, PETER FRENCH'S HEADQUARTERS

FIRST GARAGE IN HARNEY COUNTY, 1910

PIONEER MOTHER, MRS. JENNIE CLEMENS, DRIVES LAST
SPIKE AS RAILROAD REACHES BURNS,
AUGUST 16, 1924

HARNEY COUNTY'S MODERN COURT HOUSE

FEDERAL BUILDING AT BURNS

spanned a gap between the rimrock and a strong rock fence six feet high. Miller rode ahead, only to rush back with several hostiles in pursuit. In a flash, he and Smyth cut the horses loose from the wagon, to mount them and attain greater speed in flight to Diamond Valley.

The red men fired but missed their targets. Miller reined up, saying, "Boys, I am shot."

Doc said to him, "I guess not."

Miller felt of a small lump on his head, but his hand showed no blood. He gasped, "I guess it must have been that tug that hit me."

The taunting braves had difficulty in opening the gate and the delay gave the ranchers sorely needed gain as they raced downhill. Quickly, they overtook John Witzel who, with George Bollenbaugh, had been separating horses in Diamond Valley. All rushed on to Diamond Ranch. Horses had just been run into a corral preparatory to saddling. French's horse already was saddled.

While Smyth hurriedly related his story, Doc picked out a horse that was "shod all around." French advised his men to choose a good horse for each and let the others go. In a moment he had procured for himself a Springfield rifle and a belt weighty with cartridges.

From the top of a small corral, the irate leader directed the mounting of his force. Besides the pursued men, they included Henry Robie, Sid Thomas, John Dale, Charles Luce, George Bollenbaugh, Joseph and George Hichneedle, Prim Ortego, two Dixon brothers and their Indian hand called Joe, a youthful Taylor, Juniper Jack, buckaroo cook, and a Chinese cook.

As the leading hostiles hove into sight, French coolly stopped them with whizzing bullets. Two dozen red men cautiously sought protection of hillside grass and rocks. French leaped to his horse and rallied his force for the 16-mile race to P Ranch. The cowboys sped up McCoy Creek, led by Witzel.

Gunfire of the hostiles felled Sylvester Smyth's horse. The Chinaman had been slain and as the riderless steed of the cook had galloped ahead, Smyth grasped the dangling rein and, springing upward, rode furiously again.

Maurice Fitzgerald tells of further pursuit: "McCoy Creek was crossed a mile and a half from the ranch, and then the trail led up a very steep and rugged bluff." In a narrow passage at the top, French dismounted and "kept peppering away at the pursuers" until all his men had gained the bench.

In that climb Witzel was shot in the hip and his horse was killed. He, with a wounded buckaroo, escaped with the others, the Indians giving up the chase at this point. The white men, reaching P Ranch, prepared to take women and children to Fort Harney.

French and his party changed horses hurriedly, then headed for the post. The group, going by way of old Camp Wright and through the center of Harney Valley, had ridden between ninety and 100 miles by the time they dismounted at the fort.

D. H. Smyth, Frank Krugsberry and William Barton also had fled from inflamed warriors, to advise settlers. The trio joined a camp of buckaroos at the Malheur Slough, John G. South being their boss. The cowboys hastened to Fort Harney to join volunteers.

South went back to Diamond Ranch and came upon the body of the scalped Chinaman. On the road to P Ranch, he warned Tom Dixon and another man (named Nixon or Harrison), camped near the river. Disdainful of danger, the pair soon met death at the hands of Indians.

The flailing warriors cut across the sand reef dividing Malheur and Harney lakes to go on to Silver Creek and overtake the people under Egan. Forty-five miles west of Fort Harney, they pitched camp in a screened flatland of good grass. For several days raiding parties struck in various directions, committing further spoilation or returning with needful booty. An incursion 30 miles westward to Wagontire Mountain led to the driving of a herd of range cattle into a corral. Slaughter of all the stock there gave rise to the long-lasting name of "Bone Corral."

Meanwhile, Sergeant Fitzgerald had returned to Fort Harney by way of Canyon City. After resting a day, he set out for Malheur City with another dispatch. Agent Rinehart accompanied him, inspecting the abandoned agency in a pause. On the tableland above Bully Creek they met General Howard and his foot troops with a number of two- and four-horse wagons.

On June 20, while marching to Malheur Reservation,

Howard had sent on horseback to Fort Harney his aide, Lieutenant Melville C. Wilkinson, Corporal Moffat and Private Musenheimer, accompanied by Sarah and Mattie Winnemucca as guides. They were to learn if Captain Bernard had been reinforced by troops from the Harney post.

Bernard's four companies and Robbins' scouts, after striking across Barren Valley, camped near Crowley Creek, at a northern spur of Steens Mountain, June 18. Next day they camped near or on the southeast section of Malheur Reservation. By June 21, Bernard's men reached Fort Harney, entering the Harney Valley only a day or two after the pillaging of Steens Mountain settlements.

French and his volunteers were on hand to relate their experiences and to offer assistance. Company K of the Twenty-first Infantry had to guard the post. After drawing rations, the other soldiers followed the scouts and volunteers in pursuit of the enemy. There was some backtracking. From The Narrows the trail led to the OO Ranch and up Silver Creek, a trail quite betraying.

The strength of Bernard's four companies, if each averaged 40 men, was 160 cavalrymen. Robbins' 20 scouts now were assisted by a few less than that number who volunteered at Fort Harney.

In the late afternoon of Saturday, June 22, Robbins and his scouts came upon the distinctly fresh trail of the hostiles. The leader, with caution, climbed a promontory. His eye quickly caught a view of a camp lying in the jaws of Silver Creek, a few miles south of old Camp Currey. He advised his sweating party to dismount and rest while waiting for Bernard.

With thud of hoofs, slapping of horses and exchange of banter, the column of cavalry, followed by its dust-swallowing pack-train, overtook the huddled scouts long after darkness fell. While troopers and some of the citizens napped in un-rolled blankets beneath a star-blinking sky, Robbins led his scouts forward along the broad track.

Particularly pleased was W. A. Goulder, reporter for the *Idaho Statesman* of Boise City. He had come far to tell of the impending engagement.

When a sheltered position near the red men had been gained, Robbins ventured alone to a shadowed spot near the natural stronghold. The camp of the Indians, screened by black lava walls and dense willows, was calm. Unguarded stock grazed at will. Surprisingly strong, the enemy numbered between 1,200 and 2,000 persons, 700 of them capable of fighting.

Not since the June day two years previously, when Custer's force had been wiped out, had so many hostiles assembled for war. The Idahoan observed approaches that could be used, crept back to his men, and reported to Bernard.

Chapter XVIII

FIGHTING AT SILVER CREEK AND NORTHWARD

In the early hours of the Sabbath, June 23, as his officers sprang into council, Bernard dispatched a courier to tell Howard the war party of Bannocks and Paiutes had been located. Bernard yearned for action and, taking into consideration the force of the foe, he and Robbins stressed the necessity of surprise.

The resultant plan was for Bernard's troops to enter the canyon below the red people's camp. Simultaneously, the men under Robbins and French would plunge into the fight from a position upstream. The assault from both directions was to be made before the camp came to full life.

Aroused, and with dawn about to break, the cavalrymen guided their horses in a wide arc, gaining the banks of Silver Creek at an unalarming distance below the red men's lodges. A few scouts, in advance, led them to a jump-off position. The Indian camp stirred but faintly. Women and children prepared for breakfast. Men who had slept under shelter or in the open spaces rose to tend horses or to search for supplies. Dogs and puppies, curled beside tepees, raised their noses.

Robbins successfully assembled his men among the lofty willows and coppice well above the line of lodges. Then the group lunged toward the shelters, the loud explosion of repeating rifles and weighty revolvers causing the red people to tear out of their wickiups in a sudden rush. All was confusion. When the first shot had been fired, the cavalrymen also leaped forward, with hurried preparation.

Bernard, shrewd Indian fighter, had, as at other times, so arranged his command as to belie its actual power. Too, he foresaw the importance of keeping his column in contact with the department commander and forces deployed on flanks and to the rear. Only three of the four companies were to begin the charge.

Upon initiation of the battle by the scouts, the cavalry advanced in columns of fours. Above bushes in the valley, a

117

dozen war chiefs could be seen riding in a circle, rallying the warriors. The troopers were to charge as foragers, with pistols. When they had cantered to within a few hundred yards of red men threshing downstream, the usually taciturn Bernard voiced a cautious command:

"Forward — not too fast!"

The bugler caught his cue and the shrill notes of the charge rose in the air. Rocky bluffs hurled back the echoes. Half-naked warriors, though taken by surprise, speedily threw out a body of skirmishers. These were mostly chiefs and sub-chiefs, and they bore the brunt of the fighting.

Many of the Indians recoiled from the combined onslaught. They forsook their village and fortified themselves on bluffs and behind brush and boulders. A shot from the bushes wounded mortally Corporal Peter F. Grantzinger.

Mixed groups of soldiers and scouts, recklessly facing close firing from Winchester rifles with which select warriors were armed, charged twice through the camp. Carbine and six-shooter blazed alternately, stone walls echoing their metallic biting along with war whoops and blasphemy. Women and children scurried to bluffs and beyond. Some of their fathers and brothers already lay dead in the grass. Bold youths like Laughing Jake and Pointer fought on in spite of hurts that bled.   ,

Hand-to-hand encounters made for isolated display of valor. Sergeant George H. Richmond, of McGregor's troop, had his gun knocked from his hand as husky Bearskin, subchief of the Bannocks, raised his rifle to fire at close range. The sergeant whipped out his pistol and, leaning over the neck of his horse, pulled the trigger. Bearskin, severely wounded, sank to the mud but comrades rescued him.

At the height of the battle, Chief Egan and Robbins dashed at each other. The Paiute veteran used the far side of his pony for a shield. Firing from the withers, he sped several bullets in an effort to unseat the well-known scout. The lead tore through the clothing of the white challenger. Robbins, half-standing in his stirrup to overcome the excitability of his mount, took steadier aim. A bullet smashed through Egan's wrist.

The chief, in a leaning position, tumbled to the ground.

While he struggled to his feet he received a bullet in his breast, another trigger-pull by Robbins. A shot crippled the scout leader's horse, and French rushed in to rescue the rider. With unsteady aim, another scout wounded Egan in the right groin. As the chief fell to earth again, red men encircled him. They carried their fallen leader through the willows to safety.

Yells of savagery ascended from hundreds of throats. In bitter answer to the defiant whites, the Indians loosed a deadly and repetitive fire from behind rocks and humps of hazardous slopes. Their comrades in bushes held closer aim, Private E. F. Albrecht of Troop A felt a trickle of blood on his knee-cap. A bullet broke the crossbar of his horse's bridle. His company and the others felt sharper ripping of clothes and saw vacancies in some saddles. Captain McGregor had "Cease Firing" and "Recall" sounded, and he ordered Lieutenant Frank A. Edwards to bring back his men through the hail of bullets.

The men formed a skirmish line, guarding Grantzinger until he died. Bernard restrained his full command from carrying the fight through a fire too withering. Ammunition for the cavalry was running low and replenishing had been delayed. From the torn and abandoned camp the soldiers and scouts seized an abundance of property, including money and ammunition. An aged and blind Indian woman, unharmed during the melee, went across the creek to the east bluffs with the soldiers, their dead and wounded.

At a shielding distance, men unsaddled their horses and tied them to a picket line. Then they hastily aided in gathering loose rocks to construct low and semicircular breastworks. The troops stood their ground as they counted the toll.

Three were killed: Joseph Schultz, saddler in Company F; Grantzinger of Company A; and William Meyers, an enrolled scout from Idaho. Private William M. Marriott, blacksmith in Company F, bore bravely a mortal injury. Two men, Privates George Foster of Company L and Christian Hanson of Company G, sustained serious wounds. About fifteen horses had been lost.

The Indians, bearing off their wounded and some of the slain, left the troopers guessing, customarily, their losses. About ten red men "positively" were reported as killed, estimates mounting to fifty. Despite their being securely ensconced across Silver Creek and realizing they had overwhelming force, the bronzed warriors made no move to crush their foe.

Egan was borne around the protective shoulder of a bluff, his limp form placed upon a bed of brush covered with his favorite red blanket. Skilled, dark leathery hands whittled splints, and wounds were cleansed and treated. Then two braves tied Egan's splintered wrist into a rigid cast.

Of the hundreds in the war assemblage the Indians had to rely chiefly upon a dozen of them. The foremost were Oits, his son-in-law, Surger, Paddy Cap, Bannock Joe, Boss, Big John, Beads, Charley, Eagle-eye, D. E. Johnson, the wounded Bearskin and Laughing Jake.

At night sagebrush was piled high and set afire to make the soldiers believe the Indians were standing their ground. The troopers expected an attack at daybreak, and they burrowed shallowly.

At dawn, with the enemy fled, the soldiers buried Grantzinger in a martial ceremony. Bernard's dispatch to General Howard said, in part, concerning the events:

> . . . Conduct of officers and men deserves commendation; all behaved splendidly. . . . Indian losses unknown, . . . Shall locate their camp again to-night. They are moving leisurely, burdened with stock and many wounded.

General Howard had entered Malheur Agency on the 23rd, detaching part of Captain Melville C. Cochran's company of infantry to guard against pillaging there, and had left on the same day for Fort Harney. Howard and his staff arrived at Fort Harney at 11 a.m. of the 24th. Then the general and Lieutenant Wood hastened to Sage Hen Spring where they overtook Captain Evan Miles and his two infantry companies which had advanced from the post.

Under escort to the rear, the aged Bannock woman captured at Silver Creek sobbed out the story of her people's misfortune to Sarah and Mattie Winnemucca. Sarah retold this to Howard, emphasizing the opinion the hostiles were endeavoring to reach the Umatilla Reservation.

The general, on the morning of the 25th, arrived at the

scene of Bernard's fight, saying, "Lieutenant Wood delays to make a topographical sketch, while I go on to Bernard's camp, ten miles beyond." At Cecil's ranch, site of Camp Currey, where Howard joined Bernard the same morning, the general summed up the situation in a telegram sent to division head-quarters. In part, he said: "I am of opinion hostiles intend to move north, following up Silver Creek, striking nearest route to south fork John Day River, then up Granite to Bridge Creek, to join with such discontented Cayuses and other Indians that may be in that vicinity."

Howard, by his aide, Lieutenant Wilkinson, sent "letters and instructions" on the 26th to Colonel Wheaton at Walla Walla and to department headquarters. They revealed Howard's plans in distributing troops, emphasizing "the General expects the enemy to be held in check and not permitted to pass beyond the Columbia River country," with more troops to be brought from Camp McDermitt, "by rail and steamer, to Wallula, should you find the enemy coming northward in force."

At dawn of the 27th, Howard's troops started on a zigzag course across the Blue Mountains. They marched thirty miles in an all-day rain. The wagons, some pulled by oxen, after starting at 6 o'clock the next morning, made only thirteen miles by 8 o'clock that night. Part of Bernard's cavalry advanced farther.

Almost rationless, the cavalrymen left Howard's slower force behind June 29th. By day-and-night plunging, during which thirty-four horses gave out, they conquered 112 miles. At midnight of the 30th they camped near the John Day River east of Dayville, to await delivery of rations from Canyon City.

On Sunday, June 30, the soldiery plodded for a time between walls that confined roaring, icy waters of the South Fork of the John Day. When an impassable narrow barrier compelled them to withdraw from the chasm, the wagons creaked up a high ridge.

Two days later the pursuers marched thirty miles down the course of the South Fork. At Stewart's ranch, on Murderer's Creek, they saw evidence of a skirmish. Two mounds marked the burial by scouts of the bodies of two young men, herders of sheep. They were nephews of James Small, whose ranch house had been pillaged.

The cavalry, having drawn rations again, advanced through Fox Valley, and camped in Long Creek Valley where they found settlers in a stockade July 3. That day, Howard's infantry camped in John Day Valley, near the mouth of the South Fork. Pack mules, brought by way of Canyon City, replaced the wagon train.

The skirmish at Murderer's Creek had initiated a running fight participated in by volunteers who on the morning of June 29 had been searching the country west of Canyon City for hostiles. Mounted on ranch horses and led by James Clark, the group of about fifteen white men encountered fifty-odd red men who rode ahead of the main body of warriors. The advantage held by the Indians compelled the volunteers to flee to natural covering afforded by the canyon of the South Fork. While in flight, Oliver Aldrich received a fatal shot in the head. W. L. Burnham and Milton Andross, though injured, kept up with their fellow skirmishers. Three other volunteers escaped afoot after losing their horses. Several Indians were reported as wounded or slain.

Meanwhile, on the morning of the 30th, another group of volunteers of about the same number as the first had assembled at the Cummins' ranch. These men had elected J. Cummins as their leader and had exchanged fire with parties of hostiles who lurked in nearby hills. Nick Thornton and E. Shultz were wounded.

From the business section of Canyon City the citizens eyed yawning entrances to mines that had been tunneled in the mountainside. These diggings provided shelter for more than a hundred families as rumors flew thick and fast that vengeful Bannocks and Paiutes were near the settlement.

Lieutenant William C. Brown, on July 1, left his pack train, guarded by eight cavalrymen, on the town's outskirts. Accompanied by an orderly, he went into the town. Cavalryman Brown, noting the confusion, pondered the matter of recruiting volunteers to lead in an exploration of the flaming territory. He started an inquiry, quickly interrupted by a loud shout:

"Here they come! Here they come! The Indians are coming right down the road!"

Phil Metschan, the merchant, needing a shave badly, could not persuade his barber to complete the task he had started. And Metschan grew a heavier beard. Many years later, Brown wrote:

> . . . Pandemonium had broken loose. Men were yelling; dogs barking; women and children screaming; one woman was running wildly down the street with her luxuriant tresses streaming in the wind — women in those days didn't wear their hair bobbed! Hurrying to where I could see the cause of the tumult, I discovered that in my absence the chief packer had concluded to bring the train on into town, either for safety or to get a glass of beer — perhaps both. My train had been mistaken for an onslaught of the hostiles. . . .

Depredating red men did not approach the town. They hurriedly rejoined the main group which was eager to push on and augment their numbers. Moreover, the troops followed too closely. The flight in John Day Valley continued with only minor interruptions.

As the hostiles left Grant County and continued their retreat toward the Columbia River their numbers swelled. Those who joined in depredations represented malcontents from bands of Columbia Indians, some Lemhis, Shoshones, and others.

When the enemy headed toward the reservation of the neutral Umatillas, the state of alarm increased in the whole of eastern Oregon sloping to the turbulent Columbia. Volunteer groups assembled hastily. Settlers sought refuge in Pendleton, Umatilla, Heppner, Weston, Milton, Wallula, and Walla Walla, where defenses were organized. In occasional forays, red warriors dealt damage and death to cattlemen and sheepmen, and fought volunteers.

The cavalry, at the battle of Birch Creek, near Pilot Rock, on July 8 hurled backward the massed Indians, driving them from heights not easily ascended. The Indian fighters retreated toward the Wallowa country, to unite with their women and children who had been shunted from the battlefield.

Meanwhile, Governor S. F. Chadwick of Oregon and Elisha P. Ferry, governor of Washington Territory, had arrived in eastern Oregon aboard armed steamers. On the day of Howard's success at Birch Creek, well-manned boats aided in dispersing all but small parties of red men who attempted to cross the Columbia River.

The main body of hostiles swung back from flight, some to wreak death or injury upon surprised settlers. On July 13th, Captain Evan Miles, with a mixed force of artillery, infantry and volunteers, repulsed and scattered the Bannocks and Paiutes near the Umatilla Agency.

Umatilla headmen conferred with Miles during the night. They received his consent to ally themselves with the whites in chasing the foe, but they started on the trail so quickly the captain was unaware of their immediate intentions.

On July 15, about eighty Umatilla red men came upon Egan and some of his followers. The place of meeting, supposedly designated by Umapine, Umatilla chief, and the hostiles as a friendly rendezvous, was said to be two miles southeast of Meacham Station. In the course of the meeting sudden fire from betrayers brought death to Egan and a few of his partisans.

L. V. McWhorter, a highly respected authority on Indians of the Pacific Northwest, asserted: "Umapine, Umatilla chief, did not kill Egan, according to a Rock Creek Indian woman who knew the circumstances first hand. It was Chief Walsac and band of his own tribe, who were employed by Umapine to do the treacherous deed. Umapine did not want to do it because 'they' (Egan and Umapine) were of the same tribe, speaking the same language."

Near Emigrant Springs on the 15th, Lieutenant Brown saw Egan's head brought into camp in a gunnysack, and Dr. J. A. Fitzgerald, army surgeon, identified it. The battle chief, at the time of his death. was nursing injuries previously received—bullet wounds in the wrist, breast and groin.

The different bands of red people, now divested of capable guidance, and impoverished through losses incurred in their long trek, had little else ahead but further wandering, and then surrender. Yet a few more clashes marked the flight of some to and across the Snake River while the majority postponed submission by seeking the isolation of rough wastes to the south.

Chapter XIX

FAREWELL TO MALHEUR

PAIUTES DRIFTED toward Malheur Reservation. Most Bannocks endeavored to reach their allotted home in southeastern Idaho, but some escaped to the region of Yellowstone Park. More depredations and killings were added to the war's score.

On August 12, 1878, Medicine Man Oits, with a group of sixty disillusioned hostiles, surrendered at Malheur Agency. Soon these and scores of others were conducted to Fort Harney, made the central depot in Oregon.

Paiutes who had refused to joint in the far-flung conflict found refuge in southern Oregon or at the military posts in northern Nevada and California. About 300 Indians, including Chief Winnemucca's band, had been camping at Fort McDermitt since June. Chief Leggins, a subleader, also had tried to keep a goodly number off paths of war. On July 8, Chief Ochoco and five of his fellows had been welcomed at Camp Bidwell. Ochoco's band at the California post had increased to 150 Indians.

At the end of September news came that the white man's government had decided to send all Malheur Paiutes back to their reservation. Sarah Winnemucca was asked to go to Fort McDermitt with troops to bring some of the bands back to Oregon. On this journey, as on a few other occasions during the campaign, Sarah enjoyed the kind attentions of a white soldier, Corporal Lewis A. Hopkins of Troop A, First Cavalry. From the East, he was rounding out a dozen years of army service on the frontier. The courtship led, finally, to their marriage.

At Fort McDermitt arrangements were made that numbers of the immediate bands of Chief Winnemucca and Natchez would not be removed at that time. The remainder, reluctantly, went to Fort Harney. Over these, Leggins was chief.

Until the captured malcontents were properly disseminated by the Department of the Interior, they remained under military care. Mingled fears and weighing of justice went in un-

certain step. Of forty soldiers and civilians killed in the uprising, thirty-one were civilians. Fifteen soldiers survived
serious wounds. About eighty Indians had been slain. The cost
of the war, including conduct of the military establishments
in 1878, totaled $556,636.

The Malheur Agency was in a state of deterioration. Rinehart, whose resignation as agent had been accepted in the
summer of 1878, was advised to stay on until naming of a
successor. On August 13, he received instructions to re-establish the agency. A small group of employes stacked hay for
winter. Rinehart, for months, searched diligently for scattered
property. He found evidence against offenders, but little
material was recovered.

Within a month after Chief Leggins arrived at Fort Harney,
the Indian men were fitted in odd sizes of soldier's shirts,
coats, trousers and shoes. The women grumbled, because
there was no calico for dresses. Yet of food there was plenty,
some captives suffering from excessive eating.

As new days and new snows piled one upon the other, the
Paiutes kept asking: "When is our white leader at the Agency
to send for us?"

In November, 1878, General Howard received definite
word from government authorities as to the disposal of 543
Bannock and Paiute prisoners who were at Fort Harney. As
punishment, they were to be taken, at a convenient time, to
the Yakima Reservation, 350 miles north. A copy of the order
was sent to Captain Cochran, commanding officer at the Malheur Reservation post, who broke the news to Sarah and
Mattie.

The Paiute women were stunned, as were 191 Indians they
had aided Leggins in bringing from Fort McDermitt October
10. Sarah asked the captain to intervene on their behalf. Although they had been reluctant to leave Nevada, they preferred to go back to Malheur Agency rather than to a region
foreign to them. Agent Rinehart deplored the removal, estimated to cost $47,000, in the dead of winter. Cochran prom-
ised all possible help in adjustment.

But the commander of a post, isolated in a vast and barren
area swept by icy winds which cut the traveler with sagittal
sharpness, could do little for others than his soldiers. A chain

guard circled the Indian camp, permitting only women to go in or out. Broady Johnson, the agency blacksmith, had moved to the fort, and his anvil rang as he fashioned iron shackles for chief culprits. It was not yet certain that Leggins and his band would have to depart with the others.

In succeeding nights prisoners tried to escape. But the soldiers received cooperation from Leggins, Sarah, Mattie and Lee in overtaking them. On one hurried flight of several women, Mattie was thrown from her pursuing pony. The fall knocked her unconscious and the mishap left her in a weakened condition from which she was not to recover.

In the first week of the new year, 1879, preparations for the exodus were complete and the journey to Yakima was begun. Half a hundred wagons, with heavily clothed settlers in the drivers' seats, were filled with Indian men, women and children. They sat on hay and furs, tarpaulins covering the wagons. Two companies of cavalry under Captain W. H. Winters, acting as escort, lengthened the train with their mounts and supply wagons. Leggins and his band, after seeing them off, returned to their lodges with a mixed feeling of remorse and thankfulness. Thermometers registered near zero.

Sarah preferred to ride her horse, Meride. Against the weather she wore a fur hood pulled well over her ears. The long braids of her hair fell inside a thick, loose overcoat which met the top of overshoes covered with fur. Her gloves also were of dressed pelt. She had seen to it that Mattie, lying painfully ill in a jolting wagon, had likewise been clothed warmly. They were more fortunate than the blanketed majority of red people.

At Canyon City, Captain Winters received a dispatch instructing him that Leggins' band also should be conducted to Washington Territory. A courier sped back to Fort Harney to make up a wagon train for the chafing Paiutes. When Leggins' band arrived to swell the numbers to several hundred, Sarah read regretfully the piercing aggrievement as snow whirled heavily about them.

At last the wagons rolled into The Dalles and they were ferried across the Columbia River. More snowstorms defied them in final laps. Two children were born on the trek. One baby died at birth, the mother surviving only for another day. Two more children failed to reach their destination. All were buried in roadside graves dug and chopped in granite-like earth.

The spiritless caravan neared Toppenish at the end of January, going into a temporary camp about thirty miles from the agency headquarters. Agent James H. Wilbur and the Yakima chief came to extend their greetings. The wagon-drivers returned to Oregon, replaced by those of Yakima red men.

Soon they proceeded toward Fort Simcoe, near by. They battled ice in crossing Toppenish Creek. A huge shed of poles and wide boards became the temporary shelter of the charges who were to be kept separated from the other reservation Indians.

The transplanted red men received a supply of army clothes. They had the privilege of caring for a goodly number of horses, to be used in farming plots of ground. By spring all the Paiutes were more properly clothed, ready for work, but they did not find happiness with their neighbors. The Yakimas seemed to fare much better than did they.

At the end of May, 1879, Sarah and Lee sat beside Mattie as they watched her life ebb on a last tide. Before the coming of another winter a score of Paiutes were buried in the strange land.

Besides the people placed under Agent Wilbur, there were about 340 Indians who belonged on Malheur Reservation. They included 139 Weisers, former hostiles among them seen at times in the vicinity of the Agency, and a few of them hiding in Salmon River mountains in Idaho. Ochoco's band straggled around Fort Bidwell, while Winnemucca's people remained near Fort McDermitt and along the Humboldt River.

More than a year after the outbreak of war, no Indians had yielded to the government's desire that they settle upon the vacant Malheur reserve. Influential efforts were made for its abolishment. The public press reported General Howard as in agreement with opinion that "the Malheur Reservation must and shall be broken up."

In the summer of 1879 Agent Rinehart went to Fort Mc-

Dermitt to interview tribal heads. Winnemucca and Ochoco were not unhappy to have Oits kept at Yakima, but they urged strongly the return of Leggins and his people. Winnemucca made this a contingency for his own and others' return to Malheur. The treatment was unjust and it bred fears and doubts in all. Rinehart, promising to place the matter before his superiors, engaged Natchez and Jerry Long, interpreter, to round up the people of Winnemucca and Ochoco. They failed in this objective.

Such conditions were hastily weighed by some stockmen and settlers. They had taken their herds onto the reserve and had occupied portions of the best meadow lands. The military at Fort Harney had been hesitant in following orders to remove all trespassers from Malheur Reservation.

In his annual report of August 15, 1879, Rinehart set forth his belief that the reservation should be discontinued. Oregon, he declared, had too many agencies, "more than are receiving decent support." Notwithstanding the perplexities, in 1879 an appropriation of $20,000 was forthcoming for Indians of the reservation, while it was thought unsafe to have former hostiles return.

At the year's end Sarah Winnemucca, after aiding Agent Wilbur in the rehabilitation on the Washington reservation, visited briefly at Vancouver. From there she sailed for San Francisco, to lecture on behalf of the unfortunate Paiutes. On the platforms of halls, dressed in her native costume and gifted with eloquence and fervency in speech, she attracted no little attention and aid.

Early in 1880 Sarah, her father and two other Indian leaders boarded a train to Washington, there to interview high officials. They met President Rutherford B. Hayes in the White House. They elicited certain promises from the Department of the Interior: All Paiutes "heretofore entitled to live on the Malheur reservation" could return there, "each head of a family and each adult male" to be allotted 160 acres of land "to cultivate for their own benefit." No compulsion rested on Paiutes at Yakima or elsewhere to seek the right.

Sarah, again appointed as interpreter for Malheur Agency and promised an annual salary of $420, went in the spring to Yakima to persuade her people to return to the Oregon lands.

They were to procure their own transportation. Unhappily, friction resurged among authorities, some favoring departure of the Paiutes, others opposing it.

Shortly after her futile errand, Sarah was appointed interpreter and teacher for Indian prisoners transferred to Vancouver Barracks. And, at last, she received $500 for her services in the Bannock War.

Rinehart reported, October 14 of that year, that the storeroom and schoolhouse at Malheur Agency were filled with supplies serving no useful purpose. The commissioner of Indian affairs became convinced it was best to discontinue the agency. Proceeds from sale of the land, it was thought, could be used for the benefit of the Indians.

Oregon's chapters of Indian hostilities were forever sealed. Fort Harney was abandoned June 13, 1880. Company H, Twenty-first U. S. Infantry, the last of its units, hauled down the Stars and Stripes from a tall flagstaff on the parade ground, flown there for thirteen years.

Stores of the post were disposed of by transfer to other military stations or sold at auction. Buildings, for the time being, remained intact on the reserved half section of land.

Permanent peace had come to the Harney region.

Chapter XX

POSTWAR ADJUSTMENT

ALTHOUGH THERE WAS NO marked upsurge in the population of the Harney country until after the turn of the eighties, a telling number of new families gained footholds when came security. The influence of the military and Indian affairs officials dwindled. Settlers, especially those along the Silvies River, formed closer ties of mutual aid. Their purposes gave note to embryonic communities. Commercial needs had to be ' supplied more readily. Still, a market for their principal products was no nearer than the county seat of Canyon City. Barter was limited.

Increased attention was given to obtaining better roads. Rights to good land held by the Willamette Valley and Cascade Mountain Wagon Road Company were questioned by citizens. In March, 1878, they complained to the Secretary of the Interior that the road had not been constructed in accordance with provisions of the original act. The department appointed a special agent to make a report. He reported in October, 1880, the government later suing for cancellation of patents. The case, however, lingered in the courts for twelve years.

The telegraph had become commonplace in Oregon by 1878, when Portland got its first telephone exchange. It was not until the mid-eighties that the telephone became handy over a fair part of the state. Pendleton was not to acquire an exchange until 1889, with Baker City waiting until 1898, then to connect with Canyon City.

Because of uncertain economic conditions, men and families came into Grant County's lower area. A few moved out after trials. Everybody talked of horses and cattle and sheep. Indians had taken some while abandoning a few, picked up and used by ranchers.

There was the case of three self-styled heroes coming up from Linkville in August, 1878, to help win the war. Armed and dressed as dashing scouts, they identified themselves as

131

Rattlesnake Jack, Arizona Sam and Texas Dick. The so-called bad men hit upon the trail of retreating hostiles on the middle fork of the John Day River, attacking two aged Indian women. They manufactured three or four scalps to display in Canyon City and at Fort Harney. After being treated as heroes, they headed for Steens Mountain.

Within a short time, Grant County's sheriff received a telegram from the sheriff at Winnemucca, Nevada, asking that a requisition from the governor of Oregon to the governor of Nevada be obtained for the return to Oregon of one Rattlesnake Jack. The bad man was held for theft of 150 head of horses owned by Peter French. His two companions had fled to parts unknown.

Maurice Fitzgerald of Fort Harney was appointed state agent to bring back the accused desperado. Accompanied by John Riggs, Fitzgerald rode in a two-horse spring wagon to Winnemucca, a week's trip. The main-line train took them to Reno, connected with Carson City, the state capital, by a narrow-gauge railroad. Sheriff Lamb of Washoe County, disclosing an alarming record of the prisoner, queried Fitzgerald as to plans for his safe conduct to Canyon City. Oregon's agent related:

. . . I told him exactly how I intended keeping him handcuffed most of the time and always at night. He said, "You never can get that bird to Canyon City with handcuffs. He can slip them off as easy as a glove, having a remarkably small hand." I told him that was all the Sheriff gave me. He kept silent for some time, then said, "If you'll promise faithfully that you'll return it to me after you get to Canyon City, I'll let you have something to put on his leg that will hold him solid as long as you hold the key. It is a recent invention known as the Oregon Boot." I had come from Oregon, but had never even heard of it. It was solid chilled steel, in two parts, that could be put together on the leg and locked. It weighed fifteen pounds. I am satisfied that I never could have taken him to Canyon City were it not for that "Oregon Boot."

The prisoner waited in Canyon City's jail two months for his trial in circuit court. He was convicted of stealing horses, but he received a light sentence. Seemingly, members of the jury had been influenced by a feeling of sympathy for the man's "poor old father," who came across the Cascades to ask indulgence of farmers of the John Day Valley.

At this time wire fencing began replacing lumber in the enclosure of large fields. The section of land boarded in by Catlow stood out as a final reminder of the change. Catlow, now well advanced with his herds, secured Dave Shirk as manager of the property. Youths like Martin H. Brenton, native of England, yielded to the lure of Oregon's ranges. Just out of his teens, in 1878, he was on the fringe of hostilities. From Catlow Valley he drove horses back to northern Nevada, where N. H. A. (Hock) Mason was the towering figure in the cattle business. Brenton delayed his return two years.

The Hutton family soon settled in the region of Wagontire Mountain. Near them, at the "Gap", planning for stability, was William Walter Brown who, it is said, had graduated from San Jose Normal School and had tried teaching school. He had two brothers with him. Of the man who became a legendary figure of the range, former Governor Oswald West says:

Wm. W. ("Bill") Brown was born at Kenosha, Wisconsin, July 15, 1855, and with his parents, reached Oregon in 1869 — the family making settlement at Mt. Pleasant, near Oregon City.

Along in the late seventies, Bill and his brothers, George and Robert, decided to look over the opportunities offered by California — traveling, no doubt, the Central Oregon route which afforded them an opportunity to note the great expanse of open range with its lush native grasses — a stockman's paradise.

Not finding California to their liking, the Brown brothers returned to Oregon and made homestead entries in Central Oregon, near Wagontire mountain. At first, they took to sheep, grazing them in three counties — Harney, Crook and Lake. Within a few years, Bill had acquired the interests of his brothers and, to save expenses, did his own herding — fostering a band in excess of 3000 head.

Families increased in Silver Creek Valley and elsewhere. Robert J. Williams, born in Arkansas and later elected commissioner and judge of Harney County, settled on Silver Creek, thirty miles west of Burns, in 1881. He told Fred Lockley of *The Oregon Journal*:

I came to Harney County with my grandfather, my half-brother Tom, my stepfather's nephew, William Dodson, and Simon Lewis, J. C. Garrett and Thomas Jefferson Shields. We brought 330 dairy cows, worth $12 a head. I took a preemption claim, as did Tom Dodson. Shields and Garrett took homesteads. . . . I was married on January 2, 1884, to Emma Garrett, daughter of my partner, J. C. Garrett.

Shields, a native of Missouri, migrated to the Willamette Valley with his parents in 1852. He married Julia Garrett at Lakeview in 1880, they subsequently coming to Silver Creek. Mrs. Shields, whose husband became first county judge of Harney, relates:

At that time only five families lived in Silver Creek Valley — two Baker families, Cecils, Fred Oakermans, John Wilson — who remained for some time. We got mail at first, once a month, from Fort Harney, by Mr. Baker. About 1883 we got our mail at Evergreen postoffice and in 1884 started getting it at Riley on the Oakerman ranch. Most of our supplies at first came from Lakeview and Surprise Valley. We took 400 pounds of butter in kegs to Canyon City and sold it at 40 cents a pound to miners. We got logs from the hills and, like most settlers, built log houses of two rooms. Our flooring came from a mill near Fort Harney.

It was about 1880 that a postoffice was established at Egan (named for Chief Egan) by Mons Curry in his little store and saloon. Byron Terrill was a partner of Curry's. Another postoffice was placed, about the same time, in the ranch home of Rufus Witzel at Evergreen, thirty-five miles west of Egan. Tom O'Keefe carried the mail over the route between Prineville and Canyon City.

Travelers increased along road or trail.

The first business house in what is now Burns stood out of the sagebrush in the fall of 1878. Little more than a shack, it was built by Jim and Joe Fitzgerald, who came from Goose Lake with two barrels of whiskey and stocked a few staple goods. The liquid refreshments sold most readily. The winter, however, was abrasive. In the spring the water formed a lake from Fort Harney to within jumping distance of the new enterprise, at or near the site for the Burns Hotel. The Fitzgeralds sold out to a Mr. Josephson.

Within a brief time, William Curry bought Josephson's

stock. He and his brother, Mons, moved it to their home ranch, naming the location Egan. The new store, on higher ground adjacent to the future Hines, attracted more settlers than wayfarers.

New settlers as well as older ones sought further progress for their children's schooling. Minutes for District 13 of the Silvies region in 1879 recorded that a site selected for a schoolhouse was "at bunch of willows on the North side of the Harney Road, about one mile from McLeod's Bridge." Miss M. J. Forrester earned $60 for teaching six weeks. In 1880 the school site was abandoned in favor of a new site at Miller's Cove. The first pupils at Miller's Cove assembled in a house bought from Thomas Whiting for $100. George Stancliff served as district clerk and F. Mace received $188 for teaching three months. The daily attendance averaged sixteen in an enrollment of thirty-three pupils.

The financial panic of the seventies had ebbed enough to permit financiers to explore new fields. In 1879 Henry Villard organized the Oregon Railway and Navigation Company, the first step in linking the wheat and pasture lands east of the Cascade Mountains with the transcontinental railroad. From this date engineers worked toward the Harney country to make surveys for a railroad, holding the Malheur Canyon to be the feasible route. More than a few settlers were outdone by having to drive their crop 300 miles. Others remained and, with new neighbors, hoped for yielding days.

The spaciousness itself was a magnet for young and bold hands, among them Will Y. King and William Hanley, whose beginnings were typical of the final year of the seventies. Young Bill Hanley, at seventeen and with little formal schooling, chose to strike out the hard way. He left his Rogue River home with a small herd of cattle, going by way of Lakeview and Warner Valley to the Double-O ranch, on to Sage Hen Hill and to Harney Basin. He slept on his blankets and got his food from the mess wagon. The high sky and the wide reaches he greeted warmingly. Exotic like a plant, he took hold quickly. And, as he said, he "listened in the stillness."

Stranger Bill met Pete French, John Devine and others. He took his band to the "island," in the middle of level grassland pronged by the Silvies River. With the people from the

Blue Mountains to the Nevada line, he joyed in going to Fort Harney. At big celebrations soldiers paraded, horses raced and men laid down their bets. He, as many another bachelor, had high respect for the handiwork of Mrs. Kennedy, who "followed washing" at the post. This woman of kind heart had entertained folks like Sarah Winnemucca and her father, and Sarah, in gratitude, had aided her in laundering.

Bill Hanley put up hay for the first winter and built corrals. He killed deer for the meat, visited Doc Anderson's ranch and ate potatoes with him. In the spring Hanley went back to Josephine County for more cattle and, returning with them, brought a rake and a mower. Fort Harney was no more but some needs were supplied at Mons Curry's store at Egan.

In 1879, also, Ed and Frank Roberts of San Jose, California, turned about 800 head of cattle onto the range between Crane Creek and Malheur Lake. Silvies Valley attracted Tom Overfelt and Frank Sweetser, who bargained for the Rann herd. They had little time to prepare for one of the severest winters known to neighbors. Heavy snow, crusted with ice, spelled death to cattle, and in the springtime thousands of carcasses littered the ground and fouled the air.

All stockmen suffered heavily, Overfelt and Sweetser being almost wiped out. Sweetser left shortly afterward, to become a leading rancher in northern Nevada. Overfelt moved over to the country of the lower Malheur, gaining interest in property known as the Harper Ranch. The Roberts brothers, who sustained discouraging losses, remained a few years at their comfortable home on Crane Creek below the Burns Ranch before returning to California.

In spite of staggering blows dealt by winter's blasts or by economic gnawing, the kingdom of grass held new promises. Devine and Todhunter expanded holdings from Alvord into Harney Valley while Glenn and French reclaimed section after section of the Blitzen area for their increasing herds. Abbott and Whiteside, on Alvord Creek, rebuilt their lank livestock and farming business. Influence in politics came to the aspiring section at the end of its first decade. Jim Abbott, in 1880, received the Republican nomination for state senator of Grant County. He met defeat at the hands of Democratic nominee "Tommie" Davidson, another resident and stockman of the Steens Mountain region.

Winnemucca, Nevada, attracted the cow hands, 33,000 head of cattle being shipped from there in 1877 and the number mounting each year. The settlement of eastern Oregon swelled so much in the seventies, with sheep and cattle so numerous, that Oregon's surveyor-general raised his voice for railroad connections to add to the valuable resources in wealth. By 1880 farmers and sheepmen were battling for ranges possessed by cattlemen. Depleted ranges, in Umatilla County and other northern districts, compelled withdrawals and much of the Grande Ronde Valley was fenced.

Overstocked in 1879, the Steens Mountain district had 12,000 head of its cattle driven to Cheyenne, Wyoming. Also in that year, a shipment of 1,200 head of Oregon-bred steers went from Winnemucca to Iowa. An estimated total of 40,000 head of cattle were driven from Idaho Territory in 1879, annual marketing of 35,000 head being announced two years later. While farmers encroached upon rich pasturage spots of the Owyhee and Bruneau River valleys, in 1880 the ranges in Steens Mountain region showed improvement. Pasturage in Lake County, created in 1874, still was attractive.

After dropping to the lowest point early in 1880, the price of beef started to rise later in the year. With a gradual lift, the market was booming by 1882, an advance of forty-five per cent being recorded in six months. "Choice" brought up to $8.90 per hundred of live weight.

Bill Hanley, who had added to his herd, became one of the Harney crowd at roundups. He recalled: "Wagontire was not so much of a center for cattle as it was a meeting place out of the desert. Here for a week we had feasts, lassoing the mountain sheep that were plentiful around Wagontire and killing mule-tail deer . . . then we had bucking contests and horse races." Vaqueros used rawhide ropes as long as seventy feet.

Ike Foster, foreman for Riley and Hardin at the Double-O Ranch, oversaw a peppery outfit. John Devine branded his colts "CC," they becoming rangy and high-powered saddle horses known afar. Devine liked to race them, but he rode around a great deal in a high rig with a well-selected team.

The rocker springs sagged with his figure of striking length and heaviness.

After a sojourn of about two years, Bill Hanley sold his cattle to Devine, but he kept some chickens on his Poison Creek ranch. Again he returned to Rogue River, paid his debts and had $7,000 left to reinvest. Bill was only twenty-two years old then, and he remained with his father for some years. Meanwhile, his brother Ed journeyed over to Harney Valley to care for the ranch that had been selected.

Martin Brenton, when he returned in 1880 to ride for French and other cattlemen, had reason to note the changes in successive years. Water flooded Harney basin more in some years than in others, causing irrigation by natural spread. In 1881 there was plenty of water but the sand reef between Malheur and Harney lakes stood intact in the spring. The reef, twelve or fifteen feet across in the narrowest part, pretty much "up and down," did not have a uniformly straight bank. At a point where the reef was about thirty feet wide, Brenton noted the sand had pockets and the water nearly reached the top. Horses crossed and mashed down the pockets, water rushing through the outlets.

Depth of the water then was about the same as the sand reef, fifteen or twenty feet. In due course the water cleaved more of the barrier, until, as at present, it was washed out to the bottom. Throughout the years Malheur Lake continued to be shallow around the margin, with low water period from July to fall. The channel at The Narrows had been carved by outpourings from the lake. Harney Lake kept getting drier and the water of both lakes fell with each year of dryness.

These factors and others had no little influence on settlement of the Harney country, where water was of prime importance. Changes propelled people faster in the initial years of the eighties. Already there was beginning to be a "past" in historical and legendary sense. Arrival of delayed newspapers in the late fall of 1882 revealed interesting happenings.

For the moment, talk revolved around the death of Chief Winnemucca, on October 21. There was a note of sadness in columns of several Nevada editors. A widower for some time, the father of Sarah had taken a young bride in another marriage. In August they had started from Pyramid Lake to join other Paiutes in a visit to Ochoco's band near Fort Bidwell. They got only as far as the south side of Surprise Valley when the old leader, becoming gravely ill, was forced to make camp.

He lingered for a while, a hundred people, including his son Lee and a daughter, waiting and ministering. On his last day, wrapped in a rabbit-skin robe, he lay beside a fire in his wickiup. The young bride, who was left with a year-old child by a husband who had died some months before her marriage to Winnemucca, was blamed for bewitching the chief and causing his sickness. For this, or some other reason, reports disclosed, she had been taken to a rocky bluff and stoned to death.

Editor S. P. Davis, of Carson City, who more than a few times had dug deeply in his pocket to assist the chief of the Paiutes on his journeyings, wrote:

Old Winnemucca has gone over to the Shades, traveling the beaten road which royalty must tread the same as the rest of us. Nominally speaking, he was as much a king as Alexander, and also enjoyed the advantage of having died in Nevada. He turned his feet to the setting sun on Friday last, and his immense moccasins shaded his face in his dying moments. . . .

There was less of human sympathy apparent when a reader's eyes rested on an abbreviated article in Reno's *Evening Gazette* of November 3. It told of a pestilential type of man passing out his checks. John Said, alias Rattlesnake Jack, had tried to kill a barkeeper at Weiser City, Idaho. In resisting arrest, the desperado was slain in a swift exchange of shots with Deputy Sheriff Porter.

As elsewhere, most residents of the frontier fought to maintain law and order. Tragedies, shallow or deep, occurred all too frequently and suddenly. Longevity beckoned most earnestly to those of law-abiding desires. Heat and cold exacted toll.

In August, 1882, Jezreel Venator, 80-odd years old, met death from overexertion. His son, Alphena, describes the circumstances:

After we moved to Lakeview we took some mares over there and they ran off and came back to Juniper Mountain. My father found out when the buckaroos would be at Juniper Mountain or thought they would be, so he took a horse and went there and they — the buckaroos — had moved away. . . . He hobbled his horse and in the evening lost him. He started down a canyon now known as Venator Canyon (between Alkali Lake and Abert Lake) for the road, but the distance and the hot weather was too much for him and he perished about 200 yards from where the highway is now, dying under a juniper tree, which was cut down by the highway when they constructed the present highway. It was a very lonely country, very isolated and at that season of the year there was no one in it, and it took nearly two weeks to track and locate his body.

The Circle Bar ranch, according to Venator, "was located about 1879 or 1880 by Fritz Stauffer and Frank Sweetzer. The ranch was operated by Ed Stauffer. My brother-in-law, Joe Cooksey, sold out the same time we did, and for a number of years was superintendent for Devine & Todhunter."

Chapter XXI

IMPULSE OF THE EARLY EIGHTIES

In the several years preceding Villard's tying of the Pacific Northwest and Chicago by rails of the Northern Pacific, dealers in cattle and sheep created knights out of plodding herders. This period of the frontier stood virulent, bold, picturesque. In saddle or at camp fire, in weariness or in merriment, the men quaffed or gulped the freedom of the trail. From their lips rose popular songs: "The Mocking Bird," "Down Upon the Swanee River," "Darling Nellie Gray," "Auld Lang Syne."

As in communities or in bunkhouses, along with games of cards or other entertainment, riddles pursued the trailers.

As cattle drives were conducted from Yakima to Puget Sound, or between other points in the seventies and eighties, so did they attain high importance in eastern Oregon. Cattle were shipped directly from The Dalles to Astoria, as were sheep and hogs. Nevada miners were heavy buyers of beef, and Nevada's range was utilized in wintertime. Cattle and sheep went to buyers in Wyoming, and to fill the needs of rising settlements in and around the Black Hills of Dakota. Colorado procured some, others went to New York and to England. Says Oliphant: "Oregon cattle that had been grazed in Kansas were bringing much higher prices in Chicago than Texas cattle." The Harney region contributed richly in many drives.

Horses and sheep were in greater demand in some areas. Those driven to Montana went over two routes—the Mullan Road from Walla Walla to Fort Benton, and the stage route, past Baker City, Union and Boise City.

Cattle drives from Oregon eastward swept to a climax in 1880, when the main portion went to Wyoming. Washington Territory sent 62,000 head, Oregon 58,000 head, and Idaho Territory 50,000 head. They comprised less than half of the total entering Wyoming in 1880. In that year, asserts Oliphant, "as in several preceding years, the most widely adver-

141

tised cattle-buyers in the Pacific Northwest were Lang & Ryan, and they drew from the ranges of Oregon, Washington, and Idaho . . . no record has been discovered of any firm that bought as extensively as Lang & Ryan."

The price soared into 1885, falling steadily with the Chicago market from that year until 1890. Portland's *Morning Oregonian* of March 9, 1880, printed a list of the cattlemen of eastern Oregon who had sold cattle to Lang & Ryan. These ranchers sold 15,300 head, added to 9,500 head from Idaho in the procurement. Of the drive, the *Oregonian* said:

To drive these to the Yellowstone country, where they will winter, will require 800 head of horses and the services of 120 men. Most of these "cow boys" are Kansas men, who have been in the employ of this concern for the past six years. Forty wagons accompany the drive, and about 160 stand of loaded rifles will always be on hand, good for about 3,000 shots at any band of hostile Indians that may attack them. The drive will be cut up into three squads or bands of cattle, the first lot having two days start of the third. This brings them in easy range of the rear from the front. In April they will begin to gather up for the start, and by the 25th of that month the greatest body of cattle ever banded together will be slowly marching eastward. Up to the 20th of June the drive will be about nine miles per day, but as the heat of summer comes along they will decrease it to about five. Therefore a steer travels no more on a drive of this kind than he would upon the range, and is sure to be in good order when he reaches the Yellowstone, as there is abundance of bunch grass as soon as the Grande Ronde River is passed.

Multiplying of sheep in eastern Oregon in the seventies and eighties made for changes. In 1880, Oregon estimated its sheep at 1,368,162, the three southeastern counties having 130,743. Clashing with cattlemen was inevitable, some cattlemen going into the sheep business apathetically. Protests and range wars ensued, the battles multiplying in or out of courts.

In citing the opinion of Idaho's Supreme Court, Oliphant declares that in 1901 the truth still held that: "Citizens graze their stock upon the public domain by sufferance of the general government, and not by virtue of any vested right." The states and territories had their police power, but this power did not go beyond the boundaries of Indian reservations. The Federal Government had its own regulations in reserved areas.

With the transition to wethers between 1880 and 1885, sheep drivers altered policies. Breeding sheep from California numbered from 2,500 to 5,000 head in average bands, while 5,000 to 7,000 head were driven in Oregon wether bands. Expenses incurred were far under those of cattlemen. Three sheepmen could handle each band: one at the point or lead, one at the swing, near the center, and the other at the slower trail. Sheep were fondest of eating in early morning or late evening. Drinking from any kind of running water was preferred to stagnant pools or marshes. Often blossoming desert plants contained enough water for a sheep's survival.

E. N. Wentworth, an authority on early drives, tells how a herder tried to move a band for a day: Early start in morning for cool grazing; make a drive of eight to ten miles to keep sheep in proper condition; feed well with grass, stop at a stream before the sun gets too hot, and permit drinking and lying in shade, "heads under the shadow of one another's bodies" if brush growth or trees were insufficient. With the sun on decline, the sheep scattered to feed at a slow-moving pace until nightfall. Rounded up in a bunch, on good bed ground, they would generally sleep and rest quietly. Drivers preferred dry camps and a chance to get a night's sleep without taking turns at watch.

The long sheep trail from Oregon led from Umatilla County over the Blue Mountains, close to present Union, south to Powder River headwaters and beyond Baker to cross Burnt River and follow along its south bank to Snake River, entering Idaho at Old's Ferry, ten miles west of Weiser. In the 1880s it deviated farther south to follow the Malheur and cross the Snake at Nyssa.

Hartman K. Evans, with his partner Robert H. Homer, in 1882 drove three bands of sheep, totalling 23,000 head, from near Pendleton to Laramie, Wyoming. Evans, as trail foreman, supervised trailing of the three bands. "Each band," he wrote, "had a foreman, three helpers, and a cook who drove the grub wagon—five men in all." Sheep dogs aided them. Of a total of fifteen men starting, only three finished at Laramie with Evans. Foremen of bands were paid $50 a month, the cook and others $40. They had a goodly supply of food, sometimes exchanging mutton for beef when encountering cattle drives. Canned goods were carried and renewed.

"The sheep in these bands," Evans explained, "were all Merino wethers. They were purchased at an average cost of $1.50 a head and 10,000 were contracted for delivery at Laramie at $3.00 a head." Evans arrived in Laramie with a loss of only 820 sheep out of 23,000. "This was considered a very good record."

On horseback, with grub wagons and dogs, the men drove first to Baker and Burnt River, then over mountainous country to Rye Valley and to Willow Creek, crossing a bridge to the right bank at Roberts Ranch. The trail led ten miles down to Malheur River, having poor feed and water but lots of wood and sagebrush. Another bridge was crossed at the Stone House to take a left-hand road for McDowell's ferry on the Snake River. No water was to be had in the stretch of eighteen miles from the Malheur to the Snake, and grass grew sparsely "some distance off the road."

The bands and herders got into difficulties in this rugged section, in feeding sheep and procuring supplies. The sage was large, the country bad for trailing, and Evans was forced to make two dry camps. The sheep were ferried, and a desirable watering place was found in approaching the Boise stage road. Farther east, the trail came out on Little Camas Prairie and meadow lands.

The cattle and sheep drives and enlivened markets stimulated hopes long confused. Fat cattle of Wasco County sold for as high as $35 a head late in 1882. Then the high prices and scarcity of beef animals wrought great changes in the Pacific Northwest. By 1883, when the Northern Pacific Railroad was completed, the drives eastward almost wholly ceased. Wyoming was procuring thousands of young cattle from Iowa and Missouri.

After gaining control of the Northern Pacific, Villard connected the Columbia basin with the transcontinental route in Montana to St. Paul. He also built a branch from his main line at Umatilla which crossed the Blue Mountains and the Grande Ronde to meet the Oregon Short Line at Huntington. Villard's empire collapsed, partly because of overextending branch lines in opening the Northwest, but the railroads went on to triumph after the decade of much building. Minor roads and feeder lines were built, west of the Cascades and east of them, tying into the proved outlet.

Some towns forged ahead while others remained quiescent, slipped bady or shrank to senility. The Chinese cleaned up the last gleaming dust at Auburn. Henry Griffin, "discoverer of gold" in eastern Oregon, died at the age of fifty-nine, and in passing of years a stranger could hardly find a trace of the once glittering town of Auburn.

With range lands fading elsewhere, sheepmen and farmers were coming into southeastern Oregon, far from a railroad or other stabilizing factors. Ranches in the Steens Mountain district gave more attention to their fencing and boundaries. Open and free ranges were debatable, to say the least. While numbers of sheep decreased in eastern Washington, the providers of wool and mutton multiplied in eastern Oregon, where sheep increased from 855,730 in 1880 to 1,431,577 in 1890. From 1880 to 1890, cattle mounted in Idaho and Washington. In Oregon the cattle numbered 598,015 in 1880, dipping to 520,648 in 1890.

Oregon's population in the same decade increased from 174,768 to 313,767. The increase in counties east of the Cascades was from 39,100 to 73,162. Eight of the nine new counties created in Oregon in the eighties were east of the Cascades. By 1880, Dr. John T. Ganoe has pointed out, Oregon's population had been drawn chiefly from Missouri, Illinois, Iowa, Ohio, California, New York, Pennsylvania, and Kentucky. These people could be traced back to other frontiers of civilization, and by 1880 organized migrations had ended. Until this year, the area west of the Cascades had produced almost all the products for market.

The decade of the eighties, however, saw dissolution of deserts stretching far from the course of the Columbia River, the "unifying element" in the Pacific Northwest. A host of immigrants followed the building of railroads into eastern Oregon and Washington. In this Inland Empire, by 1884, wheat shipments tripled those of the once dominant valleys west of the Cascades.

Of the import of this period, Dr. Dan E. Clark is lucid:

A matter-of-fact statement in a bulletin of the United States Census for 1890 gave official recognition of the ending of what may well be called the first great epoch in American history. "Up to and including 1880," said the Superintendent of the Census, "the country had a frontier of settlement, but at present the unsettled area has been so broken into by isolated bodies of settlement that there can hardly be said to be a frontier line." The facts are so in accord with this official announcement that the closing decade of the nineteenth century is properly regarded as the period when the frontier ceased to be a vital, contemporary force in the life of the nation. Here and there, to be sure, in isolated areas of the Far West frontier conditions long continued to prevail. But, as a whole, the pioneer phase of the occupation of the land within the boundaries of the United States was finished, and the influences of that process upon the people and the nation could be studied as something that was completed.

In Grant County, and later in Harney County, there survived a frontier ignoring many phases of progress. For long years were the people there to taste of alkaline pioneering. Economic conditions forced transitions by the mid-eighties, but the Harney country held to its cattle-raising more tenaciously than did other sections. Its agricultural market, to say nothing of soil, climate or other factors, was too distant. Notwithstanding, the inevitable westward push inflicted discernible dents.

The impact of the small farmer against the big landholder was becoming crucial. Dr. Hugh J. Glenn, father-in-law and partner of Peter French, exercised powerful influence. In 1880 he ran for the governorship of California, candidate of the New Constitution party. Though his political aspirations fell short, two years later he was acclaimed as the man growing the most grain in the United States. A thousand men labored for him, and he provided them with a theater, stores and other conveniences.

Then, on a Saturday evening, February 17, 1883, the imperial rancher of Jacinto, Colusa County, met his death at the age of fifty-eight. His angered bookkeeper, Huron Miller, shot him in the head. Winnemucca's *Silver State*, probably in overstatement, said, "In Oregon there are 60,000 acres of land and 40,000 head of cattle belonging to French & Glenn . . ."

Dr. Glenn was the father of a son, Frank Glenn, and his daughter, Ella, had become the wife of Peter French. The P Ranch on the Blitzen was an extremely busy place, but Mrs. French did not occupy the attractive white-painted house for long periods. Her husband, when possible, journeyed to California to visit her in an environment freer of loneliness and where her early-day friendships had closer ties. Affairs in Oregon, accumulating and reclaiming elastic holdings, pressed French constantly.

Sarah Winnemucca had married Corporal Hopkins in 1882, living for a while in Montana, but within a year she had gone to the East with him, earnestly seeking help for her unfortunate people. She lectured in many cities. In Boston she was aided greatly by Elizabeth Peabody and her sister Mary, the widow of Horace Mann, valiant educator. Their influence among leading citizens lent sympathy to the cause of the red peoples.

Sarah had published her book, *Life Among the Piutes: Their Wrongs and Claims*, she becoming the first of her race to produce a book in America. Though lacking literary grace, the work was a sincere attempt to set forth grievances needing remedy. Her solemn and undisguised asseverations provoked reverberations from foes within and without official circles. Not always seeming to understand the ways of government by the white man, nevertheless Sarah was a credit to her people and to her friends. In her day not even the voice of a learned white woman, in want of suffrage, could be lifted high with any satisfactory results.

The Indians who were in Washington Territory dribbled southward across the Columbia in small parties, but no Indians consented to live on Malheur Reservation. The Agency had its property guarded, a needless expense. Congress, noting refusal of the red men to live on the lands held for them, was unwilling that they should reap benefits from the proceeds of sale, as hoped for by the commissioner of Indian affairs.

The last of the Malheur lands, except 320 acres upon which were situated the buildings belonging to Fort Harney reserve, was restored to the public domain by an executive order dated May 21, 1883. Two days later, the General Land Office received directions to sell the agency buildings and the two sections of land on which they had been erected.

Upon the opening of Agency Valley on the North Fork of the Malheur, Tom Overfelt looked toward increasing his holdings. A deal was made with Henry Miller whereby the latter was, as a silent partner, to advance money to bid at the public auction of the Land Office at Lakeview. Overfelt made a hurried trip from Harney Valley in his buggy, accompanied by Maurice Fitzgerald.

Overfelt outbid a single competitor, the knock-down price being $7,000. The Land Office refused to accept a Miller & Lux check for that amount. Overfelt could raise only $3,500 for the bidding next day, and his competitor's offer of $4,000 beat him. After a legal scrap, however, the first sale was declared valid.

The rich land of Agency Valley was bought with a "Bull's Head" draft, the commissioner of the General Land Office in Washington holding that it passed as sound currency in the region. And indeed it did, a draft with a picture of a bull's head on it, with which Miller & Lux made payment where money and banks were scarce. These drafts were payable at the Bank of California, cashable at all times.

Miller, through Overfelt, his superintendent, was repeating his successful methods. Gradually, his empire was creeping to the northern edge of Nevada in fact, presaging the not distant invasion of the Harney country with the full display of title. The Overfelt brand, LF, in due course, stood for Miller & Lux ownership.

The impulse of the early eighties contained no fear for any man who took a firm hold on that which gave prescience to a glowing future. Settlements, garlanded with sagebrush, sprang to life.

Chapter XXII

BEGINNINGS OF BURNS

As THE EIGHTIES got under way, the large landowner continued to press against the smaller man, by purchase or other means. Though periods produced fluctuation, the home-making tide never became refluent for long. That the whole of eastern Oregon exerted a rising power in politics was self-evident. From the fall of 1882 until mid-January, 1887, Zenas F. Moody, merchant and Republican from Wasco County, served as Oregon's governor.

Slowly but assuredly, clusters of families formed hamlets in the Harney country. The one on the west bank of the Silvies River drew blacksmith Broady Johnson after abandonment of Fort Harney, it bearing the utilitarian title of Axhandle. Owners of ranches, their hands, and homeseekers were attracted by stables, eating places and saloons. Old buildings brought down from the post helped to get the future Burns off to a start.

Johnson and John Robinson, a young man who had arrived from California in 1879, erected the first hotel, to be run by Mrs. Mary Caldwell and Mrs. Alameda Stenger. Johnson catered to those desiring buoyant refreshments and relaxation. Next to the saloon, in 1881, Robinson, a barber, opened his shop. A short time later, Wash Smelser appeared and opened another tavern for thirsty wayfarers. Mrs. M. A. Fry, a survivor of the Donner party tragedies, found space to set out food for folks with hunger. When came opportunity, a livery stable was erected to provide bed and board for horses and rigs for hire. W. C. Byrd and Martin Brenton were forerunners in this business.

Among those seeking a freer life was George McGowan of the Willamette Valley, born in Scotland thirty-seven years previously. He relished the frontier and good literature in equal measure, educating himself advantageously. As a school teacher in Lane County he boarded at the homes of scholars before marrying Mary Jane Martin, twelve years his junior, in

1873. He made a lifelong study of Robert Burns, "Poet of the People," and the worth of his poetry.

McGowan felt that fluffy and esoteric smugness clouded some earliest settled portions of Oregon by the winter of 1882. He was ready, by spring, to pursue the brighter promises of the Harney country, as a merchant. With him and his wife went their three children, daughter Jessie, eight, and two younger sons, Archie and James. By wagon, it was a wearing trip from Cottage Grove to follow the Columbia River and head south from The Dalles. They arranged for the hauling of groceries, hardware and cloth to furnish a store at Egan.

Of the journey and their future home, McGowan wrote:

What impressed us most as we moved to Eastern Oregon . . . was the "bigness" of everything. The country was alive with cattle, horses, sheep and wild animals surpassing anything in size and numbers we had ever seen. Beeves were being driven to market by the thousand, the roads were blocked with big six-horse wool wagons and we sighted great herds of deer and antelopes. The country stores carried huge stocks of merchandise and the smallest coin circulating was a twenty-five-cent piece. When we arrived in Prineville, Judge Lynch's Court was in session and Justice was being dispensed in a big primitive way. The further we penetrated the larger things grew, reaching its climax in Harney Valley where we arrived in safety, May, 1882.

. . . Although there were vast meadows of wild hay everywhere they went uncut and cattle and horses cared for themselves throughout the season. Agriculture was an untried experiment. Everything had to be hauled from the railroad, a distance of three hundred miles. As freighters' teams had to subsist on grass, the trip required from four to eight weeks, often longer. Freight rates averaged five to eight cents per pound according to season.

Quite naturally the cattlemen were hostile to settlement. They claimed all available lands as swamp, including ridges and hills, in which claim they were strenuously sustained by the State Land Department. In order to file on land the settler had to journey one hundred and fifty miles, taking his witnesses to the land office at Lakeview to initiate an expensive contest. Nor was the Land Office more favorable to the settler than was the state and decisions were uniformly against him. Everything seemed to be against him, the cost of goods, absence of building material, and lack of means of communication.

After the military had left Fort Harney, the settlers sent and received mail once a week. Tom O'Keefe, veteran of the post, carried it between Egan and Prineville by horseback and by wagon.

Of his father's start in business, Archie McGowan writes:

At Egan we found hospitality, an old house to live in, and every courtesy from the several families living in the neighborhood. Monse Curry and Byron Terrill were operating a saloon, but also had a small stock of staple merchandise for the cowboy and stockman of the county. My father, George McGowan, proposed to buy the merchandise. They wanted to sell the saloon also, but he talked them into moving the saloon into an adjoining old log building and let him operate the store. He told them he had a stock of merchandise coming, and that he wanted to have plenty of room for a good stock to take care of the settlers that were in the community.

Folks at and near Egan barricaded themselves a few times when false rumors flew around that Indians, drifting back from Washington Territory, planned attacks on settlers. The red men begged, sometimes threateningly, but they made peaceful camps.

If a white man "got out of line," his adversary took the law into his own hands, as in this instance, Archie McGowan says:

Peter Stenger was one of the outstanding characters of the community. He had a horse ranch and owned land along the river just east of the present site of Burns; . . . He had a very attractive wife who had many admirers, and of course was a favorite at the dances and public meeting places. One day someone told Pete that Rush Frazier was paying too much attenion to his wife. Pete told Rush to leave his wife alone and to get out of the country. The next time he saw Rush he told him again that he would only give him twenty-four hours to leave the community. Twenty-four hours had hardly passed when Rush Frazier was dead, Peter Stenger had killed him. This created much excitement in the community. I remember that they brought Rush down to our house and laid him out and deliberated on what to do with him. My grandfather, Lewis Martin, who had just come over the Cascade Mountains by wagon to pay us a visit, was there, and he said, "I can make him a coffin," so a coffin was soon made out of scraps of lumber that could be picked up around the community. Rush was taken to the present cemetery and laid away. I remember that at that time there were just two other graves in that locality, so this was really the beginning of the present cemetery.

About two weeks after the incident the sheriff rode over from Canyon City to Egan. "He stayed around the saloon and store for a few days, played cards with the boys, and finally got on his horse and rode back to Canyon City. That closed that incident."

George McGowan's store, doing more business than expected by the fall of 1882, had a serious shortage of flour shortly after Christmas. A group of settlers, headed by Tom Whiting, urged McGowan to procure, if possible, enough flour to last out the winter. The solution is told by Archie McGowan:

. . . there was no road open between here and Canyon City over the high mountains, and the snow was deep. It was a long ways to The Dalles . . . so my father was quite worried where this flour could be procured. My mother's brother, Uncle Ed [Martin], was working for my father in the store. . . . He had made trips with surveyors and Army Engineers into the Cedarville country, and through by Lakeview and New Pine Creek. Uncle Ed said to my father, "I believe I know where we can get the flour, and it is not so very far away."

Ed, astride a sleek horse and fortified with many sandwiches tied behind his saddle, his Winchester rifle in front of him, set out on a cold morning for New Pine Creek. He returned within seven days, cheerfully announcing, "The flour is on its way."

Delay of another week brought fear. Says Archie:

Uncle Ed was just ready to start out for the second time to see what had happened when three wagons arrived late at night loaded with flour covered with alkali mud. They were tired, hungry men, but the emergency was over and the flour in the store.

The son of the miller related the rugged experience:

. . . The country was all frozen when we left New Pine Creek. It was hard and solid, but then it began to rain, and when they reached Warner Valley and those alkali flats frost went out of the ground and they bogged down the three wagons. They had to take all the horses and put on one wagon at a time to pull them through those alkali flats which consumed several days. In the meantime they had eaten up nearly all the supplies, and had nothing but flour to live on while they were coming from Warner Valley to Egan.

In need of more capital for his mercantile business, George

McGowan accepted Peter Stenger as a partner when Stenger put up required funds and built a large store near the Stenger home in 1883. It spelled the demise of Egan and mushrooming of another town. McGowan resettled on a vacant quarter section of land now known as the Voeghtly field with the Union Pacific depot at its center. His family occupied an old house for a time.

After Mr. and Mrs. McGowan returned from a trip to Portland to buy merchandise, they awaited completion of the new store. Late in the fall a community dance was held in it just prior to removing the merchandise from Egan. That same night, the saloon at Egan went up in flames, the fire set by a vengeful poker player who had lost all his money there that day. Egan's postoffice also was relocated in the new store, and its renaming presented an absorbing problem.

Although Stenger spent most of his time in ranching, he took pride in the new improvements and suggested that the place be named for him. McGowan steered Stenger from this, arguing that too many "boys" might slap on "The Stenger town where they got stung." The storekeeper-postmaster objected to someone's suggestion it be called McGowan, and study went on. McGowan asked, "How about Burns for the immortal poet?" All agreed. McGowan wrote:

. . . What name would more readily occur to a Scotchman than that of Burns? His songs are appreciated as much here as in Scotland. Here in Harney Valley was Nature uncontaminated by art and the subjects of Burns' lays, herds, cattle, sheep, birds, beasts, all around and about me. . . .

McGowan, as first postmaster at Burns, prepared a petition for its legal establishment. Of this he said:

. . . But the circulation of this petition was not so easy. This was the heart of a big country of "magnificent distances." Ranchers were few and far between. Luckily, a cowboy with a good horse undertook the task and to our great surprise returned the petition next day freshly signed. He said his horse was a "wonderful critter" and we believed him. We did not then know he had signed most of the names himself. That came out later. However, no objections were ever made so the petition was forwarded and duly approved by the authorities at Washington.

The new postoffice was established January 22, 1884, Mc-Gowan receiving his appointment as postmaster from President Arthur.

Children assembled for schooling at Miller's Cove, now used as Burns' athletic field.

The name of George McGowan as clerk of School District 13 first appeared on the minutes March 3 of that year; he recording meticulously for the next three years. The teacher was E. W. Nevius. His pupils in 1884 included Mart Brenton, Lizzie, Frank, George and "Skip" Whiting, Sally and Erma Howser, Laura Stancliff, Charley Bedell, Ben Simpkins, Frank Baker, Rod Howser, Louie Stancliff, Charles Johnson, Ida Simpkins, and Archie, Jessie and Jim McGowan.

Soon another daughter, Gracie, came to the McGowan home.

By spring, Burns had attracted more businesses, including saloons. To the three or four dozen persons of the community were added settlers of the surrounding country. Peter Clemens took over Stenger's holdings on Poison Creek.

Alphena Venator, who now located on Deadman Creek, tells of the cattle-buying method copied by himself and others — buying cattle around Harney Valley without paying a dollar for them until after they were sold. "Pete French in the early days originated that method in this country. He would buy our cattle in November and December, usually in December, take them to San Francisco, sell them and come back in January with a satchel full of gold — the money in those days was all gold — and payment was made in the same."

In 1884 many families who had fought unsuccessfully against ravaging grasshoppers in Kansas sought locations in Harney Valley. Called "Kansas Sufferers," they wrestled stubbornly with the newer country. Legal help was needed. Into Burns moved two lawyers — Captain A. W. Waters from Salem, Oregon, and George Sizemore from Missouri.

Nathan Brown and his two sons, Ben and Leon, of San Francisco, appeared during the summer. Sam King of Surprise Valley accompanied them. The elder Brown, foreseeing advantages of the region, prepared at once to go into the general merchandising business in Burns. W. C. Byrd saw favorable opportunity for his family in Harney Valley, and his two

sons, Charles and Julian, soon aided him in laying a strong
foundation.

In the presidential election year of 1884 political fever ran
high throughout the nation.   The Republican "Plumed
Knight,," James G. Blaine of Maine, though aided tremen-
dously by his running mate, General John A. Logan of Illinois, fought a losing battle against Grover Cleveland, Democratic stalwart. On the older streets of Canyon City and on the
newer walks of Burns refrains were lifted strongly when sing-
ers had imbibed freely. Veterans of the Union Army bore
down on a pet stanza:

> Voice the loudest airs of freedom
> In the song of eighty-four,
> Till majestic in its volume
> It shall force the White House door.
> For the nation's grand uprising,
> Felt from Mexico to Maine,
> Hails a true and trusted leader
> In the standard-bearing Blaine.
>   And the slogan,
>   Blaine and Logan,
> Means no martyrs die in vain.

By the end of the year Burns had become a raw, slap-dash,
impish "burg." Although striving for dignity, at times it
became like a blister on the hand. The two mercantile stores,
a blacksmith shop and the hotel tried to maintain orderliness.
The livery stable had yet to be finished. The two saloons easily
claimed most popularity. The boisterous and the sane stood
boldly over glasses of kick-back whiskey. They patronized
avidly the card games of their choice and, sometimes, a quarrel
culminated in the drawing of guns or a slugfest. A peace-loving
citizen generally tied his horse loosely at the hitching post,
ready to ride away on quick decision.

A native Texan known as Jack Miller procured employment
on the ranch of Devine and Todhunter in the spring of 1883.
An exception to the rule, he had no fondness for intoxicating
beverages, and he worked as a reliable hand for more than a
year. With his savings, he went to the hills, getting out timbers
for fencing and buildings. In his camp, about 15 miles from

Burns, he employed half a dozen men, including a cook named Matt Egan.

Out of acerbity flared a tragedy, delineated by Maurice Fitzgerald, who tried to avert it:

For some reason best known to himself, two or three days before Christmas he [Miller] paid Egan off and installed in his place a buxom widow of middle age. The discharged cook didn't accept his discharge philosophically. He realized that he had given entire satisfaction to the members of the crew in preparing their meals, and resented the action of the boss in firing him so that a place could be found for a female friend who, Egan believed, was incapable of performing the duties required as satisfactorily for all concerned as he.

Egan came to Burns and, after imbibing a few drinks of fighting whiskey, let it be known that he considered his former employer a rotten skunk who had treated him so shabbily.

A day or two after Christmas Miller came to town to get a few things needed at the camp. He hadn't been there very long until he was accosted by Egan, who let him know in a very plain language what he thought of him for doing such a dirty trick, and added there was only one he-man's way of squaring the score between them and that was by going out behind the blacksmith shop and shooting it out. Miller, cool and collected, said:

"Matt, you've been drinking; go and take a sleep and when you're awake you'll feel different. There's no reason why you and I should have any trouble. We can always be good friends, and I hope we shall."

Miller's level-headed talk seemed to appease somewhat the wrath of Egan, for the time being, so they parted without further recriminations. But the armistice was of short duration. Egan took an additional drink or two, when his outraged feelings again flared up. Meanwhile the news had spread that trouble was brewing between Egan and Miller. Ben Brown and I happened to be standing in front of the Brown store when Egan, coming out of the Johnson saloon which was close by, seeing us, approached and said to me:

"Fritz, I'm not going to let anyone do me dirt and get away with it."

I tried to mollify his feelings and dissuade him from making trouble. While I was speaking I noticed that Matt was gazing intently down the street, although there wasn't a soul in sight. He knew that Jack had gone down in that direction and saw his horse saddled and hitched to a post on the opposite side of the street. Presently we saw Miller come out of Wash Smelser's place and start walking towards his horse. Egan stepped off the sidewalk and as Miller was nearing the hitching post, shouted, "Jack," at the same time beckoning with his hand for him to come hither. Jack stopped in his tracks, his head bent down for a few seconds, then whirled and came walking up briskly towards us, his arms swinging leisurely by his sides. He wore a heavy blue flannel jacket.

Egan stood motionless as Jack approached until he was within fifteen or twenty feet. Then he said, "Look out," at the same time drawing a pearl-handled Smith and Wesson six-shooter which he had ready for use, the long barrel inside his trousers belt in front, with the handle protruding from his vest, which had only the lower button fastened.

In drawing his weapon he had to raise his arm several inches. Just as he did, Jack crouched, then darted in like a flash, grasped Matt's wrist with his left hand, forcing it up just in the nick of time so that the bullet passed harmlessly over his shoulder. Then, reaching with his right, he drew from the breast pocket of his jacket a "Colt's Bulldog" which he raised to fire, but Egan, on the alert, with his left hand caught Jack's gun just as he pulled the trigger, forcing it down so that the bullet went into the ground. There they stood for a few seconds, each holding the other's gun hand. It made a dramatic and awe-inspiring tableau. Ben Brown and I were spellbound and never moved a step. Just then the report of the fire-arms emptied the saloons and stores so that the finish was witnessed by quite a little crowd. Both were strong men, but Miller, having the underhold, possessed the advantage. With a supreme effort of sheer strength he forced Egan's left hand upward until his own was in line with Egan's body, while still holding Matt's right aloft with his left, then sent three or four bullets into his opponent's midriff. Egan slumped to the ground, saying as he fell, "You got me, Jack," and expired immediately.

Miller, naturally excited, placed his foot on the dead man's body, wrenching the weapon from his hand, then with a gun in either hand, walked up the middle of the street in front of the saloon where seven or eight reputedly tough characters were assembled, saying:

"If any of you so-and-so's don't like what I've done, get right out here and try your hand."

None of these reputed gunmen said a word or made a move. Jack thought that there might be some friend of Egan's among them, but there wasn't. In a little while, Miller quieted down, turned Egan's gun over to the hotelman and rode to camp. Nothing was ever done to question the legality of the killing. It was generally considered justifiable homicide.

Not long after this duel, the sheriff of Baker County came to arrest Miller on the charge of stealing a team of horses from his bailiwick. The sheriff questioned McGowan in his store and learned much about Miller, including the fact that the storekeeper was holding Miller's note for a large quantity of merchandise that then was lying on the floor to be loaded in Miller's wagon that night. Of what then happened, Archie McGowan has written:

Somehow or another Jack Miller discovered the sheriff being here, so he got into his wagon with his horses, popped his whip and drove out of town, really daring the sheriff to follow him. The sheriff organized a posse and went after him, but darkness overtook them. Miller left his team and wagon and escaped in a dry slough channel. The sheriff got the horses and took them back to Baker County.

Nothing was heard of Miller for quite a number of years. In the late nineties it was learned that Jack Miller was well known as the Jack Dalton who built the Dalton Trail into the Klondike. He made a fortune, as did Ed Hanley, formerly of Harney Valley, in moving cattle to Dawson and other points in Alaska during the gold rush. Investment in a large salmon cannery later added to his wealth. When Dalton visited Seattle, McGowan sent him the note bearing his former name. Dalton paid up.

McGowan, in confidence, looked toward more settlers in the Harney country. He raised some grain and, to show benefits from irrigation, he and Peter Stenger made their first filing for water of the Silvies River and built the first dam there. It redeemed some of their sageland.

They dissolved their store partnership in two of three years, however. Stenger obtained the original store, to which he owed considerable money. McGowan founded a hardware and implement business which proved successful. Burns kept on growing despite failures in dry-land farming. McGowan and Nathan Brown, with faith in and enthusiasm for, their businesses, worked hand in hand for advancement. Together, they recruited assistance in overcoming handicaps that discouraged settlement by smaller landowners. They fought determinedly for locating a land office in Burns, opposed by large cattle interests.

In keeping with the growth of population, a new schoolhouse was built in Burns in 1885. Also, in that year, with money borrowed from McGowan to erect a building, W. E. Grace opened a drug store. He had come from Prineville and, as a Democrat, succeeded McGowan as postmaster.

Horace A. Dillard, also from Prineville, established the *Harney Valley Items,* the first paper of that region. Founded in September, 1885, it was to accrue a circulation of nearly 200 before the creation of Harney County four years later. Dillard had more space than type for the small six-column sheet. Out-of-town advertising helped to keep the enterprise alive.

Kinsfolk, like the families of T. A. and Bob McKinnon, and single brothers such as Homer and Fritz Mace, were among new settlers. Strenuously, they lent each other help in carving homes.

Tragedy reared. Two young married men, John Bland and Horace Mace, the latter father of a baby boy, became enraged at each other over what folks said was a trivial matter. Bland told McGowan the matter must be fought out. Archie McGowan recalls:

. . . My father tried to persuade Bland to forget it. He came back again to my father, after drinking more liquor, and told my father it was going to be settled that day because "Tomorrow we start to ride for cattle, and we had better settle it here than on the range." I was one of the school children coming home from school on a beautiful summer evening . . . We were following the dusty road, and came up in front of the store and the saloon. We found in the middle of the road John Bland stretched out with his arms folded and a gun in his hand. Some men were standing near. We looked over on the bench in front of the saloon and saw Horace Mace stretched out on the bench with his arms folded with a pistol in his hand. One of the remarkable things about this affair was that both men after emptying their revolvers at one another laid themselves out and folded their own arms in death. . . .

In 1884, when Fred Racine was about four years old, his parents, the Lewis Racines, came to Burns. Two popular daughters, Eugenie and Dolores, added zest to the social life. Mr. and Mrs. Racine improved an unattractive building across the street from the original Burns Hotel about 1886 and conducted the French Hotel, favorably patronized by many visitors. Lewis, speaking English, often had to rush from his cooking tasks to assist his wife, who was manager and, at first, could talk French only.

Attorney C. A. Swenk moved from Canyon City to Burns

with his family. They remained a few years before departing.

By 1886 two physicians, Drs. T. V. B. Embree and Samuel B. McPheeters, were practicing in and around Burns. They witnessed the birth of Harney County and many of its newest children. On frequent calls they rode far and defied the elements. At home, they practiced the acme of hospitality. Ofttimes they advised wayfarers, in stringent circumstances, to abide as guests and then the goodly physicians refused compensation. Embree Bridge, on the Silvies River near Burns, was named for the physician who also served as lay preacher to local Methodists.

Thuddingly known to settlers or to travelers was a trio expert with horseflesh—Henry Richardson, Tom Stevens and Sam (Scotty) Bailey. Tom and Scotty, who became operators of Burns Hotel for a breezy period, gave quick encouragement to sporting events, chief of which was to be classier horseracing.

Burns had made an impetuous beginning. It stood in scanty and drab dress, yet on its own feet. It stood ready for more business, and ready, also, to grapple with any challengers.

Chapter XXIII

DREWSEY, HARNEY CITY AND RIVALS

IN THE AREA of the great Paiute reservation which was without Indian resident after 1879 and which reverted to the public domain four years later, interest of homeseekers was more than mild. Some of the best ranches were held under squatter rights prior to actual opening of land to settlement. The best claims had settlers on them in the spring and summer of 1883.

Then a number of families, unnerved by a false Indian scare, vacated their claims. Within a year all good locations again were taken. The alarm arose from rumors that Indians who had been granted permission to depart from Yakima Reservation would seek retaliation. These red people, including those under Leggins, drifted southward peacefully in small bands. Their plight was desperate in some respects, but most of them merely sought a haven among the Paiutes of northern Nevada.

On behalf of the homeless as well as others of her tribe Sarah Winnemucca enlisted friendly help in the East before her return to the West in the fall of 1884. Again she lectured in Nevada and in San Francisco, her speech still barbed. In an interview in January, 1885, she declared:

My people do not belong to that class of Indians who are regularly provided for by the Government. At the last session of Congress Senator Dawes of Massachusetts secured an appropriation of $17,000 for the support of the Winnemucca tribe and Leggin's band during this winter, but not a cent of it has yet been spent for us, and I am afraid that it will never get farther than the hands of the rascally agents, who steal all they can get. . . .

The impoverished ones did get some help of a temporary nature, but rehabilitation posed a drawn-out problem. Natchez, in getting assistance from Senator Leland Stanford of California to buy a farm near Lovelock, Nevada, was more fortunate than others. Sarah and her husband went there to live with her brother and, by 1886, had erected a boarding

161

school for Paiute children. Elizabeth Peabody of Boston solicited funds for its maintenance, and Sarah named it for her. This was the first Indian school on record to be conducted by a full-blooded Indian. Along with elementary studies, the girls were taught domestic trades and the boys received practical instruction in agriculture.

Many Indians worked for ranchers in Oregon and Nevada. It was when they roamed, pitching camp and seeking food, that they caused fright. Sometimes, however, the settlers' fare was little better. Dire emergencies arose in wintertime when snow piled up and frigidity clamped down.

About 40 miles northeast of Burns and neighborly to 4,212-foot Drinkwater Pass, Abner Robbins held a squatter's claim. His rights to government land being exhausted, he formed a partnership with Elmer E. Perrington, who filed and made final proof on 160 acres. On this quarter-section of land the present town of Drewsey took root in the summer of 1883.

Gabe Rush built of lumber a boxlike store, 10x12 feet, in which Robbins and Perrington established a mercantile business. Wesley Miller hauled the first load of goods from The Dalles, the trip taking three months. Overalls, tobacco, and other items, therefore, were costly. No nickels appeared in change of the merchants.

A tent served as the first saloon. Its owner, Jim Ragley, soon became embroiled in an unfortunate altercation. He shot Bob Moffett, pulled up stakes and sought more placid fields. To supply the demand for red liquor—beer was frowned upon as being too tame—Al Jones and Sam Kelly set up a limited stock.

Because of sharp clawing and hard-fistedness, the sprouting cow town had the name of Gouge Eye applied to it. About a year after founding the store, Robbins submitted the name when he applied for a postoffice. Postal authorities showed understandable hesitancy. Robbins substituted a new name, Drusy, but in due course the office was called Drewsey. L. A. McArthur's *Oregon Geographic Names* cites the *Oregon Guide* as saying the permanent name "was in compliment to Drewsey Miller, the daughter of a rancher."

A different origin was accredited by I. Milton Davis, who settled in the Drewsey section in 1883, was the first regular deputy sheriff under A. A. Cowing and the first stock inspector of Harney County. He wrote: "Away back in Maine, Mr. Perrington's native state, he left a little sweetheart whose name was Drewsey, and for whom he gave to this town her name—'Drewsey'." Upon establishment of the postoffice in 1884. Mrs. Tom Howard took charge of it, Davis said, and she taught the first school in Drewsey. She was "a successful teacher with business ability, and greatly respected by those who knew her."

Although the appellation of Gouge Eye possessed color and ferocity, most local folks in time voiced appreciation for a postmark not so ruthless. "In pioneer days," explained Davis, "Drewsey was almost an exclusive cow town, and like all pioneer cow countries it was infested with its 'bad men' and a few outlaws who darkened the serenity and disturbed the peace of the good citizens. The influence of the better elements finally prevailed, settling down to law and order." In change of name, the lawless lost recognition.

Drewsey's first hotel, started by Jack Bales, burned down in its infancy. Mrs. Tom Howard operated a new hotel. Later, this was bought by Perry Rutherford, who in turn sold to Mrs. A. J. Bartlett. John Mitchell built the first feed barn, selling to Jim Hamilton. When A. I. Johnson started his blacksmith shop he had no competitor in this line, but at a later date he opened a store.

Earliest settlers in and around Drewsey came from far and near. Joe Lamb, pioneer of 1879, chose as his wife, Mary Mahon, whose father, Patrick, built a cabin near the site of Burns in 1879. Tom Dodson moved over a year or two after settling in Burns in 1882. W. M. Moffett, arriving in 1881, along with greater numbers of succeeding years, rode for range outfits far and wide. At their tasks or on the streets of their frontier towns they met expert hands like Jeff Billingsley, speaking with drawl of the Southland.

By 1886 the Drewsey section had about 60 settlers with their families. The town itself was not to grow large, but it had a wide territory to serve. Freighting by wagons steadily increased.

In passage of more time the people welcomed a physician. Young Dr. W. L. Marsden, graduate from the Kentucky School of Medicine, decided to practice in Drewsey. He obtained his license in Oregon in 1891 and was considered one of the most intellectual of pioneer doctors. His buggy was on trail or road much of the time; in months of deep snow his saddle-horse carried him in risky trips of great length. The unflagging doctor saw fruitful results.

Phil Metschan of Portland, reminiscing in his *Oregon Inn-Side News,* tells how he enjoyed Drewsey in his boyhood:

Early in the summer of 1889, Mrs. Tom Howard . . . arrived by buckboard at Canyon City to transact some business with my father, who had backed Mr. Howard and their son, Ed, at the time they moved from Canyon City to engage in the business of raising horses. I persuaded my parents to let me go to Drewsey with her, where I remained until September.

Drewsey was quite new. The rough unfinished lumber used in the construction of Mrs. Howard's little hotel, not painted, did not show any sign of weathering. There were two stores — Geo. Perrington's built of stone, Oppenheimer's of wood, with a large canvas sign stretching the full length of the building's roof, OPPOSITION STORE. One saloon, with a high porch, making it very easy for the buckaroos to dismount and remount, its ceiling shot full of holes when the boys in a festive mood tried out their pistols. Dr. W. L. Marsden, who married my red-headed Canyon City-born school teacher, Clara Bryan, began his Harney County practice in Drewsey, where I first met him. (Dr. Marsden moved to Burns. Always sympathetic with the unfortunate Paiutes, was elected their Chief.) The squaws helped Mrs. Howard in her hotel, washing, cleaning, etc., but she was the cook and Ed and I washed dishes when we were home. Bucks cut the juniper wood, delivered and split in kitchen-stove lengths. Howling coyotes kept the nights hideous in manner not rivaled by present-day Los Angeles sirens.

Every cowboy carried a pistol, not concealed, but in a holster fastened to his belt. The Howards furnished me with a horse. I was a very proud boy when I rode with the buckaroos with my .22 pistol strapped to my belt.

A number of Paiute families lived near Drewsey, maintaining for the most part the customs of their forefathers — bucks with two long braids of hair hanging, one on each side of the head over their breast — moccasins and buckskin leggins. Squaws also buckskin-clad, . . . Their papoose (baby) carried in a Hoo Pu (pronounced *Hoo,* as who, and *Pu* with *u* sound as ugh), the Paiute word for an Indian woman's convenience for carrying her baby. Made with a board shaped like a tennis racquet, covered with buckskin, fastened to it with rawhide straps, a buckskin cover with opening large enough to permit the baby to be slipped into it. Also a buckskin hood fastened to the rounded top of the board, used to cover its head and

neck, leaving only the face showing. Another opening was provided
for baby boys at their middle, with a leather shield just below the
opening — buckskin not being impervious to water. Boys were constantly ready for emergencies . . . Girls were not quite so fortunate . . . The baby was carried on the mother's back — held securely
by a strap around her forehead. At home, the Hoo Pu was leaned
against a juniper or pine tree. When the tribe was on the move,
it was strapped on the top of a pack horse's load.

One day Ed and I rode to the Howard's new homestead on Mule
Creek, Mr. Howard having recently filed on it. We found a wickiup
village on the banks of the creek, ran horses and foot races with
the Paiute boys, rode our horses up Mule Creek to the timber,
scared up a doe sleeping under the willows in the dry bed of the
creek, fired my .22 pistol — no venison that day.

At the end of August, Mrs. Howard said, "Phil, Mr. Johnson is
going to his ranch near Prairie City, on Indian Creek. He will take
you with him. Here's a dollar to pay your fare on the stage from his
ranch to Canyon City." Another long buckboard ride over the Blue
Mountains to Johnson's Ranch, where we arrived after dark.

Phil, however, was determined to save the dollar, to buy
more bullets or candy. He started to walk early the next
morning. In taking a short-cut through tall rye grass John
Kuhl spied him, and took him into Canyon City with a load
of dressed beef. Like modern youngsters, the boy had no
aversion to hitch-hiking.

Accessibility to the road from the old Agency and Drewsey,
as well as the route to Canyon City, had much to do with the
establishment of Harney, a mile and a half south of Fort
Harney. A few miles west of Drewsey the road wound up
Stinking Water Creek to the Joe Lamb place, where it forked.
One route, after crossing the Devine Flat, entered Harney
Valley near the present home of Jesse Vickers. It was a continu-
ation of rocky ridges and deep gullies. The other road, also
running westerly, climbed its high mountain, descended to the
Edwards place on Pine Creek, snaked over ridges and flats
until it eased into Harney Valley at what is now known as the
Archie McGowan ranch.

Young Rush, about a year after adandonment of Fort
Harney, settled on Cow Creek, soon to sell his interests to
James Mahon. Rush, it is said, was a son-in-law of George
James, who later took up a claim on the site of the fort. The
expanse of good land here drew settlers readily. A ceaseless

wonder to them on summer rides to Silvies River and Burns was the fertile soil stretching southward to the long and narrow benchland which, shimmering in waves of heat, appeared like a giant train of cars.

Easier was the task of transferring the Stevens store and other buildings from Fort Harney to Harney than to Burns. Also, newly milled lumber had shorter hauling. The spot was a favored one and the town became a rival of Burns overnight. Businesses, in nature and number, grew in like manner.

Prospects in Harney were lively enough in 1884 for John H. Loggan to be attracted by them. Typical of immigrants who gave impetus to the town was the Loggan family. John, a native of Indiana, and Emily Davis, born in Illinois, met and were married in Nebraska in 1869. In 1872, not long out of their teens, they moved to Kansas. By team and wagon they crossed the plains in 1879, to Island City, Oregon. John located on land along Rock Creek in Harney Valley in 1884. The next spring he moved his wife and children there and established a hardware business in Harney City.

A topographical feature impressed the boy John E. Loggan, who today recalls:

That was the Indian trail from Fort Harney to the Agency, now Beulah, Oregon. It was as distinct as a well-traveled road although only traveled by horses and on foot. It followed the foothills on the north side of the valley, through gaps in ridges in a general straight direction. It could be seen for many years but is now obliterated except in a few places.

The elder Loggan later acquired a general merchandise business in Harney, outlasting all others. The town, by 1888, attached arresting attention to its business roster. The saloon of Lessing and Coatsworth attracted many casual as well as steady patrons, while J. C. Buckland's hotel served its guests in pleasing style. Two blacksmiths, Van Curtis and J. W. Norton, worked long days over forges and anvils. E. H. King's sawmill hummed in urgent production of lumber. The clientele of Attorney Victor J. Miller grew stoutly, and the official duties of Jasper Davis, justice of the peace, kept him in the public eye.

Like Burns and Drewsey, people of Harney at this time had

their public school and a family physician. Frank Moore instructed pupils who trudged or rode baffling distances. Dr. G. W. Gilham attended the ones stricken with illness. The officially designated postoffice of Harney had W. W. Johnson as its first postmaster. In the late eighties, and for some years thereafter, John H. Loggan served as acting postmaster, under Postmaster E. B. James and his successor.

Life had its merry as well as serious side. In May of 1887, D. I. Asbury, editor and proprietor of the *Grant County News*, drove from Canyon City to Harney Valley to claim as his bride a visitor there. Justice of the Peace Davis officiated at the marriage ceremony, held in the parlors of Buckland's Hotel. It was a gala event in Harney, but a noisier reception awaited the couple on their return northward. The Canyon City Brass Band serenaded thoroughly and the bridegroom responded gallantly. The social amenities were observed with joyful refreshments in both towns. A few days later "Attaches of *The News* office" printed a report of the wedding, including verse spun about the editor:

> To the country lying southward
> By the mighty Harney Lake
> Get a woman, find a preacher,
> Some champagne and wedding cake.
>
> Thus you'll make your old life even,
> Cease from envying and strife;
> Find a way to blow your money,
> Lead a merry, jolly life.

Although tens of thousands of coyotes preyed upon poultry, cattle, sheep and wildlife, the Harney country's people accepted the risks. In 1884 Maurice Fitzgerald went about assessing the entire southern portion of Grant County, embracing the valleys of Harney, Silver Creek, Warner, Catlow, Blitzen, Diamond and Happy, and the region south of Steens Mountain to the Nevada line. He gives a glimpse of an area:

Many changes had taken place in the Trout Creek situation. Dave Shirk had quit as Catlow's superintendent and moved into Catlow

Valley, filed on some desirable land on "Home Creek" and engaged in stock raising. His brother Bill also took up a claim on Three Mile, built a nice residence and resided there with his wife for many years.

On the day I arrived at Trout Creek for assessing the Catlow property a change had taken place. John Catlow had just bargained for the sale of his interests to A. W. Sisson of California, and the latter had just arrived with a party of friends to take possession. The party consisted of Mr. Sisson, Clark Crocker, Mrs. Catlow and "Billy" Sisson.

In addition to the party which arrived in a carriage, it was followed by a large wagon carrying an ample supply of the best that California could furnish in the line of good eating and good drinking. I felt that my visit had happened at a very opportune time, for I had just ridden from the Warner country, making long rides and not very good meals.

I had a very cordial greeting, nothing was too good for my comfort and entertainment. I stayed there three days. Perhaps it was partly owing to my business there — assessing the property, which was now in the name of A. W. Sisson, and so remained for many years thereafter under the management of "Billy" Sisson.

Clark Crocker was a brother of the multi-millionaire Charles Crocker. I had very long and interesting talks with Mr. Crocker. I will never forget his saying, "Mr. Fitzgerald, I have all the money that I care for and have no desire to make any more."

Many settlers had to trade in Nevada. Aaron Denio, choosing land south of Pueblo Valley, built a home near the Nevada line in 1885. When, 12 years later, he became the first postmaster of the office named for him, he and his neighbors faced a difficult drive of more than 150 miles when visiting Burns.

Origins of other postoffices stemmed from small businesses first established at ranches in the eighties. In merchandising aid to widely spaced ranchers, the centers included White Horse Ranch, Fields, Andrews, Blitzen, Frenchglenn (near "P" Ranch), Diamond, Mule (Mahon Ranch), Princeton, Narrows, Voltage, Venator, Oakley and Crane, Lawen, Buchanan (J. W. Buchanan Ranch), Van (Tom Cleveland place), Egli (near Wagontire), Riley, Suntex, Evergreen and Camp Currey Spring (Cecil Ranch).

Catlow, typical of those who had large interests, procured fine stock whenever possible. He and John Devine vied in shrewd dealings.

Obstacles and dashed hopes were the lot of risk-farming settlers. In the eighties, the Rye Grass district east of Burns yielded disappointments to about 20 families. Of this group, only Fred Denstad, utilizing German thrift, pulled through with any degree of triumph at farming dry land. Nathan Brown gave much of his time in trying to solve settlers' problems. He was among the first men to remove large quantities of sagebrush from lands of the Harney basin. And he labored at providing irrigation.

Like many others, the Shields family in their log house at Silver Creek drove out once a year for supplies. Most of the clothing was homemade. Missionary preachers held services once a month in winter at the schoolhouse, seldom in summer. All-night dances were held in the schoolhouse, when desks were moved out and big suppers were served.

In little more than a decade after greeting its first home-seeking families, the Harney country felt that it had an assertive population. Sturdily, it grew into a purposeful entity.

Chapter XXIV

THE FEUDAL RANGE

THE NORTHERN PACIFIC RAILROAD, by the mid-eighties, was transporting thousands of head of live stock from Oregon pastures to Montana. In 1886, Montana received, over the railroad, 28,000 head of young cattle from Oregon and Washington Territory, along with 32,000 sheep. And it procured 19,500 head of young beeves from the East.

Business and settlement faced keener competition. Rivalries embittered individuals as well as companies. In the spring of 1885, Bill Brown and his brothers had about 4,000 head of sheep and had erected a cabin near a coveted water hole at Wagtontire Mountain. Joe Foster, foreman for the Double-O outfit, came near with a small band of sheep and also had a cabin. Johnny Overstreet assisted Foster as a herder and the sheep began trespassing and mixing in on Bill Brown's feeding range. Foster and Overstreet, persisting against warnings by Brown, refused to withdraw.

The quarreling soon came to a head on a bright day. Foster and Overstreet who, it was averred, threatened Bill with a pistol, stood on disputed ground. Bill rode hurriedly to his cabin and procured a rifle and cartridges from his brother. One account relates that, as Brown rode back toward his adversaries, he was fired upon by Overstreet and Foster threw rocks at him. The argument flamed as Johnny jumped in front of his boss. Bill, not venturing too close, jumped off his horse, knelt and fired at Overstreet. The shot proved fatal.

The body was to be disposed of by Foster. Bill left the scene. Early next morning he appeared at the home of Silver Creek's justice of the peace, T. J. Shields, says Mrs. Shields. He gave himself up for questioning, breakfasting with the Shields family. Shields met Foster, with Overstreet's body in a wagon, at the Gap ranch. He ordered the driver to return to the spot where the killing had occurred—for proper inquest. This done, the dead man was buried in the small cemetery at the upper end of Silver Creek Valley. Foster withdrew his sheep at once.
170

Shields conducted the preliminary trial of Brown at a near-by log schoolhouse, putting him under bond for appearance before the grand jury at Canyon City. Attorney Waters of Burns was the prosecuting attorney; C. A. Cogswell and Mark Kelton, attorneys of Lakeview, defended Brown at the school-house. Brown won acquittal in the trial at Canyon City.

The Brown brothers kept building up sheep into the winter of 1888-89, says Robert D. Baker, it being so severe that they emerged with less than 1,000 head. Bob and George returned to Oregon City, leaving Bill to continue his venture in Harney County. Gradually, he acquired watered claims of disappointed homesteaders as well as many sections of cheap wagon road land favorable to pasturing. Control of "living waters" led, also, to control of multiplied acreages of government land. Bill rebuilt his bands, for natural increase and for wool-clipping, using the Blue Mountain ranges in summer.

For six years Bill, aided only by his dogs, increased and tended his bands. Six feet or more tall, of broad shoulders, high forehead, straight nose and alert eyes, he was a pleasant-appearing man. Usually he wore overalls and boots in the field. Regretful of the killing, Brown tried to avoid close-quarter arguments and lived in sobriety. He labored hard, chewing raisins or other dried fruit as he tended sheep all day. He could be realistically stern yet generous and honest in dealings. He chose not to marry.

Tom Overfelt, who superintended for Miller & Lux, met untimely death in 1886. He was killed, most people said, by a runaway horse, or dragged when his saddle slipped. Others claimed he became the victim of a man riding with him. Miller made a settlement with Overfelt's widow and the holdings were merged with the spreading empire. Lux died in 1887, and because of a large number of heirs, there were contests in California courts for 20 years.

Meanwhile, Miller had Hock Mason extend his Nevada ranges into Quinn River Valley and Black Rock Desert. His Seven S brand was on cattle roaming over wide areas, added to the Double-H ownership, and breeding grounds were constantly improved. Large reserves in stacks of hay carried him over years of drought, 1887 to 1890, and the evil winter of 1889-90. In 1890, Miller had bought out Mason, who was put in charge of the property and advised to let other cattle-men use water holes in his range. Sheepmen were denied because they owned no land, and sheep ruined the grass.

Another move Miller wished to make was acquiring an interest in the vast domain of grassland which John Devine had gained and on which he had his cattle marked with an S Wrench brand. It took time, though, to mow down the cattle baron whose property extended from the swamp lands to the White Horse and Alvord regions—150,000 acres. Alphena Venator says:

The vast holdings of Todhunter and Devine were acquired prin-cipally with small cost to the company. Some of the men that went to work for them would take out a preemption and then sell it to them. Devine could not at times even pay his men but they would still stay on.

Charlie W. Jones succeeded Joe Cooksey as superintendent for Todhunter and Devine, serving them many years until he resigned to enter business for himself. Venator asserts that Jones "was thoroughly conversant with the country and with a large business. He knew cattle and how to take care of them."

Venator recalled much work and little play for ranch hands in the early days when "Whitings had all the dances and entertainments before Burns was located." Later, at yuletide, he says, "we would come to Harney and we would stay a week dancing, drinking and gambling. There were very few Sunday schools in those days, if any."

Miller braved the open trail along with deals in busy marts. While riding over rough country one day he was robbed of a large sum of money carried in his saddlebags. Miller's plea that he needed something to complete his long, arduous journey resulted in the bandit's giving him back $20. A short time later, Miller recognized the robber among ruffians in a saloon. The cattle baron tapped him on the elbow and, as the gunman turned, said, "This is the twenty dollars you so kindly loaned me." Miller wheeled and departed before the man could recover from his surprise.

Devine lived closer to his land, ardently watching it while

laying foundations for a great live-stock plant. Of his aggressiveness and vision, John W. Biggs explains:

. . . He could see the opportunities surrounding him, and had a strong desire to see those opportunities developed, and like men of that nature he used all means at hand to accomplish his ends. Whether those means were always right and just, it is not for us today to judge. The country he found was unsettled by white men, its resources were undeveloped, he saw the chance and he took it. Was it wrong for him to do this? If so, was it wrong for Abraham to take his flock out upon new lands and occupy them and use them, and as far as his needs were concerned adopted them as his own? . . . First we find him who sees the vision; his mind only passes over a generation, he works and develops a thing which will be necessary in his generation; others follow, see improvement, as in this case. . . .

A much-used method in acquiring land during the homesteading period was by "dummy" entry, a person living on a piece of land for the legal amount of time to acquire title, then moving his house-on-wheels to another piece. "Devine followed another course," says the guide *Oregon, End of the Trail,* explaining:

He applied for a purchase in the name of some person in the region and then certified it as a notary public. The state land office mailed the grant to Devine who immediately transferred it to the name of his partner. The persons whose names had been used never suspected that they had applied for land and Devine's partner never knew he had so much land in his name. Other parts of his holdings were properly acquired by buying out smaller ranches.

Cattlemen tried to keep abreast of changing times. Oregon's governor from January, 1887, to January, 1895, was Sylvester Pennoyer. A Democrat, lawyer and lumberman, he had to deal with economic reverses. An emergency law enacted by the Legislature of 1887 made railroad companies liable for injuries to live stock by moving trains unless railway tracks were fenced. The Oregon Pacific Railroad, trying to push eastward from Albany, promised to reach Harney Valley within 18 months. This hope died aborning. In 1889, the Corvallis and Eastern Railroad, wishing to connect Albany with rails at Ontario, ran a survey through Harney Valley. The railroad Burns finally was to greet came from the east 35 years later.

Bounties were paid for destroying predatory animals. Fence laws, including definition of lawful wire fences, were made. Eastern Oregon had a wire-fence law different from western Oregon's for horses were more likely to be injured by barbed wire.

The winter of 1887 brought disaster. An Idahoan wrote:

So intense was the cold that nearly all water courses were frozen solid. Thousands of cattle venturing out on the ice-covered rivers fell and perished. In the hills, every nook and cavern in the rim rocks was filled with dead cattle that had in their weakened condition attempted to gain a shelter that they could not have been driven into when in good flesh.

Such ordeals sharpened the fight over the ranges. Settlers of the Harney country contended more strongly that huge acreages held under provision of the Swamp Land Act were, in reality, dry lands subject to entry under the homestead laws. They sent hundreds of letters and petitions to Governor Pennoyer protesting classification that gave prior claim to such lands by big cattlemen. Plats on file at the Land Office in Lakeview designated swamp land with a large letter "S". Devine and Todhunter gained title to section after section of these lands. The name "Red S Field" stuck to a large portion of the Island Ranch down through the years, because of use of red ink for lettering.

Of further procedure, James J. Donegan remarked:

In 1887 Devine and Todhunter conveyed by a trust deed their lands to Singletary, Hayes and Brooks of California. A. W. Waters and Robert Terrell, representing 240 settlers, appeared before Governor Pennoyer on February 2, 1888 and asked that the report of Government Agent Elliott and State Agent Richmond be set aside and urged the Governor to delay the issuance of swamp land patents to the State so that Todhunter and Devine would not acquire title to the lands in question. Governor Pennoyer wrote to the Commissioner of the General Land Office asking that no further action be taken and that the claimants be given a chance for a hearing before the Register and Receiver to prove the character of each entry.

The Commissioner of the General Land Office granted the settlers time to have a hearing as to the agricultural character of the lands in dispute before final decision was rendered.

The problem was a thorny one in courts for long years, indecision carrying well beyond the generation by which the cases were instituted. More immediate remedies lacking, there was a resort to violence. Intensely bitter became the battle between cattle king and settler.

In 1889 the term "Del Norte" was applied to the area north of Malheur Lake and around Saddle Butte (vicinity of Lawen). It was populated quite fully then, many settlers having squatted on lands that were claimed as swamp by the Pacific Live Stock Company. The cattle kings were fighting to oust them. Eventually, the company won title to what is known as the Red S Field. Meanwhile, Broady Johnson, as United States deputy marshal, directed pulling down fences and removal of "nesters" because of eviction cases won by Todhunter and Devine and big landowners. The so-called Island ranch lands had been, at first, overflowed naturally, making for good hay in proper season.

Embittered settlers were accused of organizing the "101 Secret Society," promptly and always denied. This charge never merited substantiation. Some squatters, however, were recklessly tough and bent on revenge. Men set fire to buildings, corrals and hay stacks. The burning of hay in fall and winter caused a big loss in cattle to the barons. No burners were brought into court, for guilt was hard to establish. Lawless deeds, falsely blamed on the "101" organization, were, in fact, committed by men with personal grudges.

Local papers carried paid warnings against thievery. In November, 1888, Devine offered $500 reward for arrest and conviction of any person stealing any stock. He described his horses as being branded with S Wrench on the left thigh. His cattle bore the same brand on the left hip and their ear-marks were close crop off right ear and underslope on the left ear.

The heat of passion slowly cooled at the end of the decade. Acts of violence that continued sometimes were blamed upon the old secret group when enemy pounced on enemy in personal grudges. Fears and distrust lingered after creation of Harney County. Donegan declared:

. . . Henry Miller, head of the Miller and Lux Company, filed an affidavit in the General Land Office charging that he could not receive justice in the Burns Land Office in contest cases growing out of the swamp land hearings. Among other statements he charged that there had been organized in the town of Burns a society called the Settlers Mutual Home Protection Association, and that both the Register and Receiver of Burns Land Office were members. The Clerk of the Burns Land Office, M. N. Fegtley, denied every allegation of Henry Miller's affidavit.

Devine's empire dwindled when patents to the swamp land were declared illegal by the state. Devine had to rebuy them from speculators. He lost more than three-fourths of his live stock in the dry years of 1888 and 1889, including a hard winter, and his partnership went into bankruptcy. Henry Miller, as the sole bidder, took over Devine's property when it was offered for sale.

The dethroned monarch was employed as manager by Miller and it was arranged for him to regain an interest, but Devine found it irksome to work under a superior. Further, he dived in the red ink again. Miller claimed that Devine also had made many enemies, and the last straw was too weighty. Devine was "let out," but freely deeded, as consolation, to him was the Alvord Ranch of some 6,000 acres. It rippled in changing colors of the desert of mirages on one side and the rocky buttress of Steens Mountain on another.

For a dozen years before his death Devine made it an enchanted place. Previously, he and Todhunter had assembled at their headquarters a choice collection of purebred cattle, horses, dogs, chickens and every fowl and animal obtainable. Biggs says:

This same characteristic followed him on the Alvord Ranch, and at the time of his death this ranch was completely stocked with beautiful purebred cattle and horses. He also established on the Alvord Ranch a herd of elk in an enclosed park, and fenced one side of Steens Mountain as a preserve for deer, quail and other wild life, and very seldom allowed anyone to hunt therein. He loved his cattle, he loved his horses, he loved his dogs, he loved all of the deer and elk within this inclosure, he also loved men. He had enemies, and had had enemies, he was the type of man to make enemies when certain condition would arise, but he never bore a grudge. In his later years I have often heard him speak in very affectionate and endearing terms of those with whom he had in former years had very strong differences.

ARROW HEAD HOTEL

HARNEY COUNTY BRANCH,
UNITED STATES NATIONAL BANK

EDWARD HINES LUMBER CO. PLANT,

LOGGING OPERATIONS,
EDWARD HINES LUMBER CO.

BURNS UNION HIGH SCHOOL

BURNS GRADE SCHOOL

HINES GRADE SCHOOL

GRADE, HIGH SCHOOL AND DORMITORY IN THE HEART
OF THE RANGE LANDS

TRUMPETER SWAN, MALHEUR REFUGE HEADQUARTERS

MULE DEER, MALHEUR REFUGE

CATTLE ROUND-UP

SHEEP ON RANGE

PIONEER PRESBYTERIAN CHURCH IN BURNS

HOLY FAMILY CATHOLIC CHURCH, IN BURNS

It was said that with latest accretions Miller could travel from the Kern River in California, up through Nevada, to the Malheur River region and not spend a night off his land. Indomitably and astutely, he continued to build mightily. Miller had an encyclopedic mind and gave minute directions in conducting business, and at times showed surprising tolerance of competitors' rights. He urged good treatment of animals. Keenly, he discerned what soil could be reclaimed and what should be left to the desert. And he knew the wise economy of native renewing grasses as against over-costly introduction of alfalfa.

In 1889 the president of the Portland Board of Trade, deploring impairment of cattle ranges in eastern Oregon and eastern Washington, declared "that the General Government should institute experiments looking to their reseeding with varieties of grasses suitable to our soil and climate." In Harney County, cattle companies, unknown in northeastern Oregon and in Washington, controlled distribution of water and delayed irrigation development.

Peter French, hanging on to his original holdings and even adding to them, did not permit himself to be squeezed by turning of screws about him. He also was a master of reclamation and selected wisely for its application. As he felt the sting of retaliation with other cattle barons, he fought back grimly and adroitly.

In a letter signed "Harney" which appeared in the *East Oregon Herald* of Burns was a sample of vituperation. The correspondent accused French of considerable evasion of taxes, and that rumors were rife that he hired people to "freeze out" settlers. George Smyth, it was pointed out, had received a beating when he passed through one of French's gates, torn down by order.

The feuds continued, for settlers battled to maintain footholds. Some, favorably located, expanded more readily than others. "Jimmy" Donegan, coming up from Jacksonville in 1889, soon went to work for the Hanley interests. Ed Hanley controlled some of the choicest pastures in Harney Valley. Bill Hanley, accumulating enough to buy out his brother, in the next decade and thereafter was to prove a staunch exponent of uncurbed settlement.

Alphena Venator, who with Charles Peterson as his closest neighbor had settled early on Deadman Creek, tells of the full-tide years of buying and shipping cattle after the railroad had reached Ontario:

. . . I had increased my cattle to from five to six thousand and in the following years I bought and sold the same, frequently driving 2,000 steers at a time to Ontario. I along with Hanley and M. K. Parsons shipped the first steers to Omaha, Neb., by train. About 10,000 head was purchased from the Todhunter & Devine company. We would ship them down to Central City, Nebraska, and there be met by Billy Allen, representative of Wood Bros., who would take out the killer stock, and the balance would be turned to T. B. Hord, a large feeder who would prepare them for market. I kept up the shipping for probably 10 to 15 years as there was no market on the coast except San Francisco. Gradually the markets were established on the coast and the shipping as far as Omaha has almost ceased.

In relation to finances I had to go oustide, principally. A. Hanauer and the McCornick Banking Co. of Salt Lake City was my mainstay for a number of years along with the old National Bank of Spokane, and later on when banks were more numerous I would sandwich in a lot of the smaller ones. The shipping of cattle as far east as Omaha at that time was a great gamble.

Markets fluctuated sharply. A low selling price at the destination sometimes wiped out the expenditures of months of hard preparation.

Chapter XXV

FREIGHTERS AND GOINGS-ON

CARAVANS OF FREIGHT WAGONS gave pioneering no mean spurts in the eighties and nineties. Many are nostalgic memories in Harney Valley of the freighting outfits of Tom Vickers, McKinnon brothers, Ivers and Allisons. Topside drivers engineered four to ten mules and horses pulling linked-on wagons with high wheels and broad tires.

Brakes being on the left side, the jerk-line driver rode the left wheel horse. The two wheel horses were hitched next to the wagon. The pointers were hitched at the point, or end, of the tongue. The rest of the horses were hooked on to a long chain with stretchers. The pointers, slapped by the jerk line, were made to swing to left or right. The jerk line was fastened to a swing horse's collar and, by jockey-stick connection with the bit of its mate, forced the latter to move in proper direction. Sharp jerks meant a right turn, one steady pull a turn to the left.

The driver had a shiny blacksnake whip draped around his neck. Care was exercised in the wielding of vicious whips, for hard blows could bring blood. Horses learned to respond to the crack of a whip, as loud as a pistol shot. Pelting with pebbles carried in pockets often urged lagging ones.

Whips varied for teams of four to six horses, a wooden stalk being four to five and a half feet long. The lash, usually of braided leather six to eight feet in length, had a tip of silk, often replaced with a strip of buckskin. Freighters having six-horse teams or more used the stalkless blacksnake whip. Its butt, about an inch in diameter, with handle of leather sewn inside for six inches, was loaded with shot. Of minimum length of six feet, this whip tapered to a point surmounted by silk or leather.

The business demanded husky or iron-muscled men. In Grant County the freighters rumbled and the stages rattled, and Titans of the road truckled to no personage save a graduate of their rigorous school. In reference to the "best whip on the road," a Burns news item in June, 1888, said:

George W. Roberts, an old stage driver on the Oregon & California line, is visiting W. M. Levens, an old chum, he having driven a stage contemporaneous with him. Mr. Roberts' left hand shows the effect of long years of use in handling the reins, causing the hand to twist up. . . . His thrilling stories of adventures along the line show "those palmy days have passed and gone forever."

That was about the time big Bill Bonham, having reaped a pleasant income from his freighting, left Mt. Vernon. In failing health, he took his family, including the adopted Indian son Jimmy, to southern California. The flush days of high-stacked and tarpaulin-topped wagons, however, continued until the debut of motor trucks. Traffic grew heavier between the budding communities and Canyon City and its rival, John Day, called "Tiger Town." At John Day, many Chinese reworked the ground once mined by the Argonauts, and some of them lived in the county seat.

Canyon City, with half a dozen freighters, did a flourishing business in the eighties. Harney folks went there for pleasure or of necessity, from having a photograph taken by G. I. Hazeltine to attending one of the three churches or one of five lodges. All knew of the residents in Chinatown. Lay, Toy, and Git ran laundries near a general store. Sing Koon headed the street cleaning department. Chinese Jenny presided in her opium den. Spanish Rosie and a Chinese hireling, Lon, raised pigs after having quit an impolitic profession. Vinie "Red Head" and Polly Wilson had not surrendered to continence.

Friendly with everybody was jolly Sing Koon. Twice a week in the summertime he used a broom and shovel on the business streets. Back and forth he went to Canyon Creek with a wheelbarrow to dump the collections. Each business house paid him 50 cents at the day's end. He would utter a merry "Ha! Ha!" whenever he found a quarter or a whole dollar in front of a saloon.

Upon the approach of a freight caravan of covered wagons and trailers drawn by six or 10 horses, sometimes composed of three or four outfits—their arrival announced by the jingling bells which decked the collars of the lead horses of each team— old Sing was warned that he was in for a big day of work on the morrow, and no extra pay. The teamsters parked their caravans in front of every store and then unloaded onto the sidewalks, while the horses champed their bits and stood on the narrow streets, blocking all other traffic. And the next day! Sing Koon wheeled load after load to the banks of Canyon Creek—enough to fertilize many gardens. But he loved the horses and he never complained.

Teamsters seemed to know everybody and everybody seemed to know them. They relayed news for consumption all over the county. Canyon City hummed louder than its contributing towns. Groth of the City Hotel rang a dinner bell before each meal, while across the street at the Golden Eagle, Nick, the waiter, pounded an iron bar on an iron triangle. A long row of candlesticks and smudged chimneys at the hotels had to be cleaned each morning.

Brew foamed in a great copper boiler in the Brewery saloon. In its barroom dusty pictures of famous men and stirring scenes caught the eyes of men who played cards. A bucket of ice water with a tin dipper antedated fountains. The Brewery had two competing saloons. The rising sun bared their back yards littered with torn cards and, occasionally, photos of scantily draped women which helped sales of ready-made cigarettes. Most smokers bought makin's and paper to roll deftly.

Editor Asbury, who published the *Grant County News* from 1886 to 1898, hired boys to turn the crank of the printing press as he inked the type with a hand roller and fed the machine with paper. Sawing and chopping wood, peddling fruit and vegetables, and running errands yielded money to other lads showing ambition. Phil Metschan recalls vividly:

I was now old enough to read, and subscribed to the *Youth's Companion*. What a thrill and pleasure to wait with the grown-ups for the arrival of the stage at the end of a 200-mile journey from The Dalles, and get my copy!

Walking home on dark nights — father with his *Oregonian,* I with my *Youth's Companion,* guided by a few coal oil lamps encased in glass and mounted on posts about ten feet high. The friendly rays of these feeble lamps in the inky darkness will always be in my memory as well as that of the long-bearded town marshal, Mr. Moody, who, with stepladder, shears, and coal oil can, made his daily rounds to service them. All those who lived any distance from the town's business section carried lanterns. These beacons could be seen approaching and receding on every dark night on the surrounding hills. When the moon was bright and the sky cloudless, the lamps were dark and the lanterns left at home.

No women smoked except those of the shaded district. Standards and ways of living had definite patterns. Metschan says:

Why, morals — We remember the plight of the orphaned girl and the flight of the bartender who betrayed her. Thus did the community protect the weak.

We also remembered the precipitate flight of two other miscreants who invaded the homes of peaceful citizens. Divorces followed, but the two male offenders found it good for their health to depart. Thus did this pioneer community maintain its morals. The men mentioned above were nearly all bachelors — luckless miners — digging until bent with age and no longer able to mine, who never went "back east" to their waiting sweethearts, lived in their comfortless, cheerless cabins in the town and on the surrounding gold-bearing hills and Little Canyon mountains until their end. . . .

Some of them were educated and talented. White Headed Smith, flaxen hair, clean-shaven, with the exception of a Phil Sheridan flaxen goatee, always neat and well groomed, when a little under the influence of liquor, would mount a soap box and orate — quoting history, scripture, and poetry.

Gus Bittner, an expert worker in iron and steel, a native of Germany, lived alone in a one-room cabin near the Methodist Church. Henry Kuhl, son of Peter, for whom Gus worked as a blacksmith, says that Gus went back to Germany in the early '90s — returning, found Peter had sold his blacksmith shop and was farming, . . . drew the balance of wages $7,000.00. Gus dressed up on Sunday and spent the day at the brewery, whittling, playing billiards, and refreshing himself with beer. Henry also says that Wm. Overholt, a wheelright, his father and Gus built a buggy for Dr. F. C. Horsely. Kuhl and Bittner handwrought all the iron and steel, Overholt all the woodwork. The wheels, five feet in diameter, so the doctor would have clearance over the rutted pioneer roads and enabling him to cross the swollen streams in early spring. . . .

Magnetic were parades and pageants. When they were staged, whittlers forsook their benches and folks rode in from afar. On the Fourth of July, 1886, the loudest applause went to the Liberty Wagon, bearing 40 queens. They sparkled in red, white and blue costumes. Each had the name of a state painted on her paper crown. The Goddess of Liberty stood smilingly, holding aloft the nation's flag. The proud driver, dominating six colorfully decorated horses, wore a tuxedo, a stiffly starched white shirt with a white tie, and a rigid stove-pipe hat.

Men of the Harney country, inspired by Devine in breeding of race horses, constructed a mile track at Burns in June, 1888. This race course was maintained for many years, its annual Jockey Club meeting attracting the finest running horses of eastern Oregon. Donegan names some of those who ran at Burns:

Nampa, Champagen, Miss Dudley, owned by Senator Hamilton of Grant County; John D., John S. and Grey Jim, owned by Devine and raced by Tex Sillman; Jordan, Rattler, Billy Barlow, owned by John Cusoman of Long Creek; Pin Ear, a famous quarter horse, and Little Joe, owned by M. S. Keeneg of Grant County; Barbwire, owned by Bill Wood of Diamond; Grey Rooster, owned by J. H. Wadman; Cicero and Sage Hen, owned by George W. Hayes; Barney and Soda Water Jim, owned by John Newman; Bannock, owned by John Morell; Dick Whoten, Gray Dandy, and Hush, owned by Tom Stephens and Henry Richardson.

The meet drew a rollicking, boisterous crowd of men. The horses tied in front of saloons waited long hours for their masters. Sleepless citizens sought sorely needed rest when the last cowboy spurred his mount toward the range with vociferous yipping.

When came winter's chills, die-hard sportsters of Burns created new contests. One such occurred on a Saturday morning of January, 1888, staged outside the Arcade Saloon. Joe Wooley furnished 10 chickens for shooting practice at "a bit a shot" if hit in the head, or 50 cents if hit in the body. The weaving men fired Winchester rifles at a distance of 40 yards offhand or 60 yards with a rest. The promoter realized about $14.

On the saner side, the local editor read "a sure sign of business prosperity" in Attorney J. Nat Hudson's ordering of a Remington typewriter. An ad reminded housewives they could buy a high-arm Singer sewing machine on easy monthly payments.

In that year of 1888 several near and fatal tragedies enlivened the news. Items of mid-May recorded:

A shooting scrape occurred a week ago at the P Ranch . . . An old grudge existed between Gus Harrison and Dick Cooper, which culminated in an explosion . . . While Cooper was walking on a foot log he encountered Harrison, who began shooting at him, which caused him to fall into the water. In response to his exclamation, "For God's sake, don't shoot me, Gus!" the shootist fortunately desisted.

SAMPLE OF PIONEER JUSTICE

A stranger passing through Catlow Valley paused at Wm. Shirk's long enough to steal a pair of spurs, lariat and chaparajos, etc. He was hunted up Madedi's gorge, soundly kicked and sent on his way.

The Harney region was stirred deeply when, on May 5, James Bright, a quiet, well-liked young man, was slain 12 miles east of the town of Harney. Victim of a mysterious robbery yielding several hundred dollars, his body was found under a pile of stones a quarter-mile from his runaway team and wrecked wagon. His body penetrated by a rifle bullet, and with a lariat fastened to his feet, had been dragged by a horseman, stated John Robinson, deputy sheriff, at an inquest held by Judge Davis.

The hunt for the killer brooked no delay, but a baffled posse uncovered little clamping evidence. Out of circumstances, an Indian, Buckaroo Jim, was arrested and taken to Canyon City's jail. For company he had a young Irishman named Pat McGinnis, charged with horse-stealing. They awaited trial. State and federal courts had jurisdiction for punishment of crimes of varying degree by Indians off or on reservations.

In the quiet of the evening of July 4, after a day-long frontier celebration, an alarm spread that Robert Lockwood, deputy sheriff, had been shot fatally in the head while locking up the jail cells for the night. His body lay in the corridor and under his leg was found his .44-caliber Smith and Wesson pistol, two chambers empty. The prisoners had escaped.

Both were captured within a few days, McGinnis charged with the murder. The Paiute, sole eyewitness to the crime and speaking through an interpreter, accused him. He testified that Lockwood, while unlocking his cell for a few moments, had no fear of McGinnis and he put his pistol on a table. McGinnis, in stocking-feet, he said, stole up from behind,

snatched the pistol and shot the deputy. One bullet missed
its mark.

When found not guilty of Bright's murder at the November
term of court, Buckaroo Jim gained his freedom. In the same
month a jury convicted the Irishman for the murder of Lockwood, and he was sentenced to be hanged January 18, 1889.
After an unsuccessful appeal, the execution occurred Friday,
April 26, following.

Phil Metschan reflects that McGinnis might have secured
acquittal if his influential uncle who lived about 50 miles from
Canyon City could have been contacted for help. Metschan
relates:

> While Pat was in jail, and before the murder of Lockwood, I,
> then a small boy, became quite well acquainted with him. He was
> genial, good-natured, and I liked him. Much of my time was spent
> at the courthouse in those days, my father being the county clerk. I
> saw Pat every day.
> Many of the old-timers who remember this trial, myself amongst
> them, do not believe that Pat killed Lockwood.

The day that McGinnis was hanged in the courthouse yard,
wide-eyed Phil stood at the foot of the stairs up which the
sheriff led the ill-fated Irishman. Pat refused aid. He trotted
up the steps, the boy at his side. Metschan continues ruefully:

> Just before Sheriff Gray adjusted the black cap over his head, he
> looked over at me and said, "Hello, Phil." Although young and
> calloused, I couldn't take any more. I ran down the steps.

On September 8, 1888, William H. Brown met death in the
Caldwell Saloon at Burns. Testimony revealed that, in an
aggressive mood, Brown threatened William Page with a
knife, knocking him to the floor. In a struggle to regain his
feet, Page fired four bullets that felled his attacker. Trial and
acquittal followed.

Ten days after the village's unrehearsed drama, another
took the stage in Catlow Valley—the killing of James C. Isaacs
by David L. Shirk. In a preliminary hearing at Diamond
before H. M. Horton, justice of the peace, Attorneys Hudson
and Sizemore stood for the prosecution. State's testimony

claimed that Isaacs and Archey Jordan, while examining the Sam Crow timber culture claim, were accosted by Shirk, on horseback, and accused of being on land of which he had charge. The men, answering abusive language, denied knowledge of trespassing.

Then, according to the state, Shirk produced a rifle at the edge of a field and returned. Unarmed, the men retreated. Shirk advanced, hurling an epithet. This caused the men to turn, whereupon Shirk fired and Isaacs, hit in the head, fell.

Attorney Charles Parrish represented the slayer. James Donegan notes:

> The defense claimed that Isaacs had threatened Shirk's life previous to the shooting. Edward Lyons, who was grubbing sagebrush for Shirk on the Crow claim, testified that in the quarrel before the shooting Isaacs drew a pistol and told Shirk if he made a move he would kill him. Lyons said Shirk moved away to the sagebrush and picked up his gun and that at that time Isaacs had Shirk covered with his pistol. When Shirk picked up his rifle he said, "You men have threatened my life, now get off this land." Jordan said, "All right, I will go," and he did go. Isaacs crouched down on the ground with his pistol presented. Shirk fired. Shirk was held to the Grand Jury in the sum of $5,000 with John Catlow and D. H. Smyth as bondsmen. . . .

At the October term of court in 1889, the jury, after deliberating 31 hours, gave a verdict of "not guilty." In April of that year Cooper, who had dodged bullets on a log, was stabbed to death by Ben Jones, a half-breed employed by the Sisson ranch. Jones, captured quickly at Denio, saved legal expenses when he shot himself. He and his victim went to graves the same day.

While placidity seemed to be severely priced at times, emulation of propriety prevailed. The women had their social get-togethers, and they met polite men at dances. Further, they had economic problems to solve, even as did Piute Charley.

The affable Indian sold sage-hen eggs on Burns' streets at two-bits a dozen in the spring of 1889. Barnyard eggs retailed at 25 cents a dozen (20 cents at Harney), butter at 35 cents a pound, and beef at 10 cents. On the other hand, no fruits or vegetables or tea or coffee or sugar or salt were for sale in the town in April. Irate housewives and impatient grocers urged better freighting.

Teamsters took heed ere another winter closed in on Harney Valley. The local editor announced in mid-November, next:

One of the largest freight trains we have ever seen enter Burns at one time came in from the railroad Sunday evening. It was composed of the McKinnon Bros., Ivers and Allisons' 8-horse teams, eight wagons loaded to the guards with merchandise for the already heavily stocked stores of J. Durkheimer and N. Brown.

It proved to be good foresight. For three months in the winter of 1889-90 the snow blocked the road between Burns and Ontario. No mail came through except that carried by the triweekly stage from Canyon City. It encountered schedule troubles, too.

Daily papers from Portland arrived a week or more late. Then folks eased off gruffness as they glanced at pantry shelves stacked high and at an assortment of condiments in a corner.

In the mid-eighties Julius Durkheimer took over and improved the mercantile store that had been established by McGowan and Stenger.

In 1887, Nathan Brown began construction of a gristmill, which Harney County lacked. In that year, also, Paul Locher, native of Germany, came to Burns and established that section's first brewery. In lengthy residence, he acquired considerable residential and ranch property. He built and operated a large hall for the town.

In 1892, Nathan Brown tried to encourage raising of wheat in Harney County by proposing to erect a roller flouring mill of 40 to 50 barrels' daily capacity. Citizens were to subscribe $3,000 to be repaid in products, grinding and so forth. Several years went by, however, before the mill became a reality, as a private enterprise.

Meanwhile, the town of Harney was having its heyday, with a favorable postal business.

Chapter XXVI

BURNS GATHERS MOMENTUM

By the General Allotment Act of 1887, popularly known as the Dawes Act, immediate intent was to disintegrate tribal relations, making for individual holding of title to land by Indians and preparing them for admission to citizenship in the United States. They were to gain relief from paternalistic control. Individuals got, usually, 160 acres of land, title of which was held in trust by the government for twenty-five years, whereupon the Indians became owners and full citizens. Subsquent amendments, however extended the trust period and citizenship was not granted all native Indians until 1924. Still, they cannot avoid some restrictions.

At the time of enactment of the Dawes Act, Sarah Winnemucca mourned the death of her husband, and his fatal illness had drained her savings. Cooperation with her brother in running the farm and school in Nevada had become impaired. Discouraged and in ill health, Sarah went to Idaho to make her home with a married sister for the few remaining years of her life.

Some of their tribe, although not receiving allotments of land until twenty-odd years later, lingered in the region of old Malheur Reservation. They witnessed fateful changes. They watched new towns growing at the side of roads which led in from a country of expanding ranches.

The people who came to the Harney country received glad encouragement from the press in Burns which rivaled the *Items*. In November, 1887, D. L. Grace, formerly a school teacher in Missouri, and his wife Nellie, established the *East Oregon Herald*. Horses freighted in the equipment from Huntington. Mrs. Grace assisted as editor and did the typesetting. Two of the four pages were boiler-plate, type cast elsewhere.

The *Items,* a six-column folio, carried on spiritedly in a building formerly used as a "social center" for the metropolis
188

of the range. The unconventional young women had to shift to quarters in the rear of a saloon across the street. Abandoned by the girls who had made good use of many individual windows, this place, with partitions removed, afforded beneficial light for the typesetters.

Fifty per cent of the twenty-four columns of the *Items* by February, 1887 — in its second year — was advertising which included sixteen notices of final proof on land. Advertisers were hotels, general merchants, stage lines, drug stores, blacksmithing, the Prineville Boot and Shoe Company, two livery stables, a grocery store, a saloon, two barbers, a meat market, and trade-name products. Leaders were Cuticura, Electric Belts, Hall's Sarsaparilla, St. Jacob's Oil, D. M. Ferry's Seeds, Piso's cure for Consumption, Royal Baking Powder and Dr. Pierce's Pleasant Pellets. Local news compared slimly with miscellaneous matter clipped from eastern exchanges, including staid jokes of the day.

The type of journalism leaned to sharp wit and frankness. Of the marriage of William Miller and Miss Eva Cozad, the *Herald* reported in November, 1887:

We understand no slip knot was tied at their wedding, as both church and state officiated, a minister of the gospel and county judge being the respective representatives. A legal gentleman comments on this novel feature of the happy affair: "It will require the Supreme Court of the State to divorce them and that, too, without dissenting voice."

Under the head, "Journalism from Dame Rumor," the same paper said on May 9, 1888:

Last Monday as Mrs. Bates and her son, a lad about ten years old, were driving across a bridge over Silvies River near Z. L. Thomas' place, the horses shied, turning the wagon over into the stream.

The boy was caught under the wagon, and being unable to extricate himself, was drowned.

Later information is, that both Mr. and Mrs. Bates were in the wagon, and that the bridge broke down, but as the child was drowned in either case it does not make much difference.

When politicians sailed into uncharted seas, editors often shipped with them. They clung tightly to the mast in stormy days. The *Herald's* pilot, caught up in the swirl of the Fourth of July, 1889, maintained a set course:

The Corvallis *Gazette* complains that the E. O. H. received by them is filled with sand, regular Eastern Oregon sand that doubtless sifts in through the mail bags.
The answer is:
It required sand to run a newspaper here in Burns. Scott of the *Oregonian,* Hearst of the *Examiner* and Young of the *Chronicle* have for their motive power money — others Jawbone and Promises. Having none of these, pluck and good staying qualities have kept us afloat — hence the sand in our paper. "You catch on," Bro. *Gazette?*

In November of that year a Saturday weekly of independent nature was founded by Ben Brown. Named the Harney *Times,* it had Maurice Fitzgerald as editor to guide it. Early that month, a group of Burns men met to consider "ways and means for putting a straight-out Republican paper in the field" with "all-at-home print." Hank Levens, one of these townsmen, in due course headed a stock company which bought the *Items.* This paper, at the end of November, directed its sarcasm at a crowing Democratic organ:

The use of roosters in a newspaper after an election indicates a lack of editorial ability and a desire to fill up with something trashy and cheap. We have a contempt for such foolishness.

It was in December, 1889, that youthful Julian Byrd, who was to outlast all competitors in Harney County, began to learn printing in the *Herald's* office. His father, W. C. Byrd, owned a livery stable and soon became editor of the *Herald.* Charles A. Byrd, Julian's brother, published the *Items* from 1890 to 1893. In the late eighties the Byrds scanned the foundation upon which Burns stood. They liked it.

Postal service had been widening under successive postmasters. James C. Parker, replacing Postmaster Grace in 1886, gave way to Emily A. Vaughn in April, 1889. The first daily mail was secured in the latter year.

In December, 1886, the building of two schoolhouses for Silvies District 13, at $400 each, was authorized. George McGowan turned over his duties as clerk in 1887 to H. A. Dillard, who gave way to Joseph Wooley the same year. By that time the enlarged tax roll permitted fall and spring terms of three months each. The principal, M. N. Fegtly, received $75 a month, and Mrs. E. Pratt, second teacher, drew a monthly salary of $50.00. When, in 1889, L. B. Baker became the first school superintendent of Harney County, he merited an annual salary of $300.

At Burns Hall in 1887 a large throng assembled for the Grand Christmas Ball, which became an annual event. It cost the ladies nothing, but each male escort paid an admission price of $2.00 and spectators fifty cents. It being a masquerade dance, Grace's drug store furnished wire masks. Popular musicians and three floor managers had a long night of it. Those who rebelled against decorum found themselves shoved out to cheerless cold.

In this year, also, after having started plans the previous summer, Methodists tried to erect the community's first church. A resolute group of people, who had welcomed visiting preachers, realized they needed their permanent guidance as well as their officiating at weddings and funerals. The small congregation, despite financial weakness, persisted in its aims.

Quipped Canyon City's *News*, in mid-December: "Burns folks started to build a church last summer and now an enterprising citizen is building a brewery and will have it completed before the church."

Paul Locher, who was promoting the brewery plant, had it operating several months later, and his family grew with the town. People with and without a creed contributed to the church fund. The first fraternal organization came into being, enough Odd Fellows banding for installation of a chapter.

In January and May of 1888 the *East Oregon Herald* described businesses in Burns. They were: two newspapers, two hotels, three saloons, one undertaker, one meat market, two lawyers (George Sizemore and J. N. Hudson), three physicians, one surveyor, one land agent, one drug store, one jeweler (Charles Sampson), one blacksmith (P. S. Early), one saddler (J. C. Welcome), one livery stable (Byrd's), two general merchandise stores, one bath house, one hardware store (McGowan's), one barber shop, one sawmill (John Sayer's), one ladies' nurse, two carpenters, one reading room, one school. Nathan Brown, who competed with Durkheimer in mercantile lines, dreamed of turning his gristmill into the first large flour mill for the region.

Before another winter, Union veterans of the Civil War wished to have regular meetings. Welcome and D. Jameson called a meeting to establish a post of the Grand Army of the Republic. In October, attorney Hudson obtained the first money order and postal note to be issued at Burns. Postoffices were climbing into elite standing. The postmaster general established an inviolable rule that no postoffice should be kept in a saloon or in any room from which a saloon might be entered.

The determined Methodists succeeded in bringing a measure of piety to Burns by April, 1889. The Rev. William Bartholomew of Long Creek, in giving ministerial help, added a dozen persons to the membership of the completed church. The *Herald* proclaimed that "Burns has built a church, engaged a pastor, closed her saloons on Sunday, and invites Harney and all the valley to come and enjoy the legitimate pleasures of the Sabbath."

Women proved to be the mainstay of religious observance, a few men standing as pillars of support. Boys and young men who preferred to play ball on Sunday got a raking when thirty-five of the irreverent were counted about a hundred yards from the church. A "crying disgrace," said the paper, in strong exhortation for attendance at Sunday School.

Citizens of the newly incorporated town, pious or not, realized the worth of tolerance and supplanting ridicule with respect. Businessmen who joined no particular faith knew that the ignoring of rights of better living had to be defeated to bring in people who desired advantages of churches, schools and gainful fraternization. Good settlers added to the orderliness, and they came.

Dr. J. W. Ashford left Baker and, along with physicians Embree and McPheeters in 1888, gave the people of Burns and Harney County increased medical attention. Dr. Ashford moved on to Canyon City midway of the 1890's.

Coincidental with the birth of Harney County and incorporation of Burns in 1889 came relocation of the region's land office. Opposition of big cattle interests had been strong and they had influence enough to have it located at Drewsey instead of at Burns. Archie McGowan declares:

"My father was appointed receiver of the land office. This location was almost as bad as Lakeview as a mountain range had to be crossed from Harney Valley to Drewsey. It took another year to have it located at Burns."

Election of President Grover Cleveland, a Democrat, caused a change in the local office's officials. With Captain Harrison Kelly as receiver and J. B. Huntington as register, the Harney Land Office at Burns opened for transaction of public business September 2, 1889.

For the remainder of 1889, its records included sixty-nine homestead entries, totaling 3,284.16 acres, and thirty-nine timber-culture entries, 2,131.16 acres. Cash receipts were $17,-977. The business reflected the flush of the meadow and bench lands.

In step with advancement, a new library for Burns was started with fifty volumes of choice reading matter in November. Known as the Burns Circulating Library and Book Exchange, housed in the *Herald* building, it had a free reading room, and Mrs. Grace served as librarian. With funds derived from annual membership and reading fees, hopes were maintained for establishing a public library on a central lot. All revenue for the incoming year, however, was to be spent on additional books. The librarian also acted as agent for periodicals and books.

Mrs. M. A. Fry, practical nurse, received more calls than formerly. On the first day of December she was in attendance when the first twins were born in Burns. Mrs. Isaac Winters gave birth to a twelve-pound girl and an eight-pound boy.

When the people assembled for the Christmas Ball they eyed an improvement that lit up, partially, the main stem filled with horses and vehicles. In that yuletide C. M. and L. Caldwell put up in front of their saloon the first street lamp, of wick and oil. The French Hotel and other business houses soon erected posts topped by lamps giving limited but cheerful glow.

At the end of the eighties, Oregon had established itself well in radiation of culture, patterning after older regions in architecture, schools, churches and other forms of progress, but it had not won recognition for creative culture. The only man to stand forth in the creative literary field, Joaquin Miller, had strode out of Grant County to gain fame afar.

Lawmakers had copied well. Educators, including the clergy, had accomplished wonders in conquering illiteracy. Harvey Scott of the *Oregonian* towered in journalism, his profundity continuously an aid in keeping the ship of state out of shallow channels.

The seeds of all these fruits did not spread as readily in the great spaces east of the Cascade Mountains, but a worthy number did find fertile soil. Grant County had come far since the debut of the Argonauts. Its offspring, Harney County, already was proving that it had men and women capable of accepting the obligations diverted to them in self-rule.

Chapter XXVII

COUNTY DIVISION

IN THE SECOND DECADE of settlement, the two-day trip from Harney Valley to Canyon City entailed much time and expense, in fair or foul weather. Too, the way provided opportunities for robberies, some of which had resulted in murders.

Early in November, 1888, citizens were selected to attend a convention at Harney to furnish instructions to Dr. G. W. Gilham, state legislator, as to proposals for county division. George McGowan presided at the Burns meeting, and A. W. Waters served as secretary. The fourteen delegates sent to Harney precinct to represent Burns were Waters, McGowan, J. M. Vaughn, N. Brown, J. C. Wooley, George Zumwalt, A. J. Nelson, John Martin, A. Allen, John Sayer, H. Levens, J. C. Welcome, George Sizemore and P. S. Early.

Wintry sieges failed to cool the ardor of those who circulated petitions asking the Legislature to create Harney County from territory to be sliced off the south end of Grant County. Petitioning went on through January of 1889, compelling reasons being those of a large number of people who had to travel 200 miles to transact official business and attend sessions of the circuit court at Canyon City. Petitioners pointed out that the mileage cost to serve a court summons ranged from $18.00 in Burns to $54.00 in Catlow Valley.

At the Legislature in Salem, lobbyists hired by a minority group opposing county division enjoyed more warmth. On January 6, Representative Gilham introduced a bill in the House entitled, "A Bill for an Act to Create the County of Harney." Upon hammering down of the opposition, the bill passed in the course of a few weeks. Creation of Harney County became an actuality February 25. It has an area of 10,132 square miles, as large as Maryland. The Legislature designated Harney, Gilham's home town, as county seat.

At that time George McGowan was a member of the Grant County Court, being commissioner from his district. Archie McGowan says:

. . . The people or settlers in the town of Burns wanted a county seat nearer than Canyon City. This again caused a division between the people or settlers and the large cattle interests. Finally the legislature of 1889 divided the county, but again to spite Burns the big strong cattle men were influential enough to have Harney designated the county seat. Burns had taken the lead all the way through in the struggle for the division, and they were very indignant over this affair and determined to wrest the county seat away from Harney and have it set at Burns. . . .

Pending formal election, Governor Pennoyer appointed men to the offices. The first officers of Harney County were: Thomas J. Shields, judge; W. E. Grace, clerk; W. M. Miller, deputy clerk; A. A. Cowing, sheriff; V. J. Miller, acting treasurer; Thomas H. Roberts, treasurer; L. B. Baker, school superintendent; W. E. Alberson, assessor; T. B. James and Lytle Howard, commissioners; W. H. Graydon was named surveyor.

Pressing was the building of a temporary jail at Harney. It had to be completed before May 20, 1889. Specifications called for the use of 1,600 pounds of nails to guarantee security. E. H. King offered to erect a sufficiently sound lockup for $425 by using only 1,200 pounds of nails. C. F. McKinney proposed to build the jail as specified for $610. Award of the contract went to J. W. Norton, who declared he could do the job for $425, strictly in accord with official desires.

On May 6, while plenty of nails went into the shelter for prisoners, the county clerk issued the first marriage certificate. The contracting parties, Attorney Sizemore and Miss Alta McGee, spoke their marital vows before the Rev. Mr. Bartholomew, minister of the Methodist Church.

The county government functioned as best it could while preparing for its first election, to be held in June, 1890. In February of that year began the red-hot fight over permanent location of the county seat. The deep and closed ranks which had battled successfully for their infant political unit now wavered and separated. The Burns portion of the phalanx felt that its rival town had robbed it of chief honors. Resentment exploded, with Democrats and Republicans trying to define favoritism.

W. C. Byrd assumed editorship of the *East Oregon Herald* on March 6, and, with his son Charles in the saddle of the

Items, the people of Burns rallied at a gallop. The Burns papers printed issues top-heavy with arguments explaining why the county seat should be located in their town. Equally as emphatic were the papers of the city of Harney in pointing out reasons for not removing the seat of county officialdom. Hardly a man in Harney County could stay neutral. He who hesitated found himself challenged to take his stand.

When the voters cast their ballots in June they hoped they would stop the cyclone of pleadings. The storm continued with greater fury when Burns claimed victory by a narrow margin. Both camps charged fraud and illegal voting. They hired attorneys and took the matter to the courts. Eventually, the case reached Oregon's Supreme Court. Judge Shattuck handed down a final decision in November, 1892, holding that Burns had won the election by six votes. The canvassing board had determined that the votes cast totaled 1,016, from the following precincts: Burns, 512; Harney, 415; Silvies City, eighty-four; Drewsey, four; Wright's Point, one.

The Burns battlers, however, took things in their own hands after the June election. Harney folks balked at surrendering the official papers and material accumulated in their short-lived county seat. The Burns partisans, in deep secrecy, laid plans for obtaining them. A well-chosen and strong force of riders swooped down upon temporary frame quarters in Harney at nighttime. Hastily, they piled the stuff into a wagon driven by Jasper McKinnon. Then they forked into their saddles, their guns and sharp eyes assuring a safe removal to a protected building in the town of their choice.

The county court held its first session at the permanent county seat, Burns, July 7, 1890. Some of its members felt the strangeness and tenseness of the atmosphere, but their outward appearance remained unruffled. They continued to conduct business as usual while awaiting decision on legality of the freemen's votes. By no means did Harney become a town of abjection. It held its head high for many years while Burns gained business and population at its expense.

They braved adversity together. The winter of 1890 tested them with blizzards and vengeful incendiarism. Tom Howard, indomitable stage driver, bowed to the elements in trying to push through obstacles between Burns and the railroad at Ontario. He described his last trip to Drewsey in mid-February:

Drifts in the road were so high the horses would leap and plunge forward into one and when out of that into another and when I would look back I could not see any trace of those I came through, as they would close over, so that there was an unbroken trail before me and waste of snow drifts in the rear. I don't think the road will be open for stage travel till the middle of March.

In that month flames consumed 250 tons of hay bought by Devine to feed 500 head of calves in corrals on the Island. The fire was thought to be incendiary because of the damp weather and telltale tracks in the powdery snow. Hank Levens joined those who hired men to guard their stacks. An upstate paper warned: "The hay burners . . . will get caught in their nefarious work one of these nights and reach the end of their rope, as it were. "

Stockmen welcomed a chinook early in March, but it heralded greater damage. A quickly freezing spell formed a heavy crust. Then a frigid wind blew violently hour after hour. It chilled to death hundreds of sheep at a lone ranch, their blood covering the snow as they worked through the icy sheathing.

Bound by winter, leading men of Burns formed a literary club. They participated in debates, programs and criticism. The Burns Brass Band, organized in the previous November, gave a minstrel performance in March. The proceeds helped to buy their uniforms. In March, also, the Burns Fire Company effected a permanent organization, meeting at the store bought by Durkheimer. Cal Geer, president, and George Young, secretary, were among eight officers and a membership of twenty. These volunteers acquired meager equipment.

The benefits of closer fraternal binding were enhanced by members of the Free and Accepted Masons. The charter for the Burns Lodge of Freemasonry was granted June 12, 1890, with Cyrus Sweek as worshipful master; Isaac Baer, senior warden; J. B. Huntington, junior warden; T. B. Harris, secretary: J. W. Sayer became the first man to receive the degrees of the lodge.

In the summer of 1891 the county's law enforcers were accused of wearing blinkers as hands grabbed slick-ears. A Burns

writer deplored the fact there was no conviction for larceny
of animals if confined to thievery from big companies. Said
he with salinity:

> It is tit for tat and butter for fat;
> If you hurt my dog, up goes your cat.

Obliquely, the district attorney blamed the community's
diffidence.

Some men sought bracing in the open, as bared in the
printed thrust, "The Beggar and Mister:"

"Good morn' — mister!"

"Good morning, sir."

"Please give me a quarter. I'm dead broke, don't yer know?"

"Well, what of it? Why should I give you a quarter?"

"Because I want to go to Harney the 4th and get as drunk as a
lord."

"I don't think it proper to give you money for that purpose and,
besides, two-bits worth of whiskey won't make you drunk."

"I know that two-bits of Burns whiskey won't fix me, but, mister,
you don't know Harney whiskey as well as ——"

"Stop! Here is the two-bits."

In truth, each town offered the same degree of potency.
Long hauls jacked up the price. A stockman paid a Burns
liquor dealer $1,150 in gold coin for six barrels of "Crow
Bourbon" at this time.

The permanent county seat, nonetheless, took cognizance of
its responsibilities. Under the new ownership of Byrd and his
two sons in 1891, the *Herald* pursued an exemplary and ex-
hilarating course. Mrs. Grace kept enough equipment to do
job printing while continuing her library and book exchange.
Dr. Marsden left Drewsey to practice in Burns. A lodge of the
Ancient Order of United Workmen organized with twenty-
three members in November.

The Rev. Father P. B. Champagne, Catholic missionary,
visited those interested in his faith. At times he lectured in the
Methodist Church. Within a year a Christian Science Sabbath
School, like others, met at a residence.

Business tried to keep pace with politics. A livery barn in
Burns managed by William Wood for the owner, Mrs. M. A.

Fry, who also conducted a restaurant adjoining the stable, burned on May 17, 1891. The barn was located on the present site of the Safeway Store. Three horses were lost out of forty that were in the barn when the fire was discovered by Lou J. Bosenberg, who ran a saloon on the corner later occupied by the Masonic building.

From about this date to the early 1900's, Mart Brenton kept up to date his White Front Livery Stable. It stood on what is now another corner of the block containing the Arrowhead Hotel.

In July of 1891, after visiting his Harney lands, Henry Miller, head of the Pacific Live Stock Company, declared himself willing to give a liberal grant of land for a railroad and free right of way across his Harney domain. He also said he would sell at first cost to settlers the swamp lands he had improved. His running expenses on the lands at the time, he estimated to be $60,000 annually.

By the spring of 1892 the Hub of Harney County had about 300 inhabitants. This number, inferred the Ochoco *Review,* could ill afford support of another paper, urged by prohibitionists.

John W. Biggs came to Burns as principal of its school in January, 1893. Phoebe Kelly, who later married Dr. Geary, assisted him in the teaching of twelve grades. The frame building, of one story and two rooms, stood in the south part of town. Biggs taught in Canyon City in the winter of 1893-94. In the fall of the latter year he returned to Burns and established the law practice that continued prominently for many decades.

Mayor J. B. Huntington, in March of 1893, let it be known that henceforth the night watchman would enforce the law against derelict horsemen. The four-man city council, including Brenton, decreed it as unlawful to tie a horse or horses on the streets of Burns for a period of more than twelve hours. Fines ranged from $10 to $50.

In September of that year the organization of Troop A, Oregon National Guard, was perfected in this newest county seat. With A. W. Gowan as its captain, the troop gained a bristling number of expert riders for three-year enlistments.

Effervescent in nature, they enriched discipline with color and daring.

In 1893 the Harney *Times* was a five-column quarto. It had for its editor and publisher the justice of the peace at Harney, John E. Roberts, late of Ontario. Among its advertising clientele were the Tremont Hotel at Harney, the Hess Hotel at Vale, King's Lumber Mill of Harney, and the O. C. Company, catering to the needs of ranchers. Its news matter reflected the hard times, locally and elsewhere, under Cleveland's presidency.

A quarrel, none too polite (evidenced by pictures as well as by words), waged between editor Roberts and editor Charles Newell of the *Items*. Seemingly, Newell had brought a case of libel upon the head of defendant Roberts. County politics got abusive. Liveliness was injected into the ads of stores, hotels, saloons, and livery stables in the basin's towns. The publishers. who otherwise might have had a scanty cupboard, also printed pepped-up appeal in the medicine ads.

Charles Byrd then turned over the *Items* to its stock company. Dillard, the founder, came back to run the paper as a Republican organ. Later, the *News* took it in hand. When the Byrds replaced the ancient Washington hand-press with a job press to get out a better *Herald,* more rivalry ensued. Mrs. Grace felt her job printing was being challenged. She launched again into the news field in 1894 with the *News,* which, under successive owners, held its identity for thirty-six years. Douglas Mullarky, capable and tactful, who became its last editor and publisher in 1926, joined forces with the *Times-Herald* in 1930.

Judge Shields, a Democrat, did not seek office in the first election. He preferred to give attention to his ranch where, in 1890, he replaced his log house with a home built of lumber. And, when leaving the judgeship, he succeeded John E. Roberts as teacher in nearby Silver Creek school for three winters.

Populists, seeking favor of those for a middle-of-the-road policy, offered a full slate of nominees for county offices in 1894. They had little success aside from placing C. P. Rutherford in the judgeship. Old party men held their lines.

Award of the contract for building the first Courthouse went to George W. Young. The frame building, handsome and spacious, cost $6,000. Located on the eminence so pleasing to its modern descendent, facing Buena Vista Avenue, it was completed by March of 1895. Reunited folks of Harney County looked upon the symbol of their independence and saw that it was good.

Among the earliest affrays to confront functionaries of law was a much-talked-about homicide. T. H. (Till) Glaze owned a horse Wasco, favorite as a money-winner. Glaze and Loren Parker, a companion, participated in races at the Burns fair in September, 1894. Bud Howard blamed them for something that did not please him in the least in the afternoon of the fifth.

Late that night the three men met in the Tex Saloon. Bitter resentment flared and a group of onlookers scattered for safety from the trio's flashing guns. Eight shots rang out. Parker, supporting Glaze in the duel, remained unhurt, but his friend and Howard lay dead.

The coroner's jury brought in two separate verdicts, one stating that Glaze came to his death by means of a weapon in the hands of Bud Howard. The second read that Howard also died from gunshot wounds, "the weapon causing such wounds being in the hands of T. H. Glaze and Jack Parker at the time said weapons were discharged." Tried and convicted of manslaughter, Parker was sentenced to spend seven and a half years in the penitentiary.

In its story of the homicide, the *Herald* said pointedly:

. . . All three of the parties engaged in this disgraceful and wholly uncalled for tragedy are well known in sporting circles in this state and other places. Bud Howard was known to be a dangerous man when provoked, and Till Glaze was known to have been a man of the same stripe, and when angered was a terrible man to abuse and browbeat all who crossed his path. John Parker, on the other hand, is not considered bad and from an acquaintance with him we would take him to be an unoffensive and generally courteous and very well behaved young man. but when drinking we presume, like most others who indulge in that curse, strong drink, he says and does things a sane man would blush to think of.

We are truly sorry for the young man that he allowed himself to be drawn into this trouble and God knows, we hope it will be such a lesson to him that he will eternally vow, and keep the pledge, to leave the cursed stuff alone that results when taken into the stomach in crazing the brain, and not only him but all others here to take warning and be a man and not let the brutish instincts which are common to the human family get the mastery.

The editor had not merely sermonized. His words were accepted as a declaration of rights, of the warp and woof the new county chose. The spirit of the frontier asked to be clothed with greater respect.

Chapter XXVIII

THE COUNTY'S INFANCY

ALWAYS IN CLOSE COMMUNICATION with its neighboring counties, budding Harney County was shocked immeasurably by a disaster at a Christmas dance in 1894. In a crowded hall at Silver Lake, in Lake County just over the Harney line, a panic-seized crowd faced terror in sudden flames. Exits became choked quickly. Forty persons perished and sixteen received severe injuries. Among the victims were about a dozen small children.

The Lakeview *Examiner* published an extra December 27 and the news flew fast into farthest reaches. Pioneers of nearby communities, extending kindness and funds, turned to burial of the dead and care of the suffering and sorrowing.

Tumult prevailed on the streets of Burns on April 10, 1895, when the jail emitted flames and smoke. Confliction reigned as to whether or not a prisoner was locked therein while men hastened to get Marshal Tom Dodson to unlock his fortress. A fatally burned man was carried out of his cell, and conjecture was that a straw tick was accidentally fired. In July of the next year the city council purchased a first-class fire engine, the county seat's first adequate fire-fighting apparatus.

In March, 1895, the *East Oregon Herald* gave a glimpse of the composition of Burns at that time:

. . . Burns was incorporated in 1889. Present officials, D. L. Grace, Mayor; J. M. Vaughlin, Recorder; I. S. Geer, Treasurer; P. F. Stenger, M. H. Brenton, Henry Richardson, George Fry, Councilmen; Tom Dodson, Marshal. The town has a church, public school, board of trade, militia company, Masonic, Odd Fellows, and Workman Lodges; Baptist and Methodist Churches; daily mails, two newspapers, *The County News*, D. L. Grace, Editor; and *East Oregon Herald*, W. C. Byrd and Sons, Editors. Lucas and Lewis and Mrs. L. Racine, hotels; C. H. Voegtly and I. S. Geer and Company, Hardware; George Fry, boots and shoes; J. C. Welcome, harness and saddles; M. H. Brenton and Cal Geer, livery stables; McKinnon and Kenyon, blacksmiths; D. K. Matthes, meat market; Stephens and Richardson, Sam Bailey, Caldwell and Smith, and R. E. Reed, liquor dealers. Ed Walton and John Robinson, barbers; J. W. Sayers, flour and lumber mills, McKinney and Sparrow, lumber; W. L. Marsden, physician; N. Brown, general merchant and agent Canyon City Stage line; H. M. Horton, druggist; G. W. Hayes, attorney; M. Fitzgerald, land attorney; A. W. Waters, attorney; H. A. Williams, proprietor, Ontario-Burns Stage Line; J. Durkheimer, general merchant.

Ione Whiting succeeded Emily A. Vaughn as head of the Burns postoffice at that time, turning over the postmastership to Edward B. Waters in 1898.

In the spring of 1895 S. H. Foreman of Pendleton, stockholder in the Blue Mountain Telephone & Telegraph Company, sounded out Burns' citizens on the question of having a telephone line extended to their town. The matter still was being debated two years later when C. P. Johnson of John Day and businessmen of Burns considered construction of a line from Canyon City to Harney Valley.

Midway of the nineties the county seat exercised its prerogative on styles and pranks and humor. Women, riding bicycles astride, set the fashion for riding horses the same way. Local editors acknowledged the safer way was astride with short open skirt, but they yearned for the old days of long riding skirts — picturesque and becoming if not so "fast."

Perhaps there was greater need for speed, as when a bullet followed a man coming out of a Burns saloon. It narrowly missed him — "luckily for his earthly tabernacle." George Sizemore defended an Indian in Recorder's Court for running his horse through a street. The red man was to pay George a good saddle and pony for his work. When the Indian gained freedom he went to the barn, took his pony and "skedaddled." Louie, chieftain, when asked for explanation of the runaway's conduct, replied: "Sizemore only gave a $2 talk and wanted a $35 saddle and $20 pony."

That horse racing was being taken seriously as well as pleasurably was evidence by preliminary training. The Baker City *Democrat* said, "Two Harney County race horses, Dick Hooten and Red Lane, are on the fairgrounds and are being put in condition for the summer meetings. They are 'short' horses and good ones." And the Burns Brass Band, organized in November of 1889, had developed into a striking accompaniment at public events.

New chapters of fraternal organizations were chartered for Burns. Initial officers for the Maccabees in September, 1895, included a dozen leading citizens. On September 11 the Order of the Eastern Star was organized by Deputy Isaac Baer, with A. W. Waters as worthy patron. Officers included Nellie Grace and Clara Marsden, matrons, and Clara Hanley, conductress.

A lodge of Knights of Pythias was instituted in October, 1896, with a membership of thirty-three. Among its officers were J. W. Biggs and A. J. McKinnon. In June, 1897, Burns had its seventh order of fraternal societies, Harney Valley Camp of Woodmen of the World. Daughters of Rebekah were among these seven.

Membership in Burns' churches advanced steadily, although the Methodists were moving to other fields. Catholics, Baptists and Presbyterians strengthened their congregations and mission work in Harney County.

By the spring of 1895 Harney County had 805 pupils with attendance of 621 in its schools. There were twenty-eight teachers. In mid-November, County Superintendent Charles Newell held the dedicatory exercises for the new school in Burns. Chairman was Mayor Julius Durkheimer, and the band provided music. Invocation was by the Rev. W. H. Gibson, Baptist minister. G. M. Irwin, state superintendent of instruction, delivered the address.

Changes came to the newspapers. In the issue of July 22, 1896, the name of the *East Oregon Herald* gave way to *Times-Herald,* and in January, 1897, W. C. Byrd leased it to Julian and A. M. Byrd. By the next November the *Harney Items* had been purchased by M. L. Lewis and Charles H. Leonard, who took charge.

It was in August of 1896 that "Jimmie" Donegan married Margaret Louise Smyth, first native-born white child of Harney range land settlers. To this union were born three children. They are Carmen Elfving, Pat H. Donegan, Burns attorney, and Frances Williamson.

What was thought to be a fast schedule was advertised by the Burns-Ontario Stage Line in the summer of 1897. Proprietor H. A. Williams announced coverage of the distance in forty-two hours. Today, by improved transportation, the same journey can be made in two and a half hours!

The summer of 1897 marked the start of selection of lands in Harney Valley for Indians. William Casson, allotting agent, assisted by Maurice Fitzgerald, brought about allotment of 115 claims. "Conditional patents," says James J. Donegan, "were issued at a later date. During the land boom in Harney Valley in 1910-11-12 some of these Indian lands were sold to land speculators."

Labors multiplied for the physician. In 1898, Dr. Walter LaForest Marsden, who had come to Drewsey in 1887 and to Burns in 1891, needed help. He procured Dr. J. W. Geary, a co-worker with staunch pride in his profession.

Initial steps to connect the Harney region with the outside world by telephone were taken in January, 1898. J. Ennes, representing the Blue Mountain Telephone Company, interviewed the citizens of Burns. He advised that a deposit of $1,500 would be necessary to start extension of a telephone line from Canyon City. This amount was quickly subscribed and work was begun on the new grounded line. When completed on June 29, 1898, Burns boasted nineteen telephones. George Fry directed operations of the company.

About the turn of the century Joe Sturtevant operated the gristmill two miles north of Burns on Silvies River. Grain came from the north end of Harney Valley and the flour was of such good quality that no other flour was brought into Burns for a number of years. Merchants of Burns later bought the mill but, unsuccessful, they sold it to a group of farmers. They also failed in its operation. After a final attempt by Fred Denstad, pioneer rancher, the mill burned. It was the last flour mill for Burns.

Charles A. Haines, who had erected the first building at The Narrows in 1892 and had become its postmaster in 1897, became one of the most able and prominent businessmen of the county in the early 1900's. No builder forged ahead more rapidly.

Ingenious and gay as the nineties were for townfolk the pulsing of life in the byways contributed to the standards. John E. Loggan, who in 1901 married Ella Howser, daughter of Harney Valley pioneers, recalls the vitality:

I worked for French on the P Ranch in 1892. There were 15 or

20 men working on the ranch and about the same number who rode the ranges after cattle. . . . The next spring I began working for the P. L. S. [Pacific Live Stock Co.] Company at the White Horse ranch, which they had recently acquired from Devine; he was now living at the beautiful Alvord Ranch at the foot of Steens Mountain. . . . At this time there were stalls for six stallions with the name of each on the door, also a race track near by, a stone house for the game chickens.

The method of running cattle in those days was as follows: The pasture on the range and in the fields was so bountiful that only the cows with young calves and the young heifers were fed hay during the winter months. In the last days of March or early April the cattle would be driven out to the range. After that we would start to round up the horses from the range and brand the colts. Following this it was start after the cattle again to round them up and mark and brand the calves.

There would be 15 or 20 men in the crew, part of them representing other outfits who had cattle drift on this range. A chuck wagon would drive the team. As there was few corrals on the range all the branding and marking was done on the open range, by roping and dragging to the fire for branding. In the fall it was roundup time to get the steers for market. They were driven to Winnemucca, Nevada, in bunches of about 1000 in a drive. It was 135 miles and took from eight to 10 days to make the trip. . . .

The cattle foreman, a highly important man, was Juan Redon, a Mexican who came to the ranch with Mr. Devine when he first settled there. He was a small man in stature, pleasant to meet and made many friends for the company. He was a fine horseman and an excellent roper . . .

I was sent on a trip to Denio and on the way called on the Catlow family, for whom the Catlow Valley was named, was greeted by Mrs. John Catlow, an English woman, . . . Although the house was made of rough boards on the outside, it was very neat and artistically arranged on the inside. I was greatly astonished to look on a painting, life size, of Mrs. Catlow. Talking with her later on, she informed me that it had cost $5000.00 to have it painted.

Meanwhile, on the fringes of range land, had come the Basques, as sheepherders and farmers. The "Bascos," reluctant at first to be face to face with cattlemen who preferred the bellowing of cattle to the bleating of sheep, forged ahead. Gradually they became extraordinary hosts to outsiders. They led no dull life. They tended their ranches well, played well and ate well. Not to be cast off were the hereditary recipes and customs of long ago.

After their coming into eastern Oregon and western Idaho

in the eighties and nineties, they labored hard. Their holdings became fruitful and profitable. The girls, artistically inclined in decorating, kept homes of stability and cheer for their husbands. Over the spread of years, citizens of their trading towns heartily welcomed the dark-eyed and tanned neighbors. The men with high-crowned hats and blue denims leaped with merriment and generosity into beneficial enterprises. No more did the Basques move from range to range.

Piquant are the reminiscences of Dennis O'Brien who, with John McCulloch, his cousin, arrived in Burns in 1896. The twenty-year-old Dennis went to work for Mart Brenton then and remained in his employ four years. Brenton's livery stable with thirty driving horses was "in the big money," taking in as much as $1,200 a week. There being no bank available, Brenton kept his money in a safe. If Mart went away, he left Dennis in full charge of his business.

Once, Brenton forgot to close his safe as he hastened away for a trip of several days. Keys to boxes were left available, as were coins, currency and valuable papers. Dennis locked the safe, though he did not know the combination. Brenton was an excited man when he got back this time, asking, "Denny, did I leave the safe open?" For awhile Dennis kept him in suspense about the course he had pursued. Then he slid the keys over Brenton's shoulder and into his hands. Opening the safe, Brenton exclaimed, "It's all there!"

"How much money was in it?" his employe asked.

"Twenty-four thousand dollars," replied Mart, smiling.

The buffeting taken by the pioneer doctors and their adeptness at improvisation made for lasting memories. While employed by Brenton, O'Brien drove for Dr. Marsden in the years of 1897 and '98. The beloved physician and his popular red-haired wife Clara had one son, George. Dennis has written:

I think Dr. Marsden was absolutely one of the finest men I ever knew. It's worth a lot to have known a man like that.
. . . I held the light for him while he took a piece of bone out of Ira Mahon's fractured skull, and put in a silver plate. A horse had thrown him and bashed in his head. There was no such a thing as a hospital there in those days, not even down at Ontario, on the railroad, and operations had to be performed in the ranch houses, on a sheet-

covered kitchen or dining table. It was on this ranch that the Mule Postoffice was located.   .   .   .

Dr. Marsden was driven to the P Ranch where Lem Rader had a leg "broken to pieces by a wagon running over it." At the doctor's request, Augustine Berdugo, buckaroo boss, roped and killed "a fine red big calf." While it was still warm, the physician grafted a piece of the calf's leg bone into "Lem's shin bone, and it all grew back into place, as good as ever."

The worst moments and hours came when the doctor and his driver, returning to Burns in frigid weather from a visitation, would be called out almost immediately on another long journey. And the doctor's patient was not always amenable to well-meaning advice or proffered treatment. Deep personal tragedy was Dr. Marsden's lot on one wintry summons, and it bespoke keen suffering for Dennis as driver. O'Brien wrote of the experience:

Dr. Marsden, had an only brother, George, who was bookkeeper at the P Ranch. When he suddenly became ill, they sent for the doctor. But he said, when they described his illness, "I can never get there in time. There is no help after a few hours." Sure enough, when we got there at 1 A.M. his brother was already dead. He asked them to lift the sheet off his brother's face, and as he stood there looking down at that dead face, I could see the cords in his neck swell. Poor Doc — he took it hard. Later on I drove him back to Burns, and as he was worn out, he fell asleep in the rig. It was so cold, and my hands hurt me terribly, but after we changed teams at the Narrows, they didn't hurt me any more.

When we drove into Burns, it was 42° below zero. I stumbled into Broady Johnson's saloon, where there was light and a fire, and started for the stove. He tore off my gloves, and my hands were as white as chalk half way to my elbows. "Don't go near the stove. Denny!" he said, "you'll lose your hands if you do. Here, one of you fellows, go out and fetch me a pan of coal oil and one of snow. And then get out, for I have no time for customers now. I want to take care of Denny."

He rubbed my hands first with snow, then in the coal oil until about 4 in the morning, when the circulation began to come back into them — and I have no words to tell you how those hands ached. I wouldn't send for Doctor. He was all worn out and had just lost his only brother. Well, the next morning, my hands were as black as coal, and the skin peeled all off, and oh, the intolerable aching. I never held a rein again for 6 weeks, but old Broady, God bless him, had saved my hands. That man had a heart like a prince. My hands still bother me in cold weather and always will.

Dr. Marsden, like many another in his profession, held no debts over the heads of people who could not afford to pay for his services. "The wealthy," he told his driver, "who can afford it, pay me enough so I can live and care for these poor people who must somehow be taken care of."

Dennis had a warm spot in his heart for Pete French after working for him three months. He learned how the starchy little cattle king would rehire hands if they quit their jobs when a foreman asked the unreasonable.

When Bill Hanley and his wife went to Masonic and Eastern Star lodges in Burns, Dennis had their team ready for them at midnight. Mrs. Hanley would fetch some pie or cake from the Masons' lunch for the waiting youth. "Hungry, Denny?" jovial Bill would ask. Everybody liked the Hanleys, swore Dennis, but he couldn't understand Bill's choice of horses. Says he:

For years, Bill drove a runaway sorrel and a mean kicking gray mare. . . . Well, this time he wanted to go home a little earlier, as the Missus wasn't with him that evening. So I got his horses harnessed, and three tugs hitched and told a boy to watch that gray's head while I went around to hitch the other tug. The gray just took one jump and ran right over the boy. He couldn't hold them, and let them loose, and away they sailed into the fence — tore the buggy into bits and the harness into strips. About this time up came Brenton and we were busy explaining when Hanley came for his team.

"Now, don't say a word to the boys," said Hanley. "I had no business to be driving that outlaw team. My wife has told me a hundred times they'd be the death of me yet, so you've probably saved my life." Brenton offered to buy a buggy to replace the wrecked one, but again Hanley wouldn't listen to it.

It was in such circumstances and with such strong yet resilient timber that Harney County soon established for itself a formidable reputation.

Chapter XXIX

STAVING OFF RETREAT OF CATTLE INDUSTRY

IT HAS BEEN ASSUMED by more than a few qualified historians that the West's cattle industry was in retreat by 1890. For the most part, the glorious days of free range were prior to that year. Raisers of beef cattle withdrew because of hard economic times, killing winters, and because of changes to wheat-growing and sheep-raising after the debut of the Northern Pacific Railroad in 1883.

Yet there was an increase in cattle in the more remote places for in Harney County the figures tell the story. Number of beef cattle in this stronghold: 1890, 34,462; 1900, 69,531; 1910, 97,971; 1920, 67,474; 1930, 65,299; 1940, 67,000; 1950, about 80,000.

The business was good in war years, bad in the depression of market prices which followed. By 1920, Oregon had doubled Washington's number of beef cattle.

Of great importance to Oregon stockmen early in the nineties was a bill making it obligatory for them to record their brands. All brands had to be recorded in the county where the owners resided or where their animals usually ranged. No evidence of ownership by brand was permitted in any court of Oregon on or after November 1, 1894, unless the brand had been recorded. Too, in all suits of law, equity or criminal, "the brand on the animal shall be prima facie evidence of ownership of the person claiming the brand."

Among those again seeking the wider grasslands as time altered old scenes was William Hanley. Near Jacksonville, Bill had known Clara Cameron throughout her girlhood. Her folks and his were neighbors. Clara was born on the Applegate in 1868, her parents being of Scotch ancestry. Her father, after selling some land to Chinese gold miners, continued ranching there. In her early twenties Clara easily captured the heart of Bill Hanley. Though short and of slight weight, she was imbued with the alertness of outdoor living which she was always to love.

212

Clara and Bill wed on July 6, 1892, then drove a buggy over to the ranch maintained by Ed Hanley in Harney Valley. A short time later they returned for cattle, driving them back in the spring of 1893 by horseback. Clara rode in the buggy and often they made beds in snow while crossing the Cascades.

Where now stands the home at Bell A Ranch they at first had a four-room house. Their workmen boarded there. The view extended fifty miles in all directions, beyond sageland and pasture, lakes and marshes to rim-rocks, hills and table-lands. Water rose high in springtime and wild geese came to the fence near the house. To get out, the horses hitched to a buggy had to swim. In laying by supplies they bought sugar in twelve-sack lots.

They intended to pull out of debt and stay only five years. They kept adding to holdings, acquiring small pieces of state and county lands, and some homesteads. This original ranch they called the LY, using the brand brought from Jackson-ville (later the "Bell A" was applied). Ed remained till 1898 when he went to Alaska, but they kept on raising cattle and horses.

Bill's first big transaction was when he bought outright the cattle and land of the OO Ranch from Riley and Hardin, paying $6 an acre for about 16,000 acres. He used both brands, retaining the LY on his place of nearly 4,000 acres. They ran 5,000 head of stock yearly on both ranches. As always, Hanley protected the abundant wildlife, restricting hunting to a great extent and using little of the free meat for his own table.

On long cattle drives, Clara enjoyed sleeping on a bedroll in the open air or in a tent. A cook was hired for the trips as she, familiar with the region, rode in advance to pick out old camping spots.

Cattle thievery became annoying at times. In March, 1895, it was happily announced in Burns that C. W. Parrish, a law-yer of "long experience," had been appointed prosecuting attorney of that district. Soon he had on his hands the case of six Jordan brothers charged with stealing cattle. Almost two years later, a news item stated Ben and Bill Jordan had stayed in jail while Bob and John escaped the year before. John, accused of altering brands, again was behind barred windows.

Another bit of news in 1895 concerned the Miller & Lux partnership formed in 1858 with 1,000 head of cattle. "In the intervening 37 years," it was said, "the gain has been enormous. They now own 14,439,300 acres of land in California, Nevada and Oregon." In Oregon the total was "7,556,000 acres besides thousands of cattle and horses." The figures were somewhat exaggerated.

Joined by his brother Ira, Alphena Venator was building up holdings which were to include 10,000 acres of Malheur Lake range land and stretches on the South Fork of the Malheur. The Venators originally used the "JV" brand, later putting the bar below.

Bill Brown, with his headquarters at Gap Ranch in wintertime, moved around in grazing seasons. Though he carried strychnine to poison coyotes, he was known to have thrown whole hams to the dogs he treated with admiration. Brown never had much of a home at Fife on Buck Creek in being a bachelor. The frame two-story house contained extra bedrooms for his employes or guests. Dried fruits were his own standby, but he fed his men generously of food they preferred.

If occasion demanded, he made out checks on labels of cans or on a piece of paper sack — and they could be readily cashed. He had little time to keep books, collecting a debt if he thought the person able to pay. His own bills, including huge taxes, he paid as promptly as possible. His manners, congenial and courteous, were as simplified as his methods. If need be, he dressed well, but he preferred to spend most of his days in working garb.

He kept his No. 10 shoes unlaced while galloping in the saddle, a protection against getting caught in a stirrup and dragged. Sometimes, after a full day in the saddle, Bill would lace up the shoes and take a long walk in cool twilight.

In the early nineties Brown started to buy horses. First ones cost $10 a head, but he added fine Clydes and Shires. In about twelve to fifteen years he had 12,000 head of good horses. His three bands of sheep numbered 2,000 head in a band. Five to fifteen men handled his horses and four to six men cared for his sheep, to which Bill clung closely. He sold his yearly wethers and wool, freighted to The Dalles by his own or hired teams. In one early year Robert Lincoln (Link) Hutton hauled 32,000 pounds of Bill's wool to The Dalles where it brought six cents a pound. Then he returned with a year's supply of groceries and miscellaneous items. Out of his horse corrals at Lost Creek, Brown sold horses at $50 to $100 a head to California buyers and to fill Boer War demands.

In the spring of 1897 — when mail carriers used a boat to cross flood waters around Burns — the *Times-Herald* stated that the oldest taxpayer and resident "now living in the present limits of Harney County" was A. T. Clark. He had been a military trader at old Camp C. F. Smith in 1866-69 and then had spent four years at Fort Harney. His stock brand C was, in 1897, the oldest stock marking in Harney County.

With the arrival of fall in 1897 there came more bitter disputes over the meander lands of Malheur Lake. Concerning one phase of the problem, Dennis O'Brien says:

. . . A number of settlers had fenced land on the Narrows that French had bought and paid for, and the case went to the courts. The settlers continuously cut the P ranch fences. It was 75 miles long and 30 miles across and had a 30-mile lane across it, so people could cross Rock Creek and go on to town, and it was simply impossible to police that long a fence. French met a number of the settlers. . . . "I'll fight any man," he challenged. "Gentlemen, while this case is pending, come and work for me. You can work as long as you want and pay for your land." But they would not.

Christmas was celebrated with its usual good cheer and neighborliness throughout the range land. Yuletide spirit entered the home of Ed L. Oliver, located in one of the fields over which quarreling had been brewed. Oliver had a wife and several small children and it was claimed he was a peaceable man.

In the afternoon of December 26, however, Oliver had a gun in his hand as he approached a gate at which French stopped to admit his buckaroos. Wasted words were few this time, though French's workmen later testified their boss was unarmed. Oliver pressed the trigger of his weapon and the owner of P Ranch fell dead, a bullet through his head.

Dave Crow, a buckaroo, sped his horse toward Winnemucca. With change of mounts he rode straight through to send the tragic news to French's family at Red Bluff, California.

The killer retraced his steps to his home. The next morning he was placed under arrest and a coroner's jury was impaneled. O'Brien drove the coroner to the scene of the crime. James Donegan's notes declare that Oliver faced preliminary examination for the killing in the Justice Court January 5, 1898. He "was placed under $10,000.00 bail which was furnished by N. J. Simmons, J. B. Craig, H. M. Horton, A. S. Ward, H. B. Simmons, and Fred Lunaburg for the sum of $1,000.00 each and W. D. Huffman for $4,000.00." Indicted by the grand jury, his trial was set for May 19.

Of Oliver's trial, Donegan summarized:

. . . On Thursday, May 19th, 1898, the empaneling of a jury to try him for killing French began and it took until May 24th to get the required number. During this time 45 men were examined. The trial jury consisted of J. M. Ferrens, W. B. Johnson, R. E. Williams, Sam Jenkins, E. L. Beede, A. W. Howser, Milo Cushing, Wallace Capps, Carey Thornburg, A. Vanderpool, T. J. Shields and Tim Donovan. There were 16 witnesses examined for the State, and 19 for the defendant. The State was represented by District Attorney Parrish and Vic Cozad; L. R. Webster, George Hayes and Waters and Gowan appearing for Oliver. The case was given to the jury at 4 o'clock P.M. and a verdict of "Not Guilty" was returned about 7 o'clock, the jury being out three hours.

Mixed emotions swayed the many people who heard the fateful news that winter. Whether an able and fearless builder had been right in his methods continued long as a subject of debate.

In the cold that gripped the countryside, Mart Brenton and Bert French, brother of Peter, accompanied the hearse conveying the body of the slain cattle baron away from the scene of his achievements. The horses waded snow on the journey to Baker City by way of Canyon City. The casket rested in a box lined with tin and padding, well sealed against freezing. A tarpaulin gave extra cover. Poles and brakes had to be used on steep roads.

Not until they reached Baker City was the body embalmed. From that point it went by Wells Fargo Express to Red Bluff, insurance of $20,000 being procured to hasten shipment. At Red Bluff, Pete French rested in the burial plot of his parents.

F. C. Lusk, attorney of Chico and administrator of the Glenn
and French estates, reimbursed Brenton with a check for $600.

Some years after the death of French, in his forty-eighth
year, part of his ranch of 150,000 acres passed into the hands of
another live stock company. The federal government later acquired about 65,000 acres, bought in 1935 to add to the Malheur National Wildlife Refuge.

Seemingly, ulitimate irony lay in the moist acres over which
strife had ridden and blood had been shed. Improved fields
over which men thirsted again became marshes.

Meanwhile, Attorney Lusk, as administrator for the French-
Glenn properties, named the capable Bill Hanley as manager
of the P Ranch on the Blitzen River.

Chapter XXX

A NEW CENTURY AND NEW ROADS

WHEN CAME THE NEW YEAR 1900 the United States was in an expanding mood. Victories over Spanish tyranny in Cuba and in the Phillippine Islands bolstered the feeling for "manifest destiny." There were some fears for the unsteadiness that might follow, but Harney County looked ahead without trepidation.

From California and Oregon between 1885 and 1900, more than 1,500,000 head of sheep had been driven across Idaho, with an estimated 15,000,000 head driven east in the entire era. At closing of trails about 1900, Montana had more than 6,000,000 sheep while Oregon, Idaho and Utah had 3,000,000 head. Drama of the West, says Oliphant, belonged to others, but the great sheep trails assured "economic success."

Not until later, however, did sheep invade many parts of Harney County. Most of the early production came from the Jordan Valley and Basque country. Freighters reaped benefits from it. Charles Cranmer was one, driving a ten-horse team pulling three stout linked wagons, piled high with bales of wool, between Drewsey and Huntington. Drewsey was flourishing then. The trade for vehicles and horses and feed at Sim Hamilton's livery stable, next door to Carl Riley's saloon, was tremendous. Yet the country around Drewsey remained adamant to sheepmen for two more decades.

Big ranches prevailed, as Oliphant emphasizes:

. . . A news dispatch from Burns, Oregon, dated August 18, 1900, contains considerable information about such ranches as were then in operation in Harney County. This dispatch reads, in part: "Harney County contains the largest and greatest ranches in the world. She has the largest single and the largest combination of ranches in the world. This is a broad statement but it is true. The Pacific Livestock Company's combination of ranches is the greatest in the world and the French-Glenn ranch is the largest single ranch in the world. Then there are the Sisson, Devine, Riley, Shirk, Island and a dozen others that are as large as some of the largest counties in Eastern States.

218

Miller & Lux are the owners of the Pacific Livestock system of ranches. . . ."

The French-Glenn Company was building a canal and turning 25,000 acres of swamp into fine pasture and hay land. Ed Hanley, in May, 1901, came to Huntington to receive a trainload of cattle for shipping to Alaska. Bill Hanley, indeed, was sending his cattle far from home.

In 1900 Harney County raised 64,000 bushels of barley and 34,500 bushels of oats, rye and wheat. Brown's gristmill ground 3,000 bushels of wheat through the fall of 1899 to January 1, 1900. Tons of hay put up in the 1900 season totaled 45,000, and 4,000,000 feet of lumber went into local usage. Cattle sold and shipped from the county totaled 22,000 head; horses and mules, 2,500; sheep, 20,000. The wool clip came to between 700,000 and 800,000 pounds, no small amount for Harney range land.

Improvements in Burns in 1900 cost $45,715 and the town had a population of 937. In October of that year T. A. McKinnon surveyed and plotted the Burns Cemetery to meet growth. Harney County had 4,500 residents, with thirty-seven school districts employing thirty-four teachers who were paid an average of $60 a month. Registered voters in the county numbered 1,003, the same as the number of school-age children. Robert J. Williams, Democrat, began a four-year term as county commissioner.

The Harney County Fair Association had its beginnings in April, 1900. Its record of incorporation, signed by Eddie Hamerly, Harry C. Smith, and A. W. McGowan, notary public, stated:

"Harney County Fair Ass'n. formed and organized for the business and purpose of conducting a District, County and local fairs and exhibits of products of the State and to test the speed of horses and to arrange for and direct athletic sports and games. . . . "

Smith, taking a leading part in enterprises for advancement, headed the first county fair. He built Floral Hall for exhibits and it served, also, as a meeting place for the public until razed by fire in 1904.

At that time Mart Brenton owned the Red Front Livery

Stable, on ground now occupied by the Arrowhead Hotel, then next to the French Hotel. Both burned out in later years, after conversion of the Red Front into a pool hall. In the fall of 1900, John Sayer's sawmill, on the Silvies River and immediately north of the present highway out of Burns, was reduced to ashes. The news account caustically referred to incendiary fiends.

John Devine, separated at last from the flocks and herds of his Alvord Ranch, died in September, 1901. With his passing there faded many of the colorful aspects of ranching which had been part of his yesterdays. Pioneers paused in tribute as his body was interred in the Burns Cemetery. Around it was the tall sage to vie with a mound of flowers.

Harney County had, in a decade and a half, performed many official functions, but its first legal hanging of a man waited until 1904. Harry D. Egbert, alias John Frost, was indicted for the murder of John Saxon, deputy sheriff, on October 28, 1903. His trial was set for December 1. Convicted, he was hanged at the noon hour on January 29, following. He had no known relatives and his body was turned over to the dean of the medical faculty of Willamette University.

Of importance in reclaiming huge areas of arid land at the turn of the century were: The Carey Act, approved in 1894 and expiring by limitation in August, 1904, and the National Reclamation Act of 1903. After passage of the latter act, the Reclamation Department soon sent into Harney Valley engineer John T. Whistler. He, with a state engineer, John H. Lewis, studied the problem of irrigation from Silver Creek. This project died aborning because government lands embraced in the districts were too few.

Of further steps, James Donegan wrote in the 1930s:

In January, 1904, water gauges were installed in the Silvies River and have been in operation to the present time. Engineer Whistler, in his final report, said, "The Harney project contemplates the irrigation of land in the Harney Valley by means of water storage on Silvies River or its tributaries. . . . The locality is remote from railroads and the principal industry is stock grazing. At the present time there is little demand for products other than those which can be used for stock feeding."

Led by the *Times-Herald* the settlers and land owners in the Harney Valley made violent objections to Engineer Whistler's report and final conclusions. . . .

William Hanley and others proposed, under the Carey Act, to irrigate 65,000 acres of sageland from flood waters of the Silvies River. A court decision dashed their hopes. Later, pumps were employed to draw water from subsurface sources for irrigation.

Other attempts were made to organize development companies but the plans withered. Long a dream that failed of achievement was to divert water from Malheur Lake to thousands of thirsty acres. Big plans were made, and were derailed.

For some time the government had been looking askance at the manner in which certain lands had been disposed. Finally, airing came for what was called the "Oregon Land Frauds." These, wrote the late Professor R. C. Clark in the authoritative *Dictionary of American History,*

were brought to light during the administration of President Theodore Roosevelt. They were effected under the Homestead Act (1862), under the Timber and Stone Act (1878) and under exchange of state school lands for government timber lands. The device of securing state school lands of little or no value at a cost of $1.25 an acre and exchanging them for valuable timber lands was in operation as early as 1890. The system of dummy entries on homestead and timber lands under which large lumber companies, often controlled by capitalists from Wisconsin, Michigan or Minnesoto, acquired immense tracts of valuable timber land was extensively used in the period 1890 to 1904. The great increase in entries in Oregon under the Timber and Stone Act (from 464 in 1901 to 4209 in 1903, and 3260 in 1904) seems to indicate the height of the period of fraud.

These funds were made possible by the connivance and assistance of state and Federal government officials. They were exposed through the investigations of Francis J. Heney and William J. Burns. Heney secured thirty-three convictions out of thirty-four prosecutions. One of those convicted was a United States senator.

The outcome was a huge and lasting benefit for Harney and other counties in the setting aside of timber reserves. The Division of Forestry, created in 1881, was given permanent statutory rank in 1886, but it was not until 1905 that the forest reserves began to be administered by the Department of Agriculture.

The Blue Mountain Forest Reserve, proclaimed March 15, 1906, included the national forests of the Malheur, Ochoco, southeastern part of the Umatilla, and the west unit of the Whitman. In 1908 came proclamation of the Deschutes and Malheur Forests, carved from larger original reserves. The Ochocho National Forest, in nearly its present shape, was proclaimed July 1, 1911, some of its area taken from the Malheur.

Today, the area of the Malheur Forest (in Harney, Grant and Baker counties), with headquarters at John Day, has a gross area of 1,274,837 acres. In 1940 it had 7,135,203 m. feet of timber, its pasturage caring for 15,904 head of live stock and grazing 60,461 sheep.

Like so many others before and since, the Poet of the Sierras in 1907 found entrancing the scenes in and about Harney basin. Joaquin Miller, having returned to the Elkhorn Hotel in Canyon City after a stage trip to Burns, used several pages of the hotel's stationery for writing up the excursion. His picturization is in the book *A Royal Highway of the World*, published by Binfords & Mort, a few years ago.

Long-disputed grants made to the old Willamette Valley and Cascade Mountain Wagon Road Company — passing through many hands — eventually were shaken free of court process. The road company's title, affirmed in 1892, made possible passage of the lands to French interests in Paris. Colonel C. E. S. Wood, of Portland, represented the French owners as attorney, says James Donegan. The road, as described in an early chapter of this work, had its course marked eastward from Albany to Idaho, across the Harney country.

Scattered sections of this land totaling about 16,000 acres were bought by Colonel Wood, William Hanley and Drake O. Reilly, who organized the Harney Valley Improvement Company. Subsequently, the rest of the lands were acquired by Louis Hill, Watson P. Davidson and associates. Their organization was known as the Oregon and Washington Colonization Company.

Also contested were holdings of the Oregon Central Military Wagon Road Company, its road extending from the Klamath area by way of Catlow Valley and Steens Mountain to Idaho. Out of a network of drawn-out legal entanglements, declares Donegan,

its title was finally confirmed and after a number of assignments and transfers of title it finally was acquired by Martin and Borders who organized the Oregon Valley Land Company. They subdivided the land in 10, 20 and 40-acre tracts and sold it to "suckers" from all parts of the United States. A majority of the land was and is utterly worthless. A big part of the land has reverted to Harney County through the tax foreclosure suits. . . .

Development fever led to an attempted boom for dry farming between 1910 and 1914. A great number of settlers filed on the vacant lands of Harney and Catlow valleys. Donegan, who later was receiver of the Federal Land Office at Burns, declared "27 of the Indian allotments were sold for prices ranging from $10.00 to $15.00 per acre. That is one time that the Indian 'slipped something over' on his white brother." Indians retained eighty allotments that, like land taken up by newcomers, slid off in value.

Settlement in the area south of Wright's Point had started in 1906. Called Sunset Valley, its voting precinct Sunset, the district had fifty-seven registered — all male — in 1914. For a time it was the largest rural school district in the county. Its population began to dwindle rapidly in 1915. A generation later naught but a fenced cemetery, island in the sagebrush, identified the place where the striving settlement wilted despairingly.

The fight over much of the swamp land, which settlers argued the cattle kings had acquired without due regard for its proper classification, waged in courts at the same time. The Pacific Live Stock Company in 1914 compromised with the State of Oregon over the concern's possession of 18,000 acres. The P. L. S. firm paid the state $125,000 and agreed "to throw open to settlement 9,857 acres of land at a price fixed by the State, Company and a third member named by the first two." It also promised to aid in subdividing, mapping and selling the land.

In the meantime, at high or low economic tide, Harney County's goodly portion of first-line pioneers labored with stout-hoping newcomers to keep their stronghold intact. Some forsook riding of the range and lent their hand to community-building. One of such was John Loggan, who was Burns' postmaster from 1908 to 1913.

In struggles against long distances, sparse population, and lack of funds, Harney County had a gigantic task building and maintaining its roads. The present Highway Department of Oregon did not get its start until 1917, with creation of a highway commission and approval of a bond issue of $6,000,-000 for road purposes.

Oregonians possessed about 150 automobiles in 1905, but ownership climbed rapidly — to more than a thousand in 1909, ten thousand in 1912, a hundred thousand in 1920 and, a quarter of a million by 1931. Soon the truck and motor bus dominated first the secondary roads, then gradually competed with railroads on trunk routes.

Archie McGowan, infatuated with horseless carriages, in the summer of 1907 bought a 1907 Cadillac from Howard M. Covy, a pioneer automobile dealer in Portland. Archie brought it to Burns and demonstrated thoroughly that automobiles could conquer the dust, mud and ruts of Harney County. He was the first to complete several round trips to Winnemucca with a car, also blazing trails to many other points. The next year his partner drove the Cadillac to Los Angeles and sold it to a doctor.

In April, 1910, McGowan established the first garage in Burns, obtaining a contract with the Standard Motor Car Company of Portland for the sale of Ford cars. He sold four Model T's that year, the beginning of the oldest Ford dealership in Oregon.

James Lampshire, another motoring enthusiast, opened an automobile repair shop and garage in Burns the next year. In 1913 he took the agency for selling Studebaker automobiles. His was the second garage in the capital of the cow country.

Keenly alert to possibilities of the motoring age was Harry C. Smith who had come to Burns in July, 1898. A contractor and builder, he erected the first permanent brick building of the town with bricks from its first kiln. Over a virile period he constructed several fireproof buildings, including the Masonic Hall and the hardware store for Charles H. Voegtly, pioneer merchant and benefactor of Burns.

Smith, in 1911, became an associate with McGowan, his son-in-law, in the Burns Garage. In giving strong encouragement to public enterprises, he urged removal of rocks and boulders for easier travel on streets. Envisioning demands of car-owners, the partners of the Burns Garage graveled the street in front of their property, the first gravel placed on any part of Main Street. It was the beginning of a foundation necessary for what is now smooth and wide Broadway.

Better roads became essential. In 1915, Smith urged the County Court to grade a modern-type highway connecting the Silver Creek Valley settlement and Burns. The court denied the request, but Smith and McGowan resolved to support the enterprise. Many residents of Silver Creek Valley, upon being canvassed by Smith, offered financial aid. They also furnished horse-drawn equipment for construction of the road which Smith, acting as engineer, located as a new parallel route over Sage Hen Pass between Burns and Silver Creek.

Within a few months the road was graded, drained and made usable. Surprised and thoroughly pleased were the people who, for the first time, drove over the new dirt road with its long tangents and its curves reduced to a minimum.

Upon creation of Oregon's Highway Department in 1917, Smith engendered a rosier outlook. Virtually alone for awhile, he insisted that provisions of the new Highway Act include the Burns community. In meeting with the first highway commissioners and their engineer, he explained the urgency of linking Burns and Crane, terminus of the railroad. Soon he witnessed a start of highway construction on this route. It was completed as a macadam highway about 1920, the first state highway improvement in Harney County. Death overtook Harry Smith in 1922.

In 1924 appeared the Harney Good Roads Club, its "booster work" carried on mainly by McGowan, president, John Biggs, Julian Byrd, and Dr. L. E. Hibbard. A county bond issue for road-building was obtained in the mid-twenties. The money was matched by state highway funds.

Upon request of the people of Silver Creek in 1925, the club erected a monument in tribute to Harry Smith at the side of the Bend-Burns Highway on Sage Hen ridge. The committee in charge of the formal dedication included W. B.

Johnson, William Hanley and J. W. Biggs, chairman. Indicative of his neighbors' appreciation, A. W. Zoglmann planted vines around the granite block, keeping them green the past quarter of a century.

Besides this and the Devine monument, the club also dedicated a modern highway bridge to the memory of Susan Whiting, a graciously known pioneer mother of Harney County. It was named Susan's Bridge, and on the structure was placed a bronze plaque, reminder of a life contributing to community needs.

Five hundred citizens and visitors assembled on Sunday, July 22, 1928, for the dedication of a monument to John Devine — a well-designed stone fountain with basin — on the Joaquin Miller Trail, at the head of Devine Canyon north of Burns. Archie McGowan, president of the Road Club, sponsor of the monument, presided. John W. Biggs gave the dedicatory address.

After a public dinner at the Masonic-Odd Fellows Park, near by, speeches were made by Lewis A. McArthur of Portland, the Hon. Robert W. Sawyer of Bend, Colonel C. E. S. Wood, a lieutenant in the Bannock War of 1878, and William Hanley.

The trail itself had been the route of rushing gold-miners, thrusting soldiers, visionary homeseekers and laboring freighters. Attorney Biggs, in his nostalgic and discerning address, said:

The pioneer was a natural gambler, every effort on his part was a chance. . . . He was surrounded daily by danger from the elements, wild life in all its forms, starvation; in fact, if the gambling instinct had not been one of the uppermost in his mind, he would never have started upon a life of that nature. Some were hunting for gold in its natural state. Others for empires, others for a domain which could be controlled by them for one purpose or another.

John S. Devine had all these characteristics . . . And now to him and to those other early pioneers who passed along this road, 'mid hardships and dangers, whose very lives were at stake, and some of them who lost their lives along this road, which we today have traveled with ease, comfort and pleasure, to him and to them as they helped carry out this, we dedicate this monumet.

While in the State Legislature in 1927, McGowan and

others championed a resolution requesting the State Highway
Commission to locate and grade the Central Oregon Highway
(now No. 20) from Bend to Burns. Success came and work
was started at once. It proved beneficial and was maintained
by the state as a desert-type dirt road. McGowan was president
of the Road Club during its lifetime. It was absorbed by the
Yellowstone Cut-Off Association.

In a big meeting at Wagontire more than 300 representatives from Lake, Harney and Modoc (California) counties
boosted a road from Redding to Boise, by way of Alturas,
Lakeview, Paisley, Burns, Vale and Ontario. They organized
the Yellowstone Cut-Off Association, the name suggested by
Mrs. William Hanley. They joined a caravan of cars from distant California points, covering the whole route and holding
meetings. A permanent organization was formed at Boise,
with William Hanley as president and McGowan as secretary-
treasurer. Each county gave a quota to funds. V. Tanner,
hired as manager at $250 a month, resided in Burns. The
chief purposes were accomplished after spending of $10,000
in two years.

The Yellowstone Cut-Off Association became merged, in
1932, with the organization backing the Three-Flags Highway or U. S. Route 395. This road, coming into Burns from
Canyon City, followed the old route as mapped to Alturas, on
to Reno, south to the edge of the Mojave desert, into San
Diego and thence to Ensanada, Mexico.

Chapter XXXI

RAILROADS APPROACH THE WAITING RANGE LAND

THOUGH NO RAILROAD neared the cattle-producing hinterland, carriage of its live stock was eagerly sought. In the late 1890s and early 1900s Edward H. Harriman of the Union Pacific speeded service. Trains of fifteen to twenty-five stock cars, with no dead freight, were yielded right of way except for fast mail.

The Malheur Canyon, under repeated surveys of various companies, long had been considered the route to bring a railroad to tap Harney Valley and the great land area of southeastern and central Oregon. Railroad owners, however, needed tonnage and the cooperation of many people to guarantee income. A huge handicap was the indifference of the small-farm people west of the Cascade Mountains to the requirements of the ranchers to the east.

Harriman held back on the Malheur route. James J. Hill, robust builder of the Great Northern, after having completed his North Bank road on the Columbia River from Portland to Spokane, eyed a central Oregon route as a feeder. Bill Hanley joined others in Hill's strategy to follow the east shore of the Deschutes River from the Columbia River to Bend, 130 miles from Burns. The year was 1908.

Alarmed at the prospect of rivalry for earnings of the field southward to San Francisco, Harriman rose to battle. He thrust a railroad southward on the west bank. The "parallel feud" grew hot — at times violent — as the railroads advanced. When the canyon presented severe and costly hazards, the rivals agreed to a truce. Over the forty-one-mile stretch from Metolius to Bend, Harriman was permitted to run his trains on Hill's trackage.

A huge celebration marked completion of the Oregon Trunk at Bend in May, 1911. Hill, the "Empire Builder," told a depot throng of 2,500 that peace with the Union Pacific was desirable. It is said Hill gave the pulled golden spike to

228

Bill Hanley, remarking, "I was building a road to come and see you." Hill and his son, Louis W., did go on a sight-seeing tour of Harney Valley with Hanley's party. They covered the country on rutty roads, but they voiced bountiful admiration.

Prineville, the oldest town in central Oregon, had to wait seven more years before railroad trains entered its limits. The City of Prineville Railway, a municipal enterprise, connected it with the outside world by steel rails in August, 1918.

Harriman did not wait long to extend the Oregon Short Line railway, branch of the Union Pacific, from Ontario to Crane. That settlement, with its neighbors, built up high hopes for the future now that at long last a ribbon of steel had emerged from the east. Crane celebrated its new triumph July 11, 1916. Governor James Withycomb and other state dignitaries were present, with 2,000 to 3,000 Harney and Malheur county people. The Burns *Times-Herald* reported:

Chief Construction Engineer Young brought the first train in with two coaches and several flatcars filled with excursionists from Ontario, Vale, Juntura, Riverside, and other points. As soon as he had disposed of the excursion people he invited Harney County people to "take a ride" with him and his train was soon filled. It was necessary to make two trips of this special to and from the scene of the big steam shovel in Crane creek gap to accommodate all. Hundreds of Harney County people were anxious to take a ride on a train in Harney County. One man aboard was taking his first ride in 33 years.

Business life of the county seat and its sister communities persevered through changes in complexion upon entering the second decade of the 1900s. Fires and misfortunes left scars, but the blows resulted in stimulation. The citizens replaced the old with finer buildings.

Fire razed the Locher Hall, a large wooden structure erected over stone walls, on the night of January 13, 1913. Burns' worst conflagration, on the night of August 31, 1914, brought $100,000 damage. It destroyed the entire block later occupied by the Levens and Clemens building and swept onward. It had started in the R. J. McKinnon Livery Stable, consuming many wooden buildings rapidly and damaging twenty-four. Among eighteen business places devoured was Brenton's White Front feed barn, fourteen horses dying.

Brenton's remodeled building burned down the next year. On September 14, 1915, another fire in Burns ruined seven buildings, including the French Hotel. Paul Locher lost three buildings, and G. W. Clevenger lost a large furniture store. In the destruction of the Cummins Hospital in Burns, October 29, 1915, David Miller died. John Morrell, with a badly fractured leg, performed heroic rescue work. Stone and brick buildings then came faster.

The Harney Valley *News,* in 1910, introduced the first linotype (type-setting machine) into Burns. C. A. Byrd had become associated with Frank Davey, well known in state politics after lengthy service on Salem's *Oregon Statesman* and *Capital Journal.* Byrd took complete control in 1914 when Davey went to the Legislature and, in 1916, he procured a second linotype.

The *American* was set up at Crane August 18, 1916, by P. J. Gallagher and George E. Carter. Gallagher, a lawyer, soon left. Carter, formerly a publisher at White Salmon, Washington, published his *American* until 1935, giving way to Clyde B. Cornell. Initially, there was much optimism in the paper issued each Friday in Harney County's only railroad town. Of six pages, six columns to a page, the paper carried five columns of local news on page one. Two pages were of "boiler plate," and the Crane Townsite Company took a full page for an ad. This paper forsook Crane for Burns in 1936.

From 1871 was a span of forty-five years in settlement of the Harney range land. Time dictated that those who had established their homes in the "long ago" should band together and have their annual reunions. The Harney County Pioneer Association, conceived at a banquet in the Burns Masonic Hall, became an actual working organization October 5, 1916. Eligible for membership were those with thirty years' residence in the county, persons coming prior to 1887 being the first in enrollment. The charter roster was signed by 120. James F. Mahon, a settler in 1879, who had been the first to suggest creation of the association, became its first president. W. E. Huston, a resident since 1885, was named secretary. Walter Riddle was the oldest pioneer in point of residence who attended the first meeting, he having settled in 1871.

Though in varied stages of progress, Harney County had a

slump in its cattle business from 1910 to 1920, use of land for sheep and the dry seasons beginning in 1917 having an adverse effect. The homesteaders, in spite of aid given by the Strockraising Homestead Law of 1916, had too many odds against them besides drouth and distance from markets. They lacked money or land to raise cattle on a big scale. In 1931 the entire cattle region of Oregon had less than two persons to each square mile.

Winter feeding gradually replaced the risks of open range, and big hay harvests were aids with drives to better areas. Harney sent some cattle into Malheur County. Tens of thousands of dollars in bounties were paid for tens of thousands of rabbit ears, evidence of the slaughter of the pests.

Better breeding and better stock came to the fore, Shorthorns and Herefords being preferred. Yard and stall feeding of the winter made for increased herds on the open range throughout other seasons. Summer range in national forests was utilized zealously. Permits were necessary by 1900, followed by a grazing fee in January, 1906, gradually increasing to 16.6 cents per head per month in 1918. Cattlemen and the Forest Service guarded against overgrazing. In 1920, markets at Portland, Seattle and Spokane absorbed nearly all of the cattle from Oregon and Washington.

By 1907 Henry Miller was owner of the gargantuan holdings of his company, buying out Lux's heirs. the minority stockholders. His enterprises soon reached their peak. In *The Cattle King,* Edward F. Treadwell, Miller's attorney and biographer, writes:

. . . Henry Miller held a preeminent place. To own over one million acres of land situated in five states, over one million head of livestock, two banks and their branches, reservoirs, and other properties, all operated as a unit, appraised at fifty million dollars, and acquired, developed, protected, reclaimed and irrigated by the sole efforts of one man starting in life with nothing but his natural endowments, is an achievement which cannot but attract attention and wonder.

Miller, monarch of such a well-knit empire, died October 14, 1916. His corporation, headed firmly by his son-in-law, J. Leroy Nickel, carried on as before. In 1918 it could still drive its herds from Grant County to Sacramento with only two camps made off its own lands.

Shortly after the century's turn, Bill Hanley, an engaging figure under his black broadbrim Stetson, was a leading product of the old cow country. He resembled, somewhat, the Great Commoner, William Jennings Bryan. Many lent ear to his sagely spoken utterances. Far-flung contacts made him a friend of business and political leaders in the West. He helped to inspire the railways that came, finally, to the heart of Harney Valley.

In the campaign of 1912, Hanley, running on Theodore Roosevelt's "Bull Moose" ticket, was a candidate for United States senator. Later he became a leader in local and state highway work.

Prior to 1911 Bill and his wife Clara had postponed more than a few times the building of a larger home on their ranch near Burns. They had consulted an architect about a stone house to replace their pioneer abode. While her husband was absent on a selling trip to Omaha in 1911, Clara got busy. Carpenters came to the Bell A headquarters and Clara helped them. Old lumber as well as new was used. After a month's absence, Bill returned to see the framework up on a commodious two-story house.

Clara kept busy always, with the crews, or with guests, there being many of both. She had twelve beds for guests; notables like Louis Hill enjoyed visits. College boys from Portland and elsewhere were fed and bedded. Like Bill and the hands, Mrs. Hanley usually arose at five in the morning and breakfasted at six. Nine at night spelled bedtime in the normal schedule.

The Hanleys had most of their land about 1912 — twenty-odd thousand acres. They ran 6,000 or 7,000 head of cattle, but their horses diminished on distant ranges, sometimes mysteriously. Some mules were used for hauling, ditching and similar work. They drove 2,000 or more cattle for Indians at Klamath. Clara rode in a buggy on four drives a year to Ontario, taking about twenty days. Loss was incurred sometimes; in other shipments the profits came to fifty cents or more a head.

Hanley and associates completed drainage of the "P-ranch

Swamp" by 1913. In this gigantic undertaking the water was diverted to higher ground for irrigation. The dredging made it possible to cultivate some of the former swamp area and give a flow of water to soil where sagebrush had grown. Then they eyed the large Diamond Swamp. Bill had his hands full managing the ranches of P and OO, the Roaring Springs and Rock Creek, riding from his home place. He exchanged horses for an automobile.

In and out of his Model T, Hanley directed dredges and channel-digging. When, however, too many juniper trees fell in his swath, the men of the Forest Service forbade excess hauling of them to stoke the dredger's boiler. Old days of freedom waned but the dredging went on.

In 1917, Swift & Co., Chicago packers, under title of Eastern Oregon Livestock Company, took over P Ranch holdings, with division of horses. The brand of P remained for Swift, and Three Dots (in triangle) for Hanley. Bill's cattle then bore the Bell A brand; calves born on his ranch bore LY, both brands being on the left hip.

George Craddock, skillful rangeman, was a long-time foreman for Hanley before quitting in 1918. Harry Golden served as foreman on the OO for sixteen years. Among other faithful employes was William Sterling. For a lengthy period he was Hanley's bookkeeper, in the longhand days and later with the typewriter.

By this time most people in the far west had heard of Bill Brown. His wide and straightforward dealings in buying and selling of sheep, horses and cattle, and his charitable nature, had gained him a niche in the grassland's hall of fame. Bill's partiality pointed to no class. He was a ruler but not a braggadocio.

In 1912 Oregon's Governor Oswald West, himself a lover of horseflesh, rode horseback into Buck Creek, location of Brown's home-ranch buildings and mercantile store. West, who was on his way to a conference of western governors in Boise, writes:

. . . Asking his housekeeper and cook if I might find food and shelter for the night, she referred me to Brown, whom she said was cutting hay in a near-by meadow. Upon my approach Bill halted the mowing outfit and acknowledged an introduction. The fact that he was about to entertain the Governor of his state made little or no impression upon him. However, he agreed to my spending the night with him, and directed me as to where my saddle animal be stabled, and where I might wash up for supper.

The ranch house was large and roomy, but Bill's bedroom, of which I was to become a joint occupant, was quite small—hardly affording room for his double bed and a desk, which occupied one corner. The latter was littered with, and surrounded by check stubs. Such appeared to be Bill's method of keeping accounts. . . . Bill's charge, on this occasion, was 50c for my supper, 50c for bed and 50c for breakfast. A like charge was made for my saddle animal . . .

Frank M. Neth, who was employed on Brown's ranch from 1914 to 1917 and knew Bill intimately, says: "Brown was a very hospitable man and I have never known of his charging anything for meals or lodging for travelers or guests, although many of them stayed many days at a time."

Additions to his grazing kingdom made Brown possessor of between 30,000 and 40,000 acres in Harney, Crook and Lake counties; this meant control, also, of about 100,000 acres of range land because he had secured the water holes. With purchase of unused school and homestead acreages, and extensive holdings around Grindstone, were about 15,000 acres bought from the Oregon and Western Colonization Company. The peak was between 1912 and the 1920s.

Estimates of the number of animals Brown owned at any one time varied, to as high as 22,000 sheep. Neth says Brown's holdings of sheep "were about 12,000 head when he owned about the same number of horses." He wore the label "horse king" during World War I when sales were strong — 1,000 horses being sold, it is said, for $100,000. His wealth was estimated as $500,000 by the war's end.

"Bill Brown," points out Neth, "never sold horses in small quantities and always required them to be taken out of the state of Oregon so that there would be no chance of an argument about horses remaining in the state bearing his brand belonging to him."

Sincerely, quietly over the years, Brown showed due appreciation of goodness that could be wrought for others. With a feeling of indebtedness to Oregon, he at one time gave $10,-000 for a building at the old Pendleton Academy. He was absent from the dedication, and did not reply to the letter inviting him to be present. Among other donations, he gave as much as $25,000 to the Methodist Old People's Home at Salem.

With the decline of the live-stock market after World War I, Brown's holdings began to shrink. The auto and truck and motorized farm equipment spelled further doom for horses. His herds fell off. Naturally, at first, cars were unwelcome on the Buck Creek premises. Bill bought an automobile in due time, but he spent little time driving it. He faced the changes of the 1920s. By the next decade hazards were to be too numerous.

If the body politic kept substantially within the law, still the range land at times had invasion by bad men. On the morning of August 27, 1924, Arch L. Cody, forty-four-year-old native of Portland, who had served time in the California and Oregon penitentiaries, climaxed his horse-and-auto-stealing career by killing W. A. Goodman, Harney County sheriff. The fatality occurred at C. L. Pollock's place, just over the line in Malheur County, when the fugitive turned on his pursuer.

A posse, bent on swift justice, overtook Cody in a running fight. When he jumped off his horse and threw up his hands, the captors found him armed "all over." He carried a .30-.30 carbine, a .32-caliber automatic, a knife and plenty of ammunition. At first brought to Burns, the prisoner soon was taken to Vale, in Malheur County, for trial. He was convicted and executed by the State.

Funeral services for Goodman, held on the courthouse lawn in Burns, were attended by the largest crowd to assemble for such rites in Harney County. Every business house in Burns closed as a tribute to the man who gave his life in line of duty. His wife, Hester, daughter of W. W. Johnson, pioneer of Fort Harney days, was left with three children.

Chapter XXXII

A FULL SWING TO RESOURCES

WITH JUSTIFIABLE PRIDE in and admiration for its exalted position in the realm of grass, Harney County came to acknowledge the inevitability of nurturing its varied resources. It retained its primitive color while encouraging sufficiency for times that were different.

Improved methods came to the range, as did improved stock. The mustang and his fellows no longer served a useful purpose. In the 1920s hundreds of thousands of the poorly bred horses, unbranded for the most part, fed and watered where better animals were needed. Sadly, but needfully, stockmen went about the process of exterminating the horse which, of itself, had never been really the preferred cow pony.

Roundups of the wild horses — "broomtails" or "slick ears" or "oreanas" — brought out all the skill and tricks that buckaroos possessed. The animals vied with mountain goats, leaped among rocks, climbed speedily to sharp points, jumped warily into declivities, or raced for gaps in mountains and rimrocks. Once captured, they often had to be roped and hobbled on the drive-in. And it all took time. When put up at auction, these "critters" evaded the gambling spirit of cowboys. The toughest and "awnriest" got a chance in rodeos. The enfeebled and past-prime became canned meat.

More attention was drawn to irrigation, but vexatious were its many problems. Bill Hanley and the Pacific Live Stock Company, at their own expense, put forth elaborate efforts for drainage and irrigation systems. In 1917 came passage of the Oregon District Irrigation Law. In conformity with this, formation of districts in Harney Valley demanded costly bond issues and other expenses. There was scarcity of settlement on dry lands.

In 1919, Hanley, A. R. Olsen (representing the Pacific Live Stock Company) and many landowners on the Silvies River attempted to form one big district, with two reservoirs or dams, to be built at Emigrant Creek and at Silvies River sites.

Within this district, the Hanley company owned 10,000 acres, the P. L. S. 20,000 acres. In June, 1921, the Blitzen River Reclamation District was organized. It called for irrigation and drainage of 50,000 acres on the Blitzen River. Directors were C. S. Green, Nelson B. Higgs and B. B. Clark. Both undertakings fell short of actuality.

In 1922 organization of the Harney County Irrigation District was effected, with election of a board of directors. Hiring of engineers and working out of details cost $50,000. An election authorized issuance of bonds amounting to $2,-200,000, and the courts validated the voted bonds. They were never sold, however.

An unfulfilled dream to extend the railroad from Crane to Burns to tap resources enticed the curiosity of E. W. Barnes. In August, 1919, says the *Times-Herald,* he

took off his coat and got busy. The first move was to secure a county cruise of the timber in private ownership from which to base an estimate of the timber in the reserve tributary to Burns; the cruise was completed and, fortified with this together with his own estimate, he went east and succeeded in interesting a lumber company in the proposition, which expended many thousands of dollars investigating the field.

Unforeseen events caused the company to drop its plans. Barnes, himself, pushed ahead while spending much on necessary preliminary undertakings. A petition asked the Department of Agriculture for cooperation of the Forest Service and assent "to an act of Congress authorizing the exchange of lands within the exterior boundaries of the Malheur National Forest." Most signers were from Harney and Grant counties. Barnes, financed by citizens of Burns, left for Washington, D. C., in January, 1922.

He was supported earnestly by Oregon's delegation in Congress and by state and local organizations. Successfully passed, the bill was signed by the President on March 10, 1922. The Forest Service was to move quickly, at the direction of its chief, Colonel W. B. Greeley, in cruising and appraising timber of the Silvies River watershed to offer it for sale.

Much remained to be done. A Committee of Ten from the Burns Commercial Club was selected to render immediate and fullest aid to Burns' plans. Members other than William Farre, secretary-manager, were Ben Brown, Leon M. Brown, Archie McGowan, A. C. Welcome, Julian Byrd, James Lampshire, I. S. Geer, J. R. Thompson, Nollie F. Reed and E. H. Conser. These men guaranteed expenses of $200 a month for "an indefinite period."

Late in the year the open bidding for the timber was publicized by the Forest Service. Fred Herrick's bid of $2.80 per 1,000 feet, board measure on log scale — approximately 890,-000,000 feet in the Bear Valley unit of Malheur National Forest, Grant County — was awarded him June 15, 1923.

In 1924 the tireless efforts of leading citizens in bringing a railroad into Burns met with realization. Of importance since the line had ended at Crane in 1916 was the growth in value of timber resources. The pine in the hills no longer was to be hacked away in small bits. The Fred Herrick Lumber Company, cooperating with the Union Pacific, began laying of the Malheur Railroad Company's rails from Crane to Burns on May 1, 1924.

Completed September 24, a big celebration at Burns drew an assemblage of 4,000 persons, including speakers representing the Oregon Short Line, well-wishing towns and organizations. On that day a train with fourteen coaches puffed to a stop in the seat of Harney County. Enthusiastic throngs crowded around the courthouse in the afternoon to hear messages, the music of a band still in their ears and the sight of gala-dressed Paiute Indians and buckaroos lifting spirits ever higher.

James J. Donegan, chairman of the program committee, presided happily. Dr. L. E. Hibbard, pioneer dentist and president of the Burns and Harney County Commericial Club, gave a worthy, informative address of welcome. Barnes, zealous booster for timber and other developments, spoke, as did Herrick, the lumberman who wished to aid milling of timber. Messages were read from numerous well-wishers, including Carl Gray, president of the Union Pacific. Other speakers continued.

Then came the crowning event, the delightful climax — the barbecue managed by William Farre. It was "all out" with baked potatoes, tubs heaped with juicy stewed Oregon prunes, ten-gallon cans of coffee and thick cream, plus servings of beef no one dared to deny as the best in the world. It came off their ranges.

The era of the freight wagons and rattling stages had walked out with bowed head and proud memories. It would not be long until high wooden sidewalks, where so much unloading, sitting and whittling had been done, would disappear into fireboxes.

Still Burns, holding its annual three-day rodeo, was to retain its cherished title of cowtown. It had no idea of surrendering in spite of iron rails, asphalt pavements and cement walks. The hitching racks could go, too, but not the saddleries or harness shops. Horses and cattle would be at home on ranches from which more commuting was done by automobile.

Optimistic and affable, Douglas Mullarky came to Burns in 1926 as editor and publisher of the *News*, which had changed ownership several times. He gained a liking for the sagebrush capital and gave of his ability to regional advancement. Consolidation swallowed the *News* in 1930, and Burns had its stronger *Times-Herald* with Julian Byrd as editor and Mullarky as manager.

In 1926, too, Robert J. Williams, always a Democrat, was elected Harney County judge. He was to hold the office ten years. And in that time, as well as over the years since 1881, he assisted farsighted men toward judicious stability of the county.

Subsequently, a slump in the market and stiff sales competition put Herrick in financial jeopardy. His company encountered obstacles of various kinds in completing a railroad to tap the forested wealth of the Blue Mountains. The contract stipulated that the mill had to be located within five miles of Burns. The site chosen was at the warm springs two and a half miles south of Burns, forty miles from any commercial timber. Only the cement foundations stood out where the mill was to rise.

Leading citizens, wearying of what they termed unwarranted delays, became critical of Herrick's enterprise and sought reliance in a company that would, in brief time, push through the project of a lumber mill and its rail feeder. Archie Mc-

Gowan, serving in the Oregon Legislature in 1927, sponsored a memorial from that body to the Congress of the United States requesting investigation of the Herrick contract.

On January 31, 1927, a committee report to the United States Senate was embodied in a resolution stating abundance of evidence revealed Herrick's noncompliance with certain terms of the original contract and the modified contract. His lack of finances, according to testimony, had caused grievous postponements in construction. The Senate committee recommended that Herrick's sawmill near Burns be completed and in full operation on or before January 1, 1928. He had less than a year to finish the plant and begin cutting. In this, he failed.

In 1928 the Edward Hines Lumber Co. of Chicago, Illinois, took over fifty miles of railroad from the Herrick interests as well as an unfinished mill. The total cost of this and erecting the mill was $6,000,000. The railroad from Crane to Burns passed to the control of the Union Pacific. The Malheur Railroad Company's line, now known as the Oregon & Northwestern, was extended to Seneca in the Ponderosa region of southern Grant County.

The Hines company also invested $2,000,000 in the pine stands. A sixty-year cutting was planned after starting to cut 11,000,000,000 feet of timber under agreement with the United States Forest Service. The annual cut then was figured at 100,000,000 feet.

In construction of the mill, which took one and one-half years, two large turbines were installed, with a capacity of 6,000 kilowatts. The mill required 3,000 kilowatts; the surplus of 3,000 kilowatts was sold to the local power company and was the only source of power for lighting purposes until December, 1949.

In 1928, also, as a result of the Hines development, Stafford-Derbes & Roy Company of New Orleans, Louisiana, purchased a huge tract of sageland near Burns and the mill. This firm soon spent $875,000 in development of the property, building a goodly array of modern homes for the Hines employes. It purchased surplus power of the Hines company to construct power lines and develop a great amount of the sageland by pumping. The modern town of Hines elbowed the ghostly pioneer settlement of Egan.

Though the mill and railroad pushed through to success, the real estate developers were caught in the cogs of the countrywide depression that followed the dizzy collapse in Wall Street at the end of the 1920s. As had happened in other attempts to make the dry soil bloom in profit, most of their expansive acres once more remained covered with sagebrush. The sturdy and roofless walls of a large hotel stood out skeleton-like to remind, for many years after, the vision of its builders.

The Edward Hines Lumber Co. bought the Stafford-Derbes & Roy Company's holdings in real estate. Beautified homes were resold to mill employes on a time-payment plan.

At the end of three years the warm springs flooded the mill pond, the building of dikes forming a forty-acre lake. The logging train could dump thirty cars of logs at one unloading into water which would not freeze in winter. The railroad from Seneca to Burns fulfilled its obligation as a common carrier, linked with the Union Pacific at Burns which ran through Crane to Ontario to connect with eastern points.

The gigantic mill, wed by rail with the Malheur Forest and Bear Valley, was started on its operating career January 22, 1930, when Secretary of Agriculture Arthur M. Hyde touched an electric button in Washington, D. C. It was a dream come true for Harney County and the firm of builders headed by Edward Hines. He, founder and president of the lumber company, was a native of Buffalo, New York. He rose from a tallyman in a lumber yard to head his firm in Chicago, incorporated in 1892.

In the triumphal opening, the day was joyously celebrated. Present were Edward Hines, his wife, and son Ralph; Mortimer L. Hudson, general secretary of the Hines affiliated companies; F. W. Pettibone, in charge of building the mill; C. J. Pettibone, operating chief; C. E. Gregory, and other members of the organization.

Civic leaders, men who had labored hard for the undertaking that gave new life to the Harney region, included Barnes, whose promoting vision lasted through from 1919; President A. A. Bardwell of the Burns Chamber of Com-

merce; Waldo Geer, head of the celebration committee; Ben
Snowden, secretary; James J. Donegan, chairman of the program committee; Editor Julian Byrd, Archie McGowan, Wil-
lam Hanley, Doctor Hibbard and other workers. The business
houses and schools of Burns closed for the afternoon.

Congratulating guests swelled the crowd to about 3,000 at
the luncheon in a huge pavilion on the mill grounds and at
the program which followed. Mayor Grover N. Jameson gave
the address of welcome. In addition to addresses given by
Edward Hines, Hanley and leaders from far and near, were
musical and varied entertainment features. Not to be soon
forgotten was the help given the milling enterprise by Colonel
Greeley of the Forest Service and other officials. The three-
bandsaw mill was ready for its cutting of the Bunyanesque
stand of timber.

At this time the federal government owned 63.8 per cent
of the total area of Harney County, larger than the state of
Rhode Island. The bigness of the area gave each person in the
county space enough to put him one mile from his nearest
neighbor, with 3,000 square miles of acreage to spare. Dou-
bling its population in a year, Burns became a town of some
3,000 residents.

A great amount of Harney Valley's 240,000 acres of irri-
gable land started changing from brown pasture land to
green fields of feed crops. Still, out on the higher benches or
on seared flats windmills and pumps would hold forth long.
There are, too, the water holes for cattle, dug six to eight feet
deep so that the water may not get too warm or evaporate.

In full swing, the local operations of the Edward Hines
Lumber Co. spelled an investment of approximately $9,000,-
000. This firm and the WPA cooperated in constructing a rec-
reation park with a modern swimming pool near the mill.
The project was completel May 30, 1936, and named for
James J. Donegan.

E. T. F. Wohlenberg succeeded C. J. Pettibone as general
manager at Hines. Alfred D. Dewey took over this position in
January, 1945, serving also as vice president and general manager of the Oregon & Northwestern Railroad Company. In
addition to the original fifty miles of main line, forty miles of

private logging railroad and spurs are now in existence for the company's logging operations.

A private logging road of fifty-two miles which permits a direct haul of timber from the Ochoco National Forest to the mill has been constructed since 1946. Volcanic cinders have been used in the first twenty-six miles. The trucks, which have twelve-foot bunks, are powered by 265-horsepower engines. An efficient slide-ladder, designed by Carl Ries, master mechanic, is employed extensively in loading cars with logs.

The entire operation is unique in that it is on a sustained yield basis, cutting forty per cent of the volume of timber per acre. The timber taken is mature and poor thrift, harvested on a thirty-five-year cycle. The company builds between 100 and 150 miles of logging road each year, thus opening large areas for fire protection and recreation.

In 1949 the Hines mill produced 121,000,000 board feet of finished lumber. Percentage of production is ninety of Ponderosa, ten of fir and larch. All the lumber is kiln-dried, in forty dry kilns, at the local plant. There is no storage except that under shed-roofing. The lumber from each log does not see daylight from the time it enters the sawmill until the customer opens the car door at its ultimate destination. All lumber is marketed in the East save that going to local yards.

In the sawmill, which has a capacity of 25,000 board feet an hour, employes number 460. The mill works two eight-hour shifts, six days a week. There are 242 employes in logging and forty on the O. & W. railroad.

As one of Oregon's largest industries, the Hines lumber firm reciprocates the high esteem in which it is held. Mindful of the best interests of community and region, it maintains a generous and strong policy in its many contributions.

The continuity of employment is exceptional. The sawmill runs fifty weeks a year, which gives Hines employes continuous work and steady jobs. The firm shuts down two weeks in July of each year, when the employes receive their paid vacations.

The yearly pay roll of the Hines Co. is $4,000,000.

Chapter XXXIII

MALHEUR NATIONAL WILDLIFE REFUGE AND EXPERIMENT STATION

THE INTRODUCTION to a governmental leaflet issued in 1947 reads:

The Malheur Refuge, lying at the threshold of the gently tilted west slope of the Steens Mountain in Southeastern Oregon, exemplifies the Nation's effort to conserve and restore our wildlife resources. Here, 35 miles to the south of the city of Burns, and within comfortable weekend accessibility from Ontario, Pendleton, Bend, and Lakeview, slightly less than 175,000 acres (over 270 square miles) of marsh, swamp, meadow, and a limited amount of arid brush land are given over to wildlife restoration and protection, which is administered by the Fish and Wildlife Service of the United States Department of the Interior.

At the southernmost end of the Refuge the settlement of Frenchglen with its hotel, service station, and general store offers pleasant and comfortable facilities for the visitor and vacationist. Located within easy reach of good hunting and fishing in the Steens Mountains, of the unique Blitzen gorge, and of the Refuge with its easily observed waterfowl, sage hen, pheasant, quail, partridge, deer, antelope and beaver workings, Frenchglen affords ideal opportunities as a base camp for adventures in the out-of-doors.

No other waterfowl resting and nesting place on our continent has as great a variety of birds — and its history is alluring. Upon creation of the Commission of Fish and Fisheries in 1871, President Grant selected Spencer F. Baird, great ornithologist and teacher of natural history, to head it. He, like his successors, contributed unceasingly to the movement for preserving of wildlife. Field work in the Pacific Northwest grew in intensity.

At and around Fort Harney prior to the outbreak of hostilities in 1878, Captain Charles Bendire of the Regular Army spent much time in observing the teeming animal life. He kept a diary and made detailed reports. After serving with the First Cavalry in Bannock War engagements, he cooperated with the Smithsonian Institution in making topographical sur-

244

veys and in collecting specimens, chiefly mineral, in the Pacific Northwest. Lieutenant William Carey Brown accompanied his expedition and scouting group.

In passing of the years, the federal and state governments, organizations and individuals built reservoirs of findings and lent increasing encouragement to protection of wildlife. The Klamath and Harney areas, among others, received absorbing interest because of their wealth in the field of natural science. Parallel with this in time were acquisitions and attempts at development of the swamp lands by cattlemen and settlers. James Donegan points out:

In May, 1895, the Surveyor General called for bids for surveying the lands situated between the meander line of Malheur Lake, as originally surveyed and established, and the then present shore line of the lake. This created a new meander line. Due to irrigation on the Blitzen and Silvies Rivers and a series of dry years, the waters of the lake receded and a large area became to all purposes agricultural lands. Settlers filed on the lands within the new meander line and as usual a legal fight arose as to the legality of their entries. The French-glen Livestock Company claimed under the theory of riparian ownership all of the lands to the center of the lake, thereby claiming all of the lands that were within the new meander line. This new survey was made by John H. Neal and approved by the Surveyor General June 25th, 1897.

President Theodore Roosevelt, in 1908, directed that Malheur Lake be set aside as a national bird refuge. This done, the climatic changes lent emphasis to utilitarian demands. In dry years water, especially from the Blitzen River, had of necessity to be regulated at sources by dams, ponds, ditches, dikes, and canals.

Governor James Withycomb recommended to the Oregon Legislature in 1919 that Malheur and Mud lakes be ceded by the State to the United States for a permanent bird refuge. The fight then started never lessened in bitterness for sixteen years. A bill embodying the governor's recommendations was introduced in the Legislature. By provisions of the bill, government engineers were empowered to determine the lakes' "water land." Donegan tells of the controversy:

Two large irrigation districts, one on the Silvies River, and one on the Blitzen River, were in the course of formation. Each provided for the construction of storage reservoirs on the Silvies and Blitzen Rivers, and the irrigation interests feared that in the way the bill was drawn, the engineers would wait until the flood waters of the Blitzen and Silvies had flowed into the lakes before the water level had been set by the Government. If such were the case the Government would be in a position to enjoin the irrigation districts from storing the waters of the rivers. The irrigation districts put up a hard fight against the bill and succeeded in defeating it in the legislature. Dr. William L. Finley, the Audubon Society and fish and game interests led by Mr. Finley, were behind this legislation and at the next general election initiated the same bill that was defeated in the 1919 session. Both sides put up a stiff fight, but the bill was again defeated in the general election by a large majority. It was the battle of "The Babes against the Birds."

A series of droughts had begun in 1914. The aridity grew worse, culminating in a complete drought in 1934. Live stock suffered from lack of water as its sources shriveled. Hay and pasture lands became scarcer. The Works Progress Administration drilled a number of deep wells on the public range, and water was pumped from shallow wells in the oozy bed of the Silvies River. Thirsty cattle drifted through cut fences.

Water evaporated from Malheur Lake's bed. In desperation, small stockmen and farmers trespassed on the seamy bed and sowed 8,000-odd acres to grain. Water lay only a yard under surface of great patches of the fertile soil. The grain developed into a fine stand. In May armies of grasshoppers invaded it. Donegan, who had served two terms as assessor of Harney County, was chairman of its relief committee in these trying days. In answer to appeal, help came from the state relief committee and the Oregon State Agricultural College. Several carloads of bran and barrels of poison enabled WPA workers to rescue the grain.

On the morning of July 4, 1934, workers discovered that a mile of the protecting fence built by the grain-growers had been destroyed. Three thousand cattle were within a mile of the prospective feast, and the alarm sounded. Men hurriedly drove off the cattle, repaired the fence, and placed armed guards along the full length of the barrier. Relief Chairman Donegan, the sheriff and district attorney requested a talk with the grain-growers and stockmen to agree on plans to save what was "about the only crop in the Harney Valley at that time." Donegan writes:

The situation looked serious, but it was pointed out to both sides that they were trespassers, and the question of the title was in the courts, and was claimed by the government as a bird preserve, the State as swamp land and the owners of deeded lands surrounding the lake claimed ownership through the theory of riparian rights. . . . it was finally decided that the fence lines covering this 80,000 acre tract would be guarded night and day until the crops could be harvested late in the fall. Each side, stockmen and grain growers, agreed to divide the cost of the protection. This was done and the Malheur Lake saved the day for many small farmers and stockmen.

The federal government then tackled earnestly the problem of acquiring and maintaining a land-lake refuge. Burns shared with other places in the hearings and testimonies that aided attorneys to iron out all relevant matters. More than a few of the rugged, individualistic pioneers of Harney County gave valuable information from reminiscences ever sharpened by their way of life. Historical scholars and engineers, and surveyors and attorneys put in appearance or submitted lengthy transcripts.

The land wanted was a huge portion of the empire founded by Pete French. On about 200,000 acres under his control he had run 20,000 white-faced steers, he had fenced in more than 100,000 acres. He and his successors had drained, irrigated and sown to grass and grain mammoth slices of the area. Dr. W. G. Brown, well-known dentist of Burns, worked on French's P Ranch when he was a boy. He drove a hay rake over a meadow five miles long.

P Ranch once had boasted 150,000 acres. On French's death it ran seventy miles from Steens' foothills to the south edge of Malheur Lake. After its handling by land development companies, it was possessed by Swift & Co. Approximately halfway between the Frenchglen store and Malheur Lake nestled Buena Vista ranch quarters.

At last the die was cast. In 1935 the federal government purchased from the Eastern Oregon Livestock Company, subsidiary of Swift & Co., 64,717 acres in the valley of the Blitzen at a cost of $675.000. It included the White House, French's loved home.

The government soon got its Malheur Wildlife Refuge in working order — reversion of a cattle kingdom to wilds — thus completing the cycle. Prudence and awareness dictated choice of officials. Stanley M. Jewett, experienced and unflagging in the field of natural sciences, became the first superintendent of the refuge. He served from May, 1935, to November, 1936. Later he went to Portland as regional federal biologist. His initial program augured well.

John C. Scharff succeeded Jewett as superintendent. He came, after education in animal husbandry at Oregon State College, from the Fremont National Forest, Lakeview. Scharff, young and energetic, studied and labored intensively at his vocation. Still in the superintendency of the refuge, he has become a part of the recreated wilderness.

Hard by the willows, coontails and tules fringing the south shore of brackish Malheur Lake, construction of headquarters buildings began in August, 1935. They were built stoutly and fittingly of native sedimentary rock. Colored, red, brown and pink tiles went into the roofs. Green lawns, edged by leafy trees and bushes, sloped gently from sage-crested hills to the ruffled edges of the lake. A 100-foot observation tower rose on higher ground to afford a sweeping view. By 1946 a thousand visitors from this and foreign lands turned from highways to be enraptured with the primeval.

Subsequent to the original purchase of Blitzen Valley acres, other lands were added to the refuge area, bringing the total to nearly 175,000 acres. A large acquisition was the OO Ranch south of Harney Lake, coming after Ira N. Gabrielson succeeded "Ding" Darling as chief of the Federal Fish and Wildlife Bureau. The price for 14,751 acres was $116,143.

Engineering feats accomplished wonders for the sanctuary of migratory waterfowl and the haven of feathered and furry life. A concrete dam spans the Blitzen at the south end of the refuge, its water available to a large area. The Blitzen serves as a canal for twenty-eight miles, there being 100 miles of canal. Water is held at various levels, the impounding of it in a box canyon making Boco Lake. Dikes and other improvements assure proper control and protection.

The teeming life on, and the system of, the refuge demand constant surveillance, and the public is furnished with well-written and accurate bulletins. Yet a glimpse of the primitive area and its occupants is not amiss. A recent leaflet explains an important part played by the sanctuary:

The Fish and Wildlife Service has found, through live-trapping birds and affixing a very light, numbered aluminum band with return address on the foot of each temporary captive, that water-fowl use four main trunk flyways in the United States in traveling to and from their wintering areas in the south and their breeding grounds in the north. The Malheur Refuge is located within the westernmost of these trunk flyways, known as the Pacific Flyway, which in itself is made up of several individual migration routes. The vast nesting areas in Canada and Alaska lie to the north and the extensive wintering grounds of California and Mexico lie to the south.

Bands of birds have been returned from as far south as a a state of South America. The refuge's greatest population is during the spring and fall migrations. More than a million water birds alight there in the fall. The recording of 227 different species of frequenting birds has been made, 125 of them nesting and rearing their young in the area.

Mammals recorded at Malheur Refuge number fifty-odd different kinds. Among the species are antelope, mule deer, beaver, muskrat, porcupine, mink, marmot, raccoon, badger, bobcat, shrew, coyote, wood or "pack" rat, kangaroo rat, and pocket gopher. They become very possessive of their habitat and multiply rapidly.

Ofttimes the landscape is a seething mass of ducks and geese. In the fall, flocks of snow geese gaining respite on the oozy flats distantly appear as fresh drifts of snow. The rare sandhill crane, numbering sixty nesting pairs in the spring and 750 migrants in the fall, come importantly. Stately but preying birds soar searchingly, among them the golden and bald eagles, the great horned owl and prairie falcon. Squadrons of hawks help to check the too numerous rodents.

Doubtless the greatest attraction on waters near the refuge's headquarters are the trumpeter swans, of royal mien and sounding off with deep-throated imperial buglings. Snow-white except for his webbed feet, bragging bill and a black streak tapering at his eyes, the adult trumpeter is an eyeful. His weight may reach thirty-six pounds, his wing length averages twenty-six-plus inches, and he has a loop which helps give the sonorous soundings. He may attain a life span of 100 years, say some biologists, a blessed longevity compared with an average of fifteen years for a goose and ten years for a duck.

Predatory and undiving man almost exterminated the trumpeter swan, which could not fly as high as some other fowl. In 1936 only seventy-four trumpeters and forty-one cygnets (young) were counted in the United States — after traveling in large convoys. By 1945 proper care had multiplied their numbers to 300, the long-necked birds on the Malheur Refuge being thirty-two.

Conservation and preservation as practiced on the sanctuary go well beyond the ideals of nature-lovers. The management explains:

Public service in the form of economic use of those natural resources surplus to the needs of wildlife is also offered, not only for the benefit of the local livestock industry and for the revenue which accrues to the Government from the sale of grazing and haying permits, but also for the benefit of the wildlife resource itself. Whereas rank meadow growth, uncut and ungrazed, affords very limited grazing for geese, grazed or mowed meadow lands offer almost ideal conditions for the feeding of these birds, and, in addition, provides earlier spring growth. Consequently certain areas are let out to grazing and haying privileges during such time as the birds are off the nest and the young reared. It is a common occurrence in the fall to see geese and cattle grazing in the same field—a field which, ungrazed, the geese would in all likelihood use but little.

Not always did the old-timer conserve that which he found so abundantly when he settled on the frontier, but the far-sighted pioneer had scruples. Reliance on meat from the hills, fish from the streams and fowl from out of the sky impelled him to guard against the day of scarcity.

In the Malheur Refuge, Harney County heralds a triumph that is also the victory of its mother nation.

———

To assist dry-farm homesteaders of the Harney basin in problems of grain and crop production, the Harney Branch Dry Farm Experiment Station was established. Selection of the area was made prior to the fall of 1911 and L. B. Breit-hauput became superintendent. On September 11 of that year Harney County and White & Raycraft entered into a contract for construction of buildings. Farming on the station area commenced in 1912, after clearing of sagebrush in the fall of 1911 and the next spring. The crops failed. Data on the first crop were collected in 1913.

By 1916 the station gave increased attention to gathering of information for the county's dry areas. H. B. Howell, under Breithauput's supervision, began work on the use of water for irrigation. Plots were laid and plans made to irrigate a small area from the well to supply water for the farmstead.

The drilling of an eight-inch field well in 1917 marked the beginning of the station's pump irrigation program which extended to 1942, inclusive. It was well demonstrated that crops, by this means, could be grown in Harney Valley. Yet homesteaders who tried out the program discontinued it because of economic difficulties and, sometimes, because of inexperience and lack of training in irrigation. The pump irrigation program fell short of its objective — to enable the homesteader to continue to live on his homestead.

The station had John H. Martin as its superintendent during 1918. Obil Shattuck took over the superintendency on February 1, 1919, serving in that capacity until the summer of 1943.

In 1937 an experimental program on range and range livestock investigations got under way. This work was centered on the newly created cooperative government station known as Squaw Butte. Oregon State College, having cooperated with Harney County on the old Harney Branch Experiment Station, bought cattle late in 1936 to be used at Squaw Butte. R. G. Johnson directed the efforts. Cattle summered on Squaw Butte and wintered on land usually leased from the Malheur Wildlife Refuge.

Officials from Oregon State College, in 1941, made arrangements to lease a section of meadow land, with an option to buy, from Mrs. William Hanley. This provided permanent winter quarters for the station's range live stock. From 1937 to 1943, inclusive, successive superintendents were Mr. Johnson, Kenneth B. Platt and Kenneth Ikler.

In 1944 the United States Department of the Interior and Oregon State College agreed to abandon the old pump irrigation program at Harney Branch and make that unit a part of an experiment station, to be called the Squaw Butte-Harney Range and Livestock Experiment Station. W. A. Sawyer then was employed as superintendent. From that date onward, emphases were placed upon experimental work, says Sawyer, "to determine the best methods of grazing desert range lands to permit the highest sustained production of livestock and methods of management of range cattle, both on the winter feed ground and on summer range."

Under the present station are 16,000 acres of federally-owned desert range land, 660 acres of native meadow land owned by the state of Oregon, and 180 acres of pump-irrigated crop land belonging to Harney County.

Steps taken to insure a continuous betterment of the livestock industry in the region have merited wide attention. Intensive study and painstaking experiments have yielded pleasing rewards.

Chapter XXXIV

GROWTH OF THE CHURCHES

AFTER ESTABLISHMENT of a permanent Catholic parish at The
Dalles in 1848, a church was built in Canyon City in 1863,
with Father Dielman as a resident pastor. As settlement grew
in Harney Valley it received irregular attendance, as a mission
field, from Canyon City.

In 1874, while Colonel Elmer Otis, a convert to Catholi-
cism, commanded Fort Harney, Father T. Mesplie served as
post chaplain. He remained two years. Sergeant Maurice Fitzgerald wrote: "During that time I did all the altar-boy duties
for his Reverence as well as attend his correspondence. There
were quite a number of Catholics among the enlisted men, and
besides Col. Otis and family, a Capt. Patrick Collins and
family. . . . "

In 1880, Archbishop Charles John Seghers of Portland
came in a buckboard to Harney Valley and, outfitted with a
saddle horse by Fitzgerald, made ready to continue his 160-
mile journey to Lakeview. He was entertained at the home of
Mr. and Mrs. Mahon, parents of John Mahon, on the Silvies
River.

For some years the widely scattered Catholic families attended Mass intermittently when it could be celebrated in a
hall or private home. The mission at Burns was served by
priests from Canyon City in the eighties, Fathers Louis Ver
Haag and A. Hilderbrand being among them. Others, including Father Ree, from Baker, attended the Harney people's
missions in the next decade.

Burns was designated as a separate parish, and gained a
resident pastor, when Father H. J. McDevitt arrived in November, 1899. He resolved to start construction of a permanent church building at once. Of pleasing personality, he min-
istered to people of Malheur, Crook and Harney counties and
lived with them.

Help and contributions for the Burns church came from
other settlers as well as from parishioners. Father McDevitt

joined in the physical labor. Among the Catholics rendering aid were Paul Locher, the Luig brothers, J. J. Donegan, Tim Donovan, J. C. Foley and Peter Andrews. Leon Brown donated two lots for building purposes and he donated the stone from his quarry, which assured a tasteful and durable edifice.

The cornerstone was laid in October, 1900, Thornton Williams, of the Masonic Order, giving the address. The chapel was moved from Locher Hall to Burns Hotel building where Father McDevitt also had his rooms. "This building," says Father Vincent C. Egan, "had been bought by Voegtly and Welcome and moved from its original site to the lot now used by the Ranch Supply for storage on the back street. It was no longer used as a hotel and no heat was supplied. . . . Father McDevitt made his home with J. J. Donegan during the winter months."

Besides procurement of $1,116 from a fair at Locher Hall, funds and materials and furnishings for the church came from out of the state as well as from within. Upon completion of the Holy Family Church, Father McDevitt made his home in a room built where the sacristy now stands. This was accomplished "near the end of 1901 or the early part of 1902," says Father Egan.

Father McDevitt was transferred to Tillamook in October, 1902, Father George Doyle succeeded him. The Diocese of Baker City was created. Burns again became a mission in 1904. Because of repairing of the Burns public school, classes for a time were held in the Catholic Church and public buildings.

Father Maximilian Klein, of the Franciscans, came as pastor to Burns in August, 1908. He erected a small frame house behind the church. The large brick house built by the Franciscans was ready to be occupied in the spring of 1911, for Burns had increased in population while Canyon City had lost residents.

"It was the intention of the Franciscan Fathers," says Father Egan, "to build a school close to the church in Burns, and for this purpose Mr. Leon Brown donated a block of land. He accepted only the nominal sum of $10.00 for the block of eight lots. But this dream was never realized, the school was not built."

The first Mass of record in Drewsey was celebrated in October, 1910. Father Klein paid $50.00 for two lots there and immediately awarded a contract to build a church costing $1,375. Beulah and its adjacent territory were attended from Ontario. Hope for permanent service at the proposed Wellington townsite a mile north of The Narrows, in 1912, faded as no town arose in the degree expected in an oil-boom vision.

The cemetery plot located near the edge of Hines was obtained by Father Pius Nieman in 1913 when Hank Levens donated the land. The church at Drewsey, which has always been attended by priests residing in Burns, was dedicated by Bishop Charles Joseph O'Reilly in honor of St. Matthew in June, 1913. A church was built by Father Thomas Brady at Beulah in 1915, but with departure of parishioners the building was moved to Malheur City .

Father Francis Redmond became pastor at Burns in 1916, remaining several years. It was principally through his efforts that the hospital of stone was erected, later to bear the name of Valley View Hospital.

The Franciscan Fathers gave up care of the Burns parish in 1922 and in December of that year the diocesan or secular priests again attended it. Father Peter Heuel gave time to conversion of local Paiutes, working among them from 1930 onward. Father A. F. Loeser took over the Holy Family Parish in 1930. He made many improvements, erecting the attractive small frame chapel for the local Indian colony. Bishop Joseph F. McGrath preached the dedication sermon October 9, 1932.

Father Egan succeeded Father Loeser at Burns in January, 1936, staying till August, 1939, and was transferred back to Baker. He served as a chaplain in World War II, with the United States Army. His service of almost four years included operations in Africa and France. Several priests served the Burns parish until Father Egan returned to it March 1, 1946.

Quickly, he labored with his parishioners in fulfilling spiritual and physical needs. The cemetery at Burns was enlarged and a hall was built for parish groups. The present parish takes in Harney County and the southern half of Malheur County. Parishioners number about 500, nearly 350 within a ten-mile radius of Burns. The parish property includes churches in Drewsey, Juntura and in the Indian colony.

Mention has been made previously of visitations in the Harney region by Protestant ministers in the seventies and eighties. By 1886 the Methodists of Burns had two preachers, the Rev. E. R. Horner and Dr. T. V. Embree, ministering to them. The Methodists who had started planning for a church after the mid-eighties built one in Burns about 1890.

The Presbyterians, in June, 1896, were bargaining with the Church Extension Society and the Methodist Episcopal Conference and presiding elder of the local district for purchasing of the Methodist Church at Burns, the congregation of which had dwindled.

Ministers succeeded in organizing the First Presbyterian Church of Burns in August. Its charter members were Mrs. M. J. Harkey, Mrs. Amy R. Byrd, Mrs. Alice King, Mrs. Carolina Johnson and Mrs. Annie Hope Jones. Incorporated in the spring of 1897, it named as trustees W. C. Byrd, A. R. Byrd and J. B. Tipton, who estimated the value of the property at about $500. In June, the Rev. David H. Jones came from Portland to take charge. Local talented singers and the band gave a concert to raise funds.

Also in August of 1896 a Presbyterian Church was organized at Harney. Its original members were Jasper Davis, Mrs. Mary E. Bower, Mrs. E. J. Newell, Mrs. R. Irving, Miss Rose Loggan, Miss Ida J. Clark, Miss Ella Williams, Mrs. Laura Newell, Miss Alma Lillian Bower and Miss Ida Marshall.

The church bought from the Methodists soon was removed from the east side of Main Street to Washington Street, five blocks west of Main. The pastors also served Harney, Lawen, Crane and elsewhere. A church was built at Crane.

The Rev. J. C. Templeton was a pastor after the organization at Burns. The Rev. A. J. Irwin came in 1900 and remained ten years. He steadily built up the congregations. A parsonage stood next to the church. Later, faced with a series of obstacles, the church lost members for some time.

The Rev. Fred L. Swanson assumed the pastorate in 1936 and has built up the membership of the Burns church from forty to 170. It was renamed the Pioneer Presbyterian Church November 16, 1943.

On the site of their old church in its block of property, the Presbyterians broke ground for a new edifice in the fall of 1946. Work was postponed, but started again in the spring of 1948, rock from the basement being used for the walls. The cornerstone was laid November 2, 1947. Lack of funds stopped work in 1948, labor being resumed in the spring of 1950.

Estimated cost of the new church in Burns is between $55,000 and $60,000. Generous contributors have envisioned a house of worship combining beauty and service in its spiritual mission.

The Baptists of Burns organized in the summer of 1894 with half a dozen members. They met in the Methodist Church. Groundwork was laid by the Rev. C. P. Bailey, and late that year the Rev. W. H. Gibson came to the Burns pastorate with his family.

In the spring of 1895 the Baptist Church received twenty-seven additions, among these being Miss Lelah McGee. Membership reached fifty-eight by May, and in June the church entered the Grand Ronde Association.

The Rev. Mr. Gibson resigned in May, 1896. He was succeeded by the Rev. Arthur Royse. The pastor preached also at Harney, The Narrows and at Silver Creek, conquering distance astride a horse.

When the Presbyterians took over the Methodist Church, the Baptists met in the Courthouse for a period. They bought an old house for a parsonage. The Baptists of Burns occupied a building of their own by 1898. This served the congregation until erection and dedication of a new church in January, 1931.

The Rev. G. A. Johnson, pastor since 1946, has worked earnestly with seventy-odd members in their challenging field.

The First Church of the Nazarene dates from March 22, 1914. It was the outgrowth of a revival conducted by the Revs. E. A. Lewis and E. S. Mathews. Conversions numbered more than 200, and the church was organized with 90 members.

The Rev. John B. Creighton was the first pastor called to this organization. Its first trustees had A. B. Whitney as chairman. Dr. L. E. Hibbard was chairman of the stewards. W. E.

Blatt became secretary and treasurer of the church board, Dr. D. E. Standard the first Sunday School superintendent.

The first building used as a church by the congregation was next to the Palace Cafe. Previous quarters had been in the old Capitol Saloon building.

The cornerstone of a new and attractive edifice of native stone was laid in 1938, under the pastorate of the Rev. G. H. Webb. The congregation also built a modern parsonage.

The present pastor, the Rev. John H. Koch, came in May, 1949, to push forward the aims of the Nazarene Church.

Under the direction of Bishop William P. Remington, Miss Charlotte L. Brown, a United Thank Offering Worker, initiated the work of the Protestant Episcopal Church in Burns early in 1927. She soon had a church school numbering 40 members. She organized the Ladies' Guild and gave·the name of St. Andrew to the parish.

A membership canvass was made early in 1929 and in April the Missionary District of Eastern Oregon bought the old Commercial High School building. This was converted into a parish house and rectory. Meanwhile, Archdeacon S. W. Creasey had conducted eight services at the home of Mrs. James Giriard and in the Masonic Hall.

In August, 1929, the Rev. J. L. Pickells became priest-in-charge. He was succeeded on September 15, 1931, by the Rev. M. G. Tennyson, who directed the building of the impressive new church of Ponderosa pine. The Hines lumber mill furnished, at below cost, the finest selection of materials. The Diocese of Minnesota provided the funds for the labor, helping to relieve unemployment. Dedication of the church building, which cost $5,600, was in the early part of 1932.

The Rev. Archie Buchanan received appointment as missionary-in-charge, beginning his duties in September, 1932. On March 28 of the next year he was ordained to the priesthood in the church by Bishop Remington and assistants.

The Right Rev. Remington, in memory of his father, presented to the church the beautiful silver Litchfield chalice and paten for the Communion service. Mrs. Charles L. Pollock and sons of Folly Farm presented six polished brass office lights to perpetuate the memory of husband and father.

The Rev. Frederick M. Crane assumed his duties as missionary-in-charge June 1, 1935, and left the parish in July, 1937. The Rev. William R. Rush replaced him the following October. The Rev. Mr. Rush resigned March 1, 1939, to be succeeded by the Rev. Eldon W. Borell on the 18th of the same month.

At this time Archie McGowan suggested formation of a businessmen's club, interested in the church, to give aid in various ways. The club, carrying on into the stress of World War II, saw completion of a handsome stone fireplace in the parish house. A cornice stone from old St. Andrew's Church in Yorkshire, England, is imbedded in a stone under the mantelpiece. The Rev. Arthur Beckwith, who assumed his duties as priest-in-charge at St. Andrew's in Burns on April 1, 1941, explains:

> This stone is a part of old Christianity imbedded in the New World and is somewhere about twelve hundred years old. It was brought from England by Bishop Remington, who had made a trip to England in 1930, and it was presented to him by a lady who had listened to him telling about the building of St. Andrew's Church in Burns, Oregon.

The Rev. Mr. Borell became a chaplain in the 186th Infantry at Fort Lewis, Washington. The Rev. Mr. Beckwith came from St. Andrew's Church, Shellbrook, Saskatchewan, Canada. By June, 1942, indebtedness was cleared from the building and fireplace in the parish house. Grover N. Jameson and Carroll Jordan assisted Bishop Remington in burning of the mortgage.

The finishing of the interior of the church with knotty pine reminds the pew-occupant of God's walking in the forested hills not far away. The pews, also of knotty pine, and fashioned by Claude Brown, local carpenter, were first used in August, 1944.

Under the ministry of the Rev. Mr. Beckwith, other improvements have been realized.

In more recent years, a goodly number of other congregations have come to Harney County. There are now a dozen churches of different denominations in the community of Burns, and a new Lutheran edifice in Hines. Each lends a spirit of unity while achieving its goals.

Chapter XXXV

ATTAINING CIVIC STATURE

LIKE COUNTLESS OTHER TOWNS and cities at the dawn of the twentieth century, Burns labored eagerly for civic betterment.

A new bell tower was erected for the fire department in 1902, it being sturdier and taller than the one it replaced. And the city fathers bought a stouter and longer rope to insure quick and loud ringing of the bell-alarm.

Under Mayor Charles E. Kenyon, the city of Burns on January 8, 1902, granted its first franchise for an electric light and power plant, to F. N. Averill of Portland, Oregon. In June the councilmen ordered a light hung in the middle of the square between the Red Front Livery Barn and Frisch and Donegan't place, also one between the Voegtly and Jordan buildings, both on Main Street. Provision was made for installation of incandescent lights in the city council chambers and other city buildings.

The source of power was at the McGowan-Stenger board dam on Silvies River, hard by where a bridge now stands on the Oregon Central Highway. Within a short time Dr. H. M. Norton, druggist and dentist, and N. U. Carpenter, then cashier of the First National Bank of Burns, bought the franchise. They erected a plant and lines. Of these beginnings, Grover N. Jameson says:

The first plant was built on an acreage of Dr. Horton's adjoining Burns on the east. Dr. Horton was General Manager and brought a young fellow up from Los Angeles by the name of Roy Dryer, who was an electrician. In about 1904 Dr. Horton had his brother Arthur Horton, also an electrician, come up from California and take charge of the plant. Dryer continued in their employ for several years under the management of Arthur Horton.

After running the plant for a few years on the location east of the city, they moved it to a place northeast of Burns to what is known as the Sweek Dam site. It was run from there for a few years and finally dismantled and abandoned. . . . Mr. Carpenter did not stay with the concern very long and was bought out by Dr. Horton. At any rate, I do know that Dr. Horton told me many times he had lost a large sum of money in the venture.

260

Insufficient generating power made for dissatisfaction, and the plant was inoperative for several years. In August, 1911, James D. Fellows and associates were granted a franchise for general distribution of electricity in Burns. It was superseded by a franchise granted Fellows on October 3, 1912, extension of time being necessary. He filed on a power site at the rapids of Emigrant Creek 25 miles northwest of Burns. He built a large log house, but never installed any machinery or built any lines. The venture failed.

With due caution, however, the Common Council of Burns by 1912 had passed an ordinance for licensing, operating and managing of moving-picture shows or nickelodeons for proper safety of the patrons. N. E. Pardee, Fellows, and Julian Byrd operated movie machines with gas engines and electric motors. Power failure often interrupted the shows.

Because of difficulties principally at the source of electric energy, Burns had little dependable and continuous electric power in the second decade. Old-timers recall interruption of service by "too high or too low water-flow" or by "fish clogging the infernal driving, churning apparatus."

A power plant, housed in a large stone building in the southeast section of Burns, came into being. Early in May, 1924, Hodge & Letson had the "big Diesel engine" plant ready to give for the first time, steady day-and-night service in electricity. The *Times-Herald* of May 3 stated:

The lights have been furnished from the water power at the flour mill for the past winter but now the irrigation season is upon us and the shortage of the water supply for such purpose has caused them to start the engine plant earlier than had been intended.

This company developed as the Burns Power Company, a franchise being granted under that name October 28, 1925. The engine-power was used until furnishing of electric energy by the Hines mill. According to McKinley Lowe, present mayor of Burns, the People's West Coast Hydroelectric Corporation succeeded, in 1929, as producers of local electric power. This firm gave way to the California-Pacific Utilities in July of 1949.

George Fry, who directed the original telephone company

in Burns, was succeeded by James Weston, assisted by John Biggs, in 1915. In 1929 the Central Oregon Telephone Company took over from Weston. With Blaine Hallock as owner, it operated under the supervision of Ben Snowden. On July 1, 1937, control passed to the Oregon-Washington Telephone Company.

In 1940 Burns andHines had 532 telephones, the number being doubled in the last decade. In a new building in Burns on April 1, 1950, the phone company converted the switching equipment from a common battery to Relaymatic dial. This was done also in Hines and Seneca, the three communities being the first to have dial service in the section of Oregon east of Hood River Valley.

The modern building in Burns, with its new switching equipment, called for an investment of $132,000.

With completion of a 100,000-gallon elevated tank at a cost of $8,370 early in 1926, Burns got its first waterworks system. Turbine pumps were installed in wells sunk deeply to assure an ample and pure flow of water. Water was turned into mains for public use in May, 1926.

At this time the old two-story frame structure that had served as Burns' City Hall was replaced by the present and more commodious building. Much contribution of labor went into its construction. It was completed by 1926 at a cost of $12,415. In this building are the city offices, fire department, Public Library, and a room for group functions.

Conceived in purposeful foresight and carried on by determination and generosity, the Public Library grew apace with Burns. A dozen women, each with a book, met in Dr. Marsden's home—opposite the present City Hall—February 23, 1903, forming the Ladies' Afternoon Club. Each donated a book and paid a dollar as dues to start a library for the town and county.

The club's 12 charter members were Mesdames Clara Marsden, Maggie Levens, Dorothy Irwin, Mary E. Foley, Lelah Miller, Dorcas Neal, Phoebe Geary, Clara Hanley, Katherine Buoy, Eunice Thompson, Marie Carpenter and Minnie Woldenburg. The limit of 20 members soon was taken.

Books, bought with dues and gained otherwise, were kept in the home of Mrs. J. W. Geary, the librarian. As the library grew, citizens could use books by payment of a dollar a year. The money was invested in books, the club having 91 volumes for circulation by the spring of 1905. Then local talent staged the opera "Mikado" in Locher Hall and netted $200 from two performances. Most of the proceeds were deposited in the bank at interest.

Two years later, when the club became affiliated with the Oregon Federated Women's Clubs, the books totaled 600. Quarters were procured in the City Hall and, after members had alternated as librarian, a librarian was hired for two afternoons a week at $5.00 a month. The library, with a fine donation of children's books by the Mothers' Club, went on in this manner till 1914.

The group changed its name to the Ladies' Library Club in 1913. The books were turned over to the city in the hope of obtaining a Carnegie library building. The hope was unrealized, although the club bought two building lots in 1916.

In completing the new City Hall in 1927, space on the ground floor was given to the library, which had become the Burns Public Library in name June 13, 1923. The club's full collection of books was placed there. The sum of $1,000 had been contributed to the new building by the Library Club, the Mothers' Club and the American Legion with the understanding that they would have a room for meetings. This space was gained above the library.

The Library Club donated a book for each member on its twenty-fifth anniversary in 1928, and since then has continued to purchase books for the library in increasing numbers.

Purchase of five $100 war bonds was made during World War II, and the Library Club was credited with the sale of war bonds valued at $17,260. In November, 1943, Mrs. Agnes Kennedy, Mrs. Theresa Guinee and Mrs. Jessie Richey, sisters, gave 15 children's books, with promise of others to the number of 100 within five years, in honor of their mother, Mary E. Foley, the first president of the club.

The Ladies' Library Club now has more than 60 members. It donated yearly to the Scholarship Loan Fund, Doernbecker Hospital and the Endowment Fund, besides helping other projects.

Support of the library comes, also, from city and county

funds. Five directors, appointed by the mayor and confirmed by the city council, serve on the library board. The board elects its officers.

By 1934 the Public Library had 1,042 registered borrowers, the town's population being about 1,800 and the county's about 4,000. For the year ending June 30, 1949, with estimated population of 2,500 in the city and 5,000 in the county, the Burns Public Library registered 1,684 borrowers, 33 per cent of the population. The library possessed 6,905 volumes. Its expenditures totaled $2,370.

Step by step, progress has been made in school affairs over the county. The residents of the widely separated communities rallied with taxes to support the elementary and high schools. The high school at Burns was initially maintained and operated by the County Court through taxation. The modern Burns Union High School, completed in the fall of 1928, cost $100,000. The last of the bonds sold for this were paid off in the spring of 1948.

In the medical field, meanwhile, physicians had been using patients' homes or their own quarters for surgeries. Dr. Carl C. Griffith came to Burns in 1908. The next year he and Dr. Marsden formed a partnership which lasted until the latter's death in 1913.

Youthful Dr. B. F. Smith arrived in the Harney County seat in 1918. His broadbrim and Model T Ford car became familiarly known in the region. Like his predecessors and contemporaries, he grew fond of the people. They were reciprocal in their respect for him.

The Sisters of Mercy of the Archdiocese of Oregon City were deeded property in Brown's Addition of Burns in 1919 for the purpose of erecting a hospital. The deed later was conveyed to the Sisters of St. Joseph and the hospital was conducted under the St. Joseph Building Association. Construction was started on the St. Joseph Hospital in 1920, and popular subscriptions were accepted to help finance it.

After the hospital had encountered financial reverses in 1923, it was acquired by the Stoddard Lumber Company for about $12,000. In January, 1924, this firm sold it to Dr. D. F. Smith, U. S. Hackney, A. H. Folkestead and E. L. Smith, who reopened the hospital under the name Valley View. In 1929 it became the property of the Edward Hines Lumber Co., Dr. Holland T. Ground being in charge for more than two years.

Dr. B. F. Smith took over Valley View Hospital in 1937 and he remained in charge until his death in March, 1950.

The hospital, which averaged about eight beds and a four-to-six-bed ward in addition, became obsolete. After much service, it gave way in 1950 to the county hospital up to date in size and in equipment.

The complacent red men of the Harney region numbered 1,200, some 200 of them in and near Burns and about 1,000 on Duck Valley Reservation. For the Indians near Burns there was little agricultural value in the few land allotments they possessed. They still were in a sorely neglected condition in 1924 because of lack of supervision. At that time James J. Donegan was receiver of the United States Land Office at Burns. Of the Indians' plight, he says:

. . . Captain Rastall, a new agent at the Warm Springs, made a visit to his wards living at Burns. He found them in a deplorable condition. They were ragged, partly naked, suffering from hunger and disease, and were living in the primitive wigwam, made from willows and cast-off parts of sacks, canvases, and old carpets.

The local land office, like the Indian office, was under the Department of the Interior. In subsequent cooperation, Donegan accompanied Captain Rastall to Bend and explained to Congressman N. J. (Nick) Sinnott of The Dalles the condition of the Burns Indians. The government sent 19 large army tents from Fort Knox, Kentucky, to provide shelter at once. These sufficed for some time.

J. B. Mortsolf, succeeding Rastall as agent, initiated measures to replace the frayed tents with 20 two-room houses. They were built of lumber on acreages a short distance northwest of Burns. Inhabitants of the Indian village took pride in maintenance of their home and their small farming plots. Much needed was an Indian school. Under Mortsolf's recommendation, the Harney County Court, in 1928, designated Donegan to present the facts personally to the Commission of Indian Affairs and members of Congress at Washington. The local Paiutes objected to sending their children to distant Warm Springs or Fort Bidwell schools.

A number of citizens had lent help to their unfortunate neighbors. Dr. D. A. Thompson, synodical secretary of the Presbyterian Church, gave medical aid. The Catholic Church steadily went ahead with its spiritual and welfare guidance. The Burns and Harney County Commercial Club was in agreement with Donegan and his helpers, and other commercial chambers, including Portland's, expressed approval for an Indian school and betterment.

With assistance from Congressman Sinnott and Senator Charles McNary, a governmental appropriation of $25,000 was obtained to build the Indian colony school near Burns. The *Times-Herald* said:

> Mr. Donegan deserves much credit for his efforts in trying to aid the Piute Indians who make Burns their home. He has acted as their white chief for several years and through his efforts and correspondence . . . he has accomplished good.

The school got off to a successful start, but soon was closed when the Commission of Indian Affairs ruled that Indian children were to be sent to citizens' public schools. People of Burns objected on grounds of health hazards, but the government remained adamant. The board of directors of the Burns schools, facing a compelling suit, sent Donegan to Washington to offer full explanation. He obtained, in February, 1934, Commissioner John Collier's assent for a thorough medical examination of the Paiutes before they be admitted to the Burns schools.

Dr. J. G. Townsend, director of health, and four other doctors examined 35 Paiutes under 21 years of age. Donegan relates:

> Dr. Townsend reported that of the 35 children examined, 33 had trachoma, and the remaining two were suffering from tuberculosis. On May 25th, Commissioner Collier wrote Senator McNary, saying that he had received Dr. Townsend's report, and said it would be evident that with the extremely high percentage of active trachoma it would not be reasonable to insist upon admission of these children to the public school at the time. . . .   ,

The Indian school was reopened and the government, with especial help from the local medical profession, proceeded to correct the ailments as found.

On June 18, 1934, President Franklin D. Roosevelt signed the Wheeler-Howard Act. This aimed at restoration and revival of Indian tribal life, and ending of any further allotment of lands to individuals. It gave the red men "the right to form business and other organizations; to establish a credit system for Indians; to grant certain rights of home rule to Indians; to provide for vocational education for Indians; and for other purposes." Any surplus lands were to be restored to tribal ownership. The act applied only to tribes voting to accept it.

An order by Commissioner Collier in 1933 read, in part:

No interference with Indian religious life or expression will hereafter be tolerated. The cultural history of Indians is in all respects to be considered equal to that of any non-Indian group. And it is desirable that Indians be bilingual. . . . The Indian arts are to be prized, nourished, and honored.

Thus, in example, Indian children were more hastily transferred from boarding schools to day schools within easier reach of their homes. Boarding schools became institutions for specialization, orphanage, vocational and high schools.

The modern school and community hall built for the Indians burned to the ground in 1938. The children were taught as a group in other quarters until 1948 by Mrs. Theresa F. Guinee. Then they began to attend school with the white pupils in Burns.

Chapter XXXVI

A GOOD PACE MAINTAINED

All the world loves Bobby Burns,
His Banks o' Doon an' a' that,
He was a bard of much regard
'Mong humble folks an' a' that.
For a' that an' a' that
His man's man for a' that.
Tho' he's not here to taste our cheer
His spirit is for a' that.

And now his namesake Burns the town
Is waking up an' a' that.
With poet's vision looking down
The glowing years an' a' that.
For a' that an' a' that.
Its timbered fields an' a' that.
Its wide domain will well maintain
Ten thousand homes for a' that.

The weary years of hope and fears
Are past and gone for a' that;
The golden dream of fifty years
Is coming true for a' that.
For a' that an' a' that
The humming mill an' a' that,
It's broke its shell and left its cell
With iron horse an' a' that.

Then let us pray to haste the day
As come it will for a' that
When watered fields with banner yields
Will dot the vale for a' that.
For a' that an' a' that.
The air is health, the soil is wealth,
Its men are men for a' that.

The town of Burns was striding through its fifth decade and its Sagebrush Orchestra had won statewide acclaim when George McGowan penned the verses above. He who had suggested the name for the town died in his eighty-fifth year,
268

on January 31, 1930, in Portland. He had lived to rejoice at the good pace maintained by Harney County.

There were setbacks—disappointments—in the harsh economy of the 1930s, but new resolutions were formed. Issued daily, five times a week, the *Times-Herald* was greatly strengthened with a wire news service in August, 1933. The progress of the Hines Lumber Company's holdings gave new inspiration, but in 1939 the paper went back to an improved weekly basis.

Syd Pearce started up the weekly Burns *Free Press* in 1930 but moved to Bend in 1935. Leo A. Mars shifted from Crane in 1936 to publish the *Harney County American* at Burns. Its life was brief. In the *Oregon Journal* of October 17, 1936, Julian Byrd, long at the helm of the *Times-Herald*, mentioned a Burns *Tribune* as a paper at one time merged with his, and that the *News*, absorbed in 1930, was his thirty-second competitor. He had built solidly and securely.

James Donegan became closely connected with the Hines lumber interests and its employes at the commencement of their operations in Harney County. He helped the firm of Stafford, Derbes & Roy in acquiring land on which rose the town of Hines. Early in 1935 he entered the office of the Hines company, handling taxation problems and public relations. Prior to his death on July 12, 1943, he had observed studiously the region's metamorphosis.

He had spent many years collecting and compiling notes on the history of Harney basin. Often he stressed the unfortunate results of dry farming—how nearly 700 persons who once lived in Catlow Valley were starved out in trying to grow grain on the fertile soil. The previously thriving town of Harney had become but a memory. Its main street, overgrown with sagebrush, had a rickety two-story saloon, empty, along with a forlorn locksmith shop and blacksmith shop. The only sizable building left after the hegira to Burns was a long and high-roofed community meeting house, used for dances. Ghosts trod warily.

The Taylor Grazing Act of 1934 and its amendment of 1936 knifed away 13,000,000 acres of public domain in Oregon from uncontrolleed use — elimination of huge unrestricted grazing lands. Individuals or stockmen's groups took charge of range areas, and grazing fees were collected for use of the domain. Also, the federal Division of Grazing, Department of the Interior, used 16,000 acres near Burns to fence and improve with reservoirs, wells and equipment to experiment scientifically for stock and range handling.

In earlier days, bitter contests had been waged by wool associations to protect their lands against encroachers not having permanent homes and not sharing taxation. The Basques had become the chief herders in Nevada in the 1890s. Some had driven stock to eastern Oregon, struggling to gain footholds. Many cattlemen soon discerned the desirability of combining sheep and cattle raising.

Forest Service regulations boosted the sheep business after 1900. Passage of the Taylor Grazing Act ended nomadic ways of sheep-tending. The act requires "all persons who feed livestock to possess grazing lands equal to the feed the home ranch produces."

Meanwhile, though the cattle ranches discarded old methods for new and employes forsook some of the garb of yesteryears, the industry claimed "know how" and full-day routine. Typical was the day-to-day life of Gus C. Willard, who went to work as a chore boy on the original twelve-section Bell A Ranch in November, 1918. He continued in the Hanley interests as foreman and cook for thirty years.

Initially, lanky Willard rousted out at 4:30 in the morning, wrangling and "choring" before breakfast at 6 o'clock. He procured a team from the corral and, like other men, changed to a fresh team after an elastic-hour layoff at noon. He quit field work at 5:30 in the afternoon, eating supper at 6 o'clock. Then free for his own diversions, he was soon ready for his bunk. After toiling a full day on Saturday, he usually went to town to spend that night in recreation.

In the older days the ranch's normal complement was eight or ten men, boosted to seventy-five in haying peaks. Later, new equipment gave a big advantage over hand labor, Hanley stacking about 120 tons of field hay in a day. Seventy horses and mules worked on the Bell A and OO ranches.

In addition to his ranching, Bill Hanley became a leader in the construction of the Central Oregon and Three Flags highways. He was a member of Oregon's Highway Commission under Governor Julius Meier. He remained active manager of his ranch properties until his health broke in 1933.

Still, "Uncle Bill" was a sagebrush man to his last day — a man stamped indelibly with the brands of cattle and of horses which made his baronetcy one long to be recalled. The "Sage of Harney County" died in the morn of Sunday, September 15, 1933, in the Pendleton home of Dr. Wilson D. McNary, president of the Pendleton Roundup.

Saturday, the day before his death, was designated "Hanley Day" at the colorful event which claimed his presence and aid so often. Throughout most of the afternoon, Bill sat with Mrs. Hanley in Dr. McNary's box. His tired eyes sparkled, the tang of the sageland was in his nostrils. Dr. McNary, however, noticed the pallor that swept across his face whenever he was helped to his feet to acknowledge plaudits of the huge throng. The cowhands, riding for the old master, outperformed previous feats.

The moment came when, despite Hanley's protests, Dr. McNary ordered a car driven to the front of the grandstand. Hanley was bundled into it. The crowd roared in a tumultuous tribute as the automobile left the arena, an hour before the close of the program. At 6 o'clock that evening, Hanley went to bed, never to rise.

The Ontario train conveying Hanley's body was met at hushed Burns by a group of Masons and townsmen. The grieving Clara Hanley and Robert M. Duncan of Burns, attorney for Hanley, accompanied the body. The people of the far-flung cattle country mourned the loss of a leader.

Duncan, until his death, continued to serve Mrs. Hanley as attorney, secretary and accountant. She, however, had a keen working knowledge of the cattle business. She read avidly the live-stock journals. Of the OO Ranch she sold 14,751 acres at $7.00 to $8.00 an acre in 1942-43 to the government for expansion of the Wildlife Refuge.

James L. Poteet, originally from Texas and an able cattleman, was head foreman for Mrs. Hanley for four years. Early in 1946, he, with O. E. Weed of Portland as a partner, leased the Bell A lands for three years and bought the stock. Although the LY brand was dropped, the Hereford cattle continued to be preferred. Five thousand head wintered on the ranch, being cut to about 1,200 in summertime.

Clara Hanley, nevertheless, could not divorce herself from cattle and lands. Ardently, she kept close to them, at her home on the Bell A, in contact with 7,000 acres of Hanley title.

The depression of the 1930s caught Bill Brown with an oversupply of cattle, sheep and horses. He had been gradually selling them because of a declining market in the age of the automobile. He had given many thousands of dollars to churches and institutions, lost much through too liberal management and unkind purloining by folks he had trusted. Loss of range land on reserves came. His possessions diminished critically.

In 1935, Brown signed a blanket mortgage by which his creditors took over his holdings. Alone, he had taken the long chance of the frontier. He had tasted long of hard-earned success. And his benevolence assured him rewarding rest as he turned, finally, away from broad pastures. He went to his reserved place in the Methodist Old People's Home in Salem, to which he had contributed heavily. There he enjoyed golden memories of a half century spent facing horizons dotted with his herds and wildlife.

Bill Brown was summoned away from his dreams, into the beyond, January 11, 1941. He had not known wife or children, and his passing was unobtrusive. But news of his death, reaching into far corners of the Golden West, induced heart-tugging for a man of rugged honesty and genuine simplicity.

Smaller became the ranches of the Harney country. So much had been taken from P Ranch for a bird sanctuary that Swift's property was well pruned. The Gill Cattle Company (Fred Gill and sons) took over Swift's holdings in 1944, moving into the headquarters at Roaring Springs maintained by its predecessor since 1935.

Joe Fine, who had performed responsible duties for the Eastern Oregon Livestock Company, became superintendent. He, like his father, B. Fine. was a well-trained buckaroo of the old school. And Joe's sons, too, quickly learned the easy and natural way that makes masters with rope and leather.

The Gill firm's main headquarters was at their Exeter

Ranch in California. To the newly acquired range in Oregon they added adjoining properties.

In April, 1937, after having been county judge for ten years, Robert Williams died. At the time of his demise he owned 2,250 acres, having bought his father-in-law's homestead and Tom Dodson's preemption claim, along with other land.

Affectionately known to all citizens as "Billy," William M. Carroll, an irradiant Democrat, has been clerk of Harney County since January 22, 1929. When but a youth, Billy fell into a dry well he had been digging on his ranch. No rescuers came until a week had passed. His legs were broken. He licked at damp earth to appease the fever of his wasting body. After his rescue and loss of the legs by amputation, he looked toward kindly neighbors with increased admiration.

Forgetful of any handicap there might be, Carroll entered public office with the aim of fully carrying out the duties devolving upon him. Never failing of re-election, he is going beyond two decades in a familiar position.

Also widely known among Harney County people at this time was Charles W. Frazier, their sheriff from 1927 to 1942. Frazier, unalterably western, had come to Harney County in 1908. After serving ten years as ranch foreman for the Pacific Live Stock Company on the Diamond and P ranches, he had his own ranch at Diamond. He was Harney County's roadmaster prior to being elected sheriff.

The cornerstone of the new and modernly equipped post-office at Burns was laid June 8, 1940. Walter R. Powell, postmaster, was the thirteenth to hold that office since 1884. With County Judge Robert M. Duncan as master of ceremonies, a fitting program included music by the Burns High School Band and laying of the cornerstone by the Masonic Lodge. Mayor J. C. Welcome gave the address of greeting preceding the speech by A. D. Lawrence, division superintendent, Railway Mail Service. J. W. Biggs spoke in appreciation for the city. The Federal building cost $143,546 and the site $6,000.

A large portrait of George McGowan, first postmaster of Burns, was hung in the private office of the postmaster in June, 1941. Suggestion for this honor came initially from Grover N. Jameson. Congressman Walter M. Pierce, in efforts to gain special permission for the hanging, succeeded in having regulations waived. Stressed was the fact that McGowan had been a pioneer merchant of the town and was the first man to pronounce it "Burns, Oregon."

Darrell L. Howser, of one of the county's first pioneer families, became the fourteenth postmaster at Burns in September, 1945. Increasing business brought additions to the staff. The office's receipts illustrate the growth of half a century: 1899, $1918.21; 1917, $6031.81; 1927, $10,525.92; 1937, $16,675.75; 1947, $21,841. Money orders issued in 1947 totaled nearly $204,000.

In November, 1938, the voters of Harney County granted permission to the County Court to expend $55,000 on a courthouse. This amount was from an accumulation of tax funds, and the Federal Government proposed a grant of $45,-000 on the building. Before the county got started, however, the government withdrew its proposal. The County Court submitted to the people another ballot, in May, 1940, authorizing a levy over a three-year period to raise $45,000. Both elections were carried successfully by a large majority.

The new Harney County Courthouse, on the site of its predecessor, was completed in the early summer of 1942, under the administration of County Judge Nelson B. Higgs. The stately building costing $100,000 combines the ideal of beauty and efficiency throughout. Imbedded in the marble floor of its spacious lobby is a bronze plaque picturing a man on his mount, dedicated to the pioneers. A large mural on the wall depicts a cattle-grazing scene typical of the region.

Veterans of military and naval service meet in a hall at Burns suitable to their needs, and lend support to civic projects. Immediately after World War I servicemen returned home they formed the Harney Valley Military Association. From this mutual benefit group they went into the local American Legion post.

The Harney County Post No. 63, American Legion, organized December 16, 1918. Members signing the charter numbered twenty-nine, and about fifty more were not present for signing. Dr. J. Shelby Saurman served as the post's first commander, F. A. Fessler as the first adjutant. The Legion post had thirty-four members in November, 1924.

A charter, with sixteen members signing, was granted to the Burns-Hines Post No. 1328, Veterans of Foreign Wars, on October 2, 1937. Subsequently, the women's auxiliary was organized and membership in both groups increased steadily. Harney County had more than 600 service men and women participating in World War II.

The Paiute families of Burns played their part in the second global war of the century.

Rightfully, they find it prideful. The Indians of the United States made enviable contributions toward winning the last conflict.

Though by Act of Congress in 1924 all native Indians were granted citizenship, they received no actual emancipation. In spite of the Indian Reorganization Act of 1934, providing means of gaining land for exclusive tribal use, the ruling tribal power has handicaps.

Nevertheless, more and more Indians are finding their way into the world, and playing increasingly successful roles. Gainfully employed in local industries, some of the Paiutes exert purchasing power at times equal to that of white neighbors.

Chapter XXXVII

IN LENGTHY STRIDE

THE SINEWS that now make Harney County unwavering in its forward movement derive their strength not from just a few sources. Closely related are the religious, social and economic elements. The adult county does not hesitate to take long strides.

There are thirty-odd community groups in Harney County. The list is appended to this chapter. Men and women join hands in spirited groups like the Valley Golf Club, the Square Dance Club, and the Robert Burns Society, which perpetuates memory of the bard for whom the county seat was named.

The degree of civic betterment cannot be accurately gauged by mere enumeration of labors contributed by women in organizations like the Mothers' Club and the Ladies' Library Club. And much more than commercial success emanates from members of groups which include the Chambers of Commerce or the Boosters' or Kiwanis or Lions or Soroptomists' clubs. From them comes stimulation.

In the period from 1939 to 1948 retail sales in Harney County increased 200 per cent, to $7.2 million. The trade volume in wholesale and service establishments of the county also showed substantial expansion. In 1948, wholesale sales totaled $1.8 million and the service trades recorded receipts of $185,000.

A combined total of 299 paid employes was reported for 1948 in these three trade classifications. Virtually all of Oregon's counties set new employment marks during 1950.

Including only the firms covered by the State Unemployment Commission, Harney County pay rolls in 1950 stood at a new high of approximately $4,000,000. Deposits at the Burns branch of the United States National Bank of Portland increased a million dollars in 1950 over 1949 year-end deposits, which had totaled $5,600,000.

Few statistics were given, however, when in January, 1948, *The Saturday Evening Post* printed E. R. Jackman's article,

"Burns, Oregon" in the cities of America series. The author portrayed, in vital Western style, the impulsive life of the town as the hub of its cow country. Enriched qualities of the peoples were set off against those possessed by inhabitants of a typical metropolis. The fate-winking folks of Burns capitalized on the stories of their pranks.

And the road boosters, come summertime, got down to business. A group of county officials and Julian Byrd, the editor from way back, joined the State Highway Commission's engineer, J. D. Walker, in a tour of newly oiled sections of road. They viewed with nostalgia the country made accessible by the Idaho, Oregon and Nevada highway. On approach to Folly Farm they had the rare view of snow-topped Steens Mountain surrounded by its purple hills. Then, out of nowhere, they would see a green meadow and shade trees with a home, such as the Hugh Tudor ranch on Crooked Creek — an oasis of 800 acres.

They entered Nevada, then the town of McDermitt. The sun shone hot. John Loggan hadn't seen that town for fifty years. Its past he related. And, according to ye ed, "while Mr. Walker looked after his business, some members of the group showed remarkable fortitude and self-control by visiting only one bar — there are five — and temperately sampled its wares, over the bar with one foot on the rail."

Harney County took bigger steps in education and hospitalization. Under the superintendency of Mrs. Myra Weittenhiller, the new Burns Grade School, District 1, was completed in the spring of 1948, at a cost of approximately $370,000. It now houses 542 pupils with twenty-one teachers. Facilities costing $60,000 were added in 1950.

In Harney County with a population of 6,000 at present, there are 1,520 students of school age — over four and under twenty years. There are fifty-seven grade and high-school teachers, assigned to fifteen active districts. Each district has its grade school. Three grade schools have more than one teacher.

There are 224 students in the Burns High School and fifty-four at Crane. Each has its own principal in charge. Crane, in 1948-49, spent $90,000 on its dormitory, and spent $20,000 on its school plant in 1950. The Crane School, combining elementary and high-school students in a recent plant with dormitory facilities, is unique. Up to date in its system, it does away with costly transportation and scores of one-room schools. Taxpayers find it cheaper and wiser to provide board and room for students traveling as far as 165 miles.

In April of 1950, Richard L. Neuberger wrote informingly of the Crane School in *The Saturday Evening Post*. Of the institution built below tall lava bluffs, he says, in part:

Today the Crane School is considered an outstanding example of how to handle public education in the wide open spaces of the West. Interested educators from dormitory schools in Colorado and the Dakotas come to Crane to see the latest developments in this field; envious residents of Idaho and Nevada, where ranch mothers often must move to the nearest town so that their children can attend school, yearn for Crane-type institutions.

A new gymnasium costing $60,000 has been built for the Hines Grade School. According to C. L. Dalton, county school superintendent, building plans are being studied for improvement of both schools in Burns.

Two years after voters had approved funds for a thirty-two-patient Harney County Hospital at Burns, it was opened for the public, May 1, 1950. With aid of a federal grant of $106,-687, the total cost of $322,000 assured a standard institution meeting every demand of federal and state medical associations.

Although the hospital is county-owned, it is managed by a board of five directors who are responsible for its functions. A hired administrator assists the directors. W. B. Johnson served in this capacity for two months after the hospital's opening. Then Nelson B. Higgs resigned his Harney County judgeship to assume duties of full-time administrator. The brick building, one floor, was erected on the west side of Egan Street, which separates it from a new clinic owned by Drs. John and Clifford Weare. Ambulance service is operated by Harold Olsen.

The hospital now serves a population of about 7,000 in the area comprising all of Harney County and the southern part of Grant County. All physicians in Burns are on the staff. Ready for any emergency, with a standby generator in event of power failure, the hospital is a far cry from the pioneer's table or cot where the travel-weary doctor operated by lamplight.

Burdens of the presiding officers of both the county and circuit courts have increased over the years. Circuit Judge M. A. Biggs, who lives in Ontario, greets many acquaintances of his earlier career when he comes to Burns for terms of circuit court.

Chester W. Craddock, after a successful career in the industry of ranching and cattle-raising, was elected Harney County judge in November, 1950.

Closer became the ties between raisers of live stock. Although they had cooperated with state and national associations, they went long with little organization in Harney County. The only group was the Burns Cattle and Horse Raisers Association, which had been formed to conduct business of its members with forest officials soon after establishment of national forests. Comprised of some fifteen holders in the national forest, representing only about four per cent of the live-stock population of the county, the group frequently had to decide for and represent the entire live-stock business of Harney County.

These men helped to form the Harney County Livestock Association in April, 1947. Henry Otley, a large operator in the Diamond Valley, became its first president. Within three years it counted 180 members. In 1950 Pete Obiague succeeded Harley S. Hotchkiss as the association's president; Lloyd Hill became first vice president, and Joe Altnow second vice president.

The county association started early to re-establish the county's tuberculosis - free accreditation and made possible shipment of its cattle anywhere in the nation without any further test. It took other health-guarding measures and secured a county veterinary. Among its outstanding activities is the sponsoring of a graded sale of registered bulls at the county fair each fall. A marked improvement in the quality of cattle throughout the region has resulted.

That the Harney County Livestock Association advanced its work rapidly is evidenced by the fact that the president, secretary, and treasurer of the state association are all residents of

Harney County. In March, 1950, fifty cattlemen from all parts of Oregon attended the meeting of the state association's executive committee at Burns.   All groups work closely on legislative and other matters.

At present Malheur County, with some 68,000 cattle, is the only county in Oregon running neck-and-neck with Harney County for leadership in production of live stock. Harney County's assessment roll for 1948 counts 71,729 cattle. Following is the county assessor's summary of live stock for 1949:

Classification	Number	Value
Horses and mules	4,475	$ 93,095.00
Cattle, 6 months to 1 year	19,544	390,880.00
Cattle, 1 year and over	52,185	2,087,400.00
Sheep and goats	22,125	149,515.00
Swine	180	1,765.00

Modernity may have stepped into the cattle kingdom of eastern Oregon, but the ranchers and the cowhands defy anybody to outclass some old methods for downright efficiency. For instance, the unexcelled quality of beef kept fresh in the old-fashioned way once summer comes. The fresh meat, wiped dry and wrapped in burlap or canvas, is covered with a hefty quantity of hay in daytime. At night it hangs high and dry for chilling — safe from things predatory. Such steaks make the cow-puncher's whistling exuberant.

And the old-timers get annoyed at newfangled ways of conservation or extermination. They claim scattering of poison by an airplane is hardly a commendable way to rid Harney County of its destructive coyotes. They contend, ably and vociferously, that the rugged, individualistic trapper-hunter does a more thorough job when he is assured a just bounty.

W. L. Lowe, speaking from long experience, avers, "The game is on the decrease and the coyote is on the increase." Poor market for the fur and lack of sufficient bounty caused him to shelve 2,100 coyote traps. To the *Times-Herald's* editor in March, 1948, he wrote:

. . . I love wild life and love to see it thrive. In the last 30 years I have caught 18,000 coyotes in Harney County and naturally while I was doing that I was living outside with wild life and making a study of it all the time and I hate to see it destroyed by predatory animals . . .

Last week I spent 2 days in the hills on the deer wintering grounds in what is known as the Badger country east of Silver Creek. The first day I counted 6 deer, killed by coyotes, and the second day 8 kills; I figured they had been killed in the last 2 weeks. I even saw coyotes running deer. . . . The history of the bounty money is it acts as a revolving fund, it helps the small rancher, the trappers and everybody concerned.

For example, I have been in this country for 32 years, been in the fur business all the time. I have sold $90,000 worth of furs since I have been here and all of it has been spent in the county.

Years and decades march on. What had occurred in its past became of increasing interest to Harney County, and its people desired to preserve it for posterity. Today's Harney County Historical Society had its origins October 23, 1946, one of its chief aims being the compilation of an authentic history of the county. Officers are: President, Archie McGowan; vice president, John E. Loggan; secretary, Leland Duncan; treasurer, Mrs. J. D. Walker. Grover N. Jameson, Judge Nelson B. Higgs and Julian Byrd became directors.

The organization is affiliated with the Oregon Historical Society. Efforts are being made to place markers at points of pioneering significance. Preservation of documents and landmarks receives attention.

Keneth G. Young, superintendent of the schools at Moro and a native son of Harney County, has shown a deep interest in the early history of the ranchers and livestock growers. He carries with him a leather brief case on which are tooled historical brands. In his unique manner of recording he has designed a map of Harney and Grant counties, stamping around it the brands of many old-time rangemen.

The big event each year for the Harney County Pioneers Association is the June day of reunion in Burns. More than 300 persons registered last year. The old-timers come from far and near, some from distant states. From morn till night they greet each other and chat of the past and present.

The high light is the noon-hour picnic on the courthouse lawn. Groups of relatives and friends sit in family style to eat food brought from their homes. The neighboring Paiutes are there, dressed in their best garb and in jovial mood.

An entertainment program follows in the high-school audi-

torium. It is as informal as possible, with speaking, instru-
mental and vocal music. The audience joins in songs of yester-
year and, sometimes, vies for prizes by telling tall tales. Each
year a new queen mother sits among those on the platform.

At night come privileges to attend the local theatres and
separate dances for young and old. The revived spirit carries
them strongly through the chock-full day and on into dark
hours as homeward they wend their way.

Each year, however, the ranks of the oldest settlers grow
thinner. Each year they revere more staunchly the past of
which they are a part. And the reverence is inherited as an
invaluable legacy by their offspring.

What is past is a guide to the future.

APPENDICES

APPENDIX

Community Groups of Harney County

Ladies' Library Club
Mothers' Club
Venture Club
Garden Club
Sagebrush Club
Harney County Chamber of Commerce
Junior Chamber of Commerce
Boosters' Club
Kiwanis
Lions
Soroptomists
Harney County Post No. 63, American Legion, and Auxiliary
Burns-Hines Post No. 1328, Veterans of Foreign Wars,
    V. F. W. Auxiliary
Independent Order of Odd Fellows, No. 77
Rebekahs
Masonic Lodge, No. 97
Order of Eastern Star, No. 40
Benevolent and Protective Order of Elks
Harney County Historical Society
Harney County Pulblic Health Association
Harney County Pioneer Association
Hines Community Club
Robert Burns Society, Inc.
Harney County Livestock Association
4-H Leader Association
County Agent's organization
Grange Home Economics
Poison Creek Grange
Valley Golf Club
Band Uniform Club
Square Dance Club
Episcopal Guild
First Lutheran Ladies' Aid Society
Camp Fire Girls
Boy Scouts of America

SOURCES

Note: All interviews, unless otherwise designated, were given to the author. All undesignated letters were those received by the author. Items in undesignated papers refer to clippings filed without titles.

BIOGRAPHICAL

L. U. Reavis, *The Life and Military Services of General William Selby Harney,* (St. Louis, 1878).

Harvey W. Scott, *History of the Oregon Country* (compiled by Leslie M. Scott, Cambridge, 1924), vol. V, 212-214.

Sketch of William Selby Harney in *Dictionary of American Biography* (Charles Scribner's Sons, New York, 1933), vol. VIII, 280-281.

Obituary in *Army and Navy Journal,* May 11, 1889.

Obituary in *Globe-Democrat* (St. Louis, Mo.), May 10, 1889.

F. B. Heitman, *Historical Register and Dictionary of the United States Army* (Government Printing office, Washington, 1903).

Data from Barbara Kell, librarian, Missouri Historical Society, St. Louis, April 25, 1951.

Data from Edward S. Luce, superintendent, Custer Battlefield National Monument, Crow Agency, Montana, April 22, 1951.

CHAPTER I

L. S. Cressman, H. P. Hansen and Ira S. Allison, "Early Men in Oregon," in *Scientific Monthly,* LXII (January, 1946), 45-58.

N. G. Seaman, "An Amateur Archaeologist's 50 Years in Oregon," in *Oregon Historical Quarterly,* XLI (June, 1940), 147-159.

Chester Stock, "Oregon's Wonderland of the Past—The John Day," in *Scientific Monthly,* LXIII (July, 1946), 57-65.

Ms., files of G. N. Jameson, Burns, Ore., 1948.

CHAPTER II

R. Ross Arnold, *Indian Wars of Idaho* (Caxton Printers, Ltd., Caldwell, Idaho, 1932), 171.

Frederick W. Hodge, editor, *Handbook of American Indians North of Mexico* (1912), vol. II, 186.

Sarah Winnemucca Hopkins, *Life Among the Piutes: Their Wrongs and Claims* (Putnam, Boston, 1883), 5, 9.

Janet Woodruff, as told to Cecil Dryden, *Indian Oasis* (Caxton Printers, Caldwell, Idaho, 1939), 162-178, 203-210.

Richard P. Erwin, "Indian Rock Writing in Idaho," in *Twelfth Biennial Report—1929-30* (State Historical Society of Idaho), 35-111.

John E. Rees, letter to Robert N. Bell, Boise, Idaho, in *Eleventh Biennial Report—1927-28* (State Historical Society of Idaho), 17-19.

Julian H. Steward, "Changes in Shoshonean Culture." in *Scientific Monthly*, XLIX (December, 1939), 527-528.

CHAPTER III

Stephen Hall Meek, *The Autobiography of a Mountain Man;* Introduction and Notes by Arthur Woodward (Pasadena, Calif., 1948), 6.

R. C. Clark, "Harney Basin Exploration, 1826-60," in *Oregon Historical Quarterly*, XXXIII (June, 1932), 101-114.

Frederick Merk, "Snake Country Expedition, 1824-25," in *Mississippi Valley Historical Review* (June, 1934), 49-77.

Carl P. Russell, "Wilderness Rendezvous Period of the American Fur Trade," in *Oregon Historical Quarterly*, XLII (March, 1941), 1-47.

Ms., thesis for doctorate, by James Orin Oliphant, *The Range-Cattle Industry in the Oregon Country to* 1890 (in Widener Library, Harvard University, 1930), 10, 14, 18, 31. (Hereafter cited as Ms., thesis, by Oliphant.)

CHAPTER IV

Catherine Cornwall DeMoss, *Blue Bucket Nuggets* (Binfords & Mort, Portland, Ore., 1939).

Dan E. Clark, *The West in American History* (Thos. Y. Crowell, New York, 1937), 419-420.

Meek, *Autobiography* (cited in Chapter III), 9.

Walter H. McIntosh, *Allen and Rachel* (Caxton Printers, Caldwell, Idaho, 1938), 31-33, 73-78, 86-99, 104-111, 155-156.

Lancaster Pollard, *Oregon and the Pacific Northwest* (Binfords & Mort, Portland, Ore., 1946), 141.

Colonel William Thompson, *Reminiscences of a Pioneer* (San Francisco, 1912), 28.

Margaret Booth, editor, "The Dinwiddie Journal," in *The Frontier*, VIII (March, 1928), 115-116.

Leah S. Brickett, "Lines," in *Frontier and Midland*, XVIII (Spring, 1938), 151.

Clark, "Harney Basin Exploration, 1826-60" (cited in Chapter III), 108-110.

"Journal of Pierson Barton Reading," with notes by Philip B. Beheart, in *Quarterly of The Society of California Pioneers*, VII (September, 1930), 174-196.

Ms. and notes by James J. Donegan, Burns, Ore., 1939.

Ms., thesis for M.A., by William G. Ledbetter, *Military History of the Oregon Country*, 1804-1859 (University of Oregon, 1935), 65-79.

CHAPTER V

George F. Brimlow, *The Bannock Indian War of* 1878 (Caxton Printers, Caldwell, Idaho, 1938), 17-26.

Clark, "Harney Basin Exploration, 1826-60" (cited in Chapter III) 110-114.

Jonas A. Jonasson, "Local Road Legislation in Early Oregon," in *Oregon Historical Quarterly,* XLII (June, 1941) , 163.

Ms., thesis, by Ledbetter (cited in Chapter IV) , 64-65, 71-73, 81.

CHAPTER VI

Ms., *History of Baker, Grant, Malheur and Harney Counties* (published in 1902) .

Hopkins, *Life Among the Piutes* (cited in Chapter II) , 9 ff.

Rufus Rockwell Wilson, *Out of the West* (Press of the Pioneers, New York, 1933) , 163-176.

Pioneers, O Pioneers, Old Oregon Trail Centennial Celebration, pamphlet (Boise, Idaho, 1930) .

W. J. Ghent, *The Road to Oregon* (Longmans, Green, New York, 1929) , 217-218.

Verne Bright, "Auburn—The Story of an Oregon Ghost Town," in *Commonwealth Review,* XXI (May, 1939) , 60-69.

George F. Brimlow, "Goings-on in Canyon City, Oregon," in *Middle Border Bulletin,* V (Fall, 1945; Winter, 1946). Friends of the Middle Border, Mitchell, S. D.

H. M. Corning, "Joaquin Miller, Lawyer, Poet, Judge in Canyon City," in *Oregon Historical Quarterly,* XLVII (June, 1946) , 165-180.

Alfred Powers and Mary-Jane Finke, "Survey of First Half-Century of Oregon Hotels," in *Oregon Historical Quarterly,* XLIII (September, 1942) , 245.

H. C. Thompson, "Reminiscences of Joaquin Miller and Canyon City," in *Oregon Historical Quarterly,* XLV (December, 1944) , 326-330.

A. L. Veazie, "Address at the Dedication of a Monument to the Pioneers of Crook County at Prineville, August 7, 1938," in *Oregon Historical Quarterly,* XXXIX (December, 1938) , 374-377.

"The Metamorphosis of Idaho," in *Seventeenth Biennial Report—* 1939-40 (Idaho State Historical Society) , 40-42.

Ms., thesis for M.A., by Ethel Peterson, *Oregon Indians and Indian Policy,* 1849-1871 (University of Oregon, 1934) , 63-66.

Letters and copies of *Oregon Inn-Side News* from Phil Metschan, Portland, Ore., 1944-49.

Letters from Mrs. Effie Sweetser Tobin, Eureka, Nev., 1944-45.

Interview with Mrs. Birdie Dave, Paiute relative of Sarah Winnemucca, July 8, 1946.

CHAPTER VII

Arnold, *Indian Wars of Idaho* (cited in Chapter II) , 90-104.

Brimlow, *Bannock Indian War of* 1878 (cited in Chapter V) , 29, 37-43.

Charles H. Carey, *History of Oregon* (Chicago-Portland, Pioneer Publishing Co., 1922) , 671-672.

O. O. Howard, *Famous Indian Chiefs I Have Known* (Century, New York, 1908) , 259-269.

Don Russell, *103 Fights and Scrimmages: Story of General Reuben Frank Bernard* (U. S. Cavalry Assn., Washington, 1936), 59-61.

Meek, *Autobiography* (cited in Chapter III), 10.

History of Baker, Grant, Malheur and Harney Counties (Western Historical Publishing Co., 1902). See also ms.

Col. Thompson, *Reminiscences* (cited in Chapter IV), 63-63.

Thompson and West, *History of Nevada* (1881), 173.

Effie M. Mack and B. W. Sawyer, *Our State: Nevada* (Caxton, Caldwell, Idaho, 1940), 78-80, 148-149.

Blue Mountain Eagle (Canyon City, Ore.), April 9, 1948.

Times-Herald (Burns, Ore.), June 5, 1931.

Charles A. Sprague, "Willamette Highway—the Seventh Across the High Cascades," in *Oregon Historical Quarterly,* XLI (September, 1940), 244-245.

Veazie, "Address at Dedication" (cited in Chapter VI), 376-377, 380-382.

Miscellaneous notes of Harney County Historical Society.

Ms. by J. J. Donegan (cited).

Ms. and notes by Maurice Fitzgerald, Burns, Ore. (no date).

Oregon, M-1045, Letters Received, 1870, Office of Indian Affairs (The National Archives, Washington). Copy from Attorney C. B. McConnell, Burns, Ore., with copy of 1868 preliminary treaty.

Report of Sam Parrish to Commissioner of Indian Affairs, November 25, 1875 (O.I.A., filed as *Oregon,* P 1/1875).

Letter from J. C. Cecil, Suntex, Ore., Jan. 25, 1948, enclosing copy of letter from Adjutant General's Office, Washington, April 23, 1930.

Letter from E. C. D. Marriage, Nevada State Librarian, Carson City, May 29, 1940.

CHAPTER VIII

Mack and Sawyer, *Our State: Nevada* (cited in Chapter VII), 188.

Albert Burch, "Development of Metal Mining in Oregon," in *Oregon Historical Quarterly,* XLIII (June, 1941), 110, 115.

Fairfax Downey, "Stagecoach Stickups," in *Reader's Digest,* XLVI (June, 1945), 91-94.

J. R. Keith, "When the Long Horned Cattle of Texas Came to Idaho," in *Sixteenth Biennial Report—1937-38* (Idaho State Historical Society), 42-46.

Joe D. Thomison, "Old U. S. Mint at The Dalles Is Monument to Argonaut Era," in *Oregon Historical Quarterly,* XLI (March, 1940), 72-73.

E. N. Wentworth, "Eastward Sheep Drives From California and Oregon," in *Mississippi Valley Historical Review,* XXVIII (March, 1942), 508-513.

Ms., thesis, by Oliphant (cited in Chapter III), 88, 105, 276.

Ms., *History of Baker, Grant, Malheur and Harney Counties.*

CHAPTER IX

George S. Turnbull, *History of Oregon Newspapers* (Binfords & Mort, Portland, Ore., 1939), 339-341.

Oswald West, "Famous Horses and Horsemen of the Pioneer Period," in *Oregon Historical Quarterly*, XLVI (June, 1945), 146.

City Journal (Canyon City, Ore.), Jan. 1, April 17, June 28, July 12, 1869.

Grant County Express (Canyon City, Ore.), Oct. 21, 1876.

Miscellaneous notes of Harney County Historical Society.

Letters and papers from Mrs. W. W. Nickell of McMinnville, Ore., 1945-46.

Letters and copies of *Oregon Inn-Side News* from Phil Metschan.

Copy of letter from William V. Rinehart, Jr., of Seattle, Wash., to Phil Metschan, Dec. 29, 1945.

CHAPTER X

Oregon, American Guide Series, T. J. Edmonds, state supervisor (Binfords & Mort, Portland, 1940), 422-423.

Randall V. Mills, "A History of Transportation in the Pacific Northwest," in *Oregon Historical Quarterly*, XLVII (September, 1946), 281-290.

Dexter K. Strong, "Beef Cattle Industry in Oregon, 1890-1938," in *Oregon Historical Quarterly*, XLI (September, 1940), 252.

Ms., thesis, by Oliphant (cited in Chapter III).

Ms. and notes from E. M. Rowland, Eugene, Ore.

Ms. and notes by Maurice Fitzgerald, Burns, Ore.

Ms. and notes by J. J. Donegan, Burns, Ore.

Miscellaneous notes, Harney County Historical Society.

Letter from Archie McGowan, Burns, Ore., Nov. 28, 1947.

Interviews with Martin H. Brenton, Burns, Ore., June, 1949.

Interviews with Alphena Venator, Burns, Ore., June 14, 1949.

CHAPTER XI

Brimlow, *Bannock Indian War of* 1878, 31-32.

Minutes of First School Meetings, Silvies River District, No. 13, in Grant County, Feb. 10, 1875, to March 5, 1888 (in custody of Mrs. Hester Goodman, Burns, Ore.).

Testimony of W. D. (Doc) Kiger in water rights case transcript in Circuit Court at Ontario, Ore., June 7, 1924. (True copy to Brimlow from Judge Nelson B. Higgs, Burns, Ore., June 10, 1947.)

Ms. and notes by J. J. Donegan.

Ms. and notes by Maurice Fitzgerald.

Interview with J. C. Cecil, Burns, Ore., June 14, 1947.

Interview with Robert Baker, Burns, Ore., June 13, 1949.

Interview with Schuyler (Skip) Whiting, Burns, Ore., June, 1947.

CHAPTER XII

Arnold J. Toynbee, *A Study of History* (abridgment of vols. I-VI by D. C. Somervell, editor; Oxford University Press, New York and London, 1947), 168-169.

"Necrology," in *Eleventh Biennial Report*—1927-1928, State Historical Society of Idaho.

Oswald West, "Famous Horses and Horsemen of the Pioneer Period" (cited in Chapter IX), 141-146.

Grant County Express (Canyon City), Oct. 21, 1876.

Ms., thesis, by Oliphant (cited in Chapter III), 11, 123, 128-133, 160, 229, 253, 265-267, 290, 296.

Ms. and notes from E. M. Rowland, Eugene, Ore.

Ms. and notes by J. J. Donegan.

Ms. and notes by Maurice Fitzgerald.

Letters and notes from Phil Metschan.

CHAPTER XIII

Edward F. Treadwell, *The Cattle King* (Macmillan, New York, 1931), 42 ff., 57, 60.

Oregon, American Guide Series (cited in Chapter X), 423.

John W. Biggs, address, *Devine Monument Dedication*, July 22, 1928 (reprint from *Oregon Historical Quarterly*, XXIX, 1928), 4.

John T. Ganoe, "The Beginnings of Irrigation in the United States," in *Mississippi Valley Historical Review*, XXV (June, 1938), 59, 64-66, 70, 77.

Account Book—1876-79 of Peter French (provided by John C. Scharff, Malheur National Wildlife Refuge, June, 1947; also interview with same).

Ms., thesis by Oliphant (cited in Chapter III), 187, 193, 198.

Ms. and notes by J. J. Donegan.

CHAPTER XIV

Brimlow, *Bannock Indian War of* 1878, 142, 151, 168, 171, 176.

George F. Brimlow, *Cavalryman Out of the West* (Caxton Printers, Caldwell, Idaho, 1944), 93-95.

Claude E. Fuller, *The Breech-Loader in the Service* (Arms Reference Club of America, New York, 1933).

Col. Thompson, *Reminiscences* (cited in Chapter IV).

Reminiscences of Mrs. Eugenie M. Bacon in *Winners of the West* (St. Joseph, Mo.), Feb. 28, 1933.

Grant County Express (Canyon City), Oct. 21, 1876.

Letters and copies of *Oregon Inn-Side News* from Phil Metschan.

Annual Report of Brig.-Gen. O. O. Howard, Dept. of the Columbia, Oct. 15, 1878 (booklet revision, Assistant Adjutant General's Office, Fort Vancouver, Washington Territory, 1879).

Report of Quartermaster-General, War Dept., Oct. 9, 1878, 45th congress, 3rd session, *House Executive Document 1*, Pt. II, 247-399.

Diary of Mrs. W. W. Johnson; copy from Archie McGowan.

Miscellaneous notes, Harney County Historical Society.

Ms. and letter from Frank Whiting, Burns, Ore., Jan. 23, 1946.

Letter from Allen M. Ross (for director, Industrial Records Division), The National Archives, Washington, to Archie McGowan, Nov. 2, 1949.

Interview with Mrs. Minnie Allsup, Gervais, Ore., Jan. 16, 1946.

CHAPTER XV

Brimlow, *Bannock Indian War of* 1878, 31-32, 46-48.

Hopkins, *Life Among the Piutes* (cited in Chapter II), 90-109.

William C. MacLeod, *The American Indian Frontier* (Alfred A. Knopf, New York, 1928), 536, 540.

Charles L. Slattery, *Felix Reville Brunot* (Longmans, Green, New York, 1901), 142-146, 152-153, 177, 224-226.

J. F. Santee, "Christian College 1866-1882 and Its Presidents," in *Oregon Historical Quarterly*, XLII (December, 1941), 306-307. See also letter from Dr. L. L. Rowland to Senator J. H. Mitchell of Oregon, April 30, 1874, Office of Indian Affairs, *Oregon*, R 328/1874.

James G. Townsend, "Disease and the Indians," in *Scientific Monthly*, XLVII (December, 1938), 483.

Ms., thesis by Peterson (cited in Chapter VI), 70.

Letters and copies of *Oregon Inn-Side News* from Phil Metschan.

Reports of Commissioner of Indian Affairs, Sept. 4, 1872, 47th congress, 2nd session, *House Executive Document 1*, 346.

Report of Sam B. Parrish to Commissioner of Indian Affairs, Feb. 7, 1874, Office of Indian Affairs, letters received, General Files, *Oregon*, S 127/1874.

Statements of Sam B. Parrish and H. Linville, O.I.A., *Oregon*, P 754/1874.

Report of Major E. S. Otis to Assistant Adjutant General, Dept. of Columbia, March 15, 1874 (copy from War Dept. to Interior Dept., April 16, 1874), O.I.A., *Oregon*, W 578/1874.

Report of Lieutenant Charles C. Cresson to Post Adjutant, Camp Harney, May 30, 1874 (copy), O.I.A., *Oregon*, W 1041/1874.

Letter from Commissioner of Indian Affairs (with enclosures) to Secretary of Interior, April 17, 1874, O.I.A., *Oregon*, W 578/1874.

Letters of William Vanderver, Sept. 13, 1874, Inspector File, No. 1430, Dept. of Interior, O.I.A., *Oregon*, M 155/1874.

Letter from H. Linville to Commissioner of Indian Affairs, March 7, 1874, O.I.A., *Oregon*, L 132/1874.

Report of H. R. Clum, Acting Commissioner of Indian Affairs, to Secretary of Interior, May 13, 1876, O.I.A.

Interview with Birdie Dave, Paiute, July 8, 1946.

CHAPTER XVI

Brimlow, *Bannock Indian War of* 1878, 51, 56, 107.

Chester A. Fee, *Chief Joseph: The Biography of a Great Indian* (Wilson-Erickson, New York, 1936), Chapters 1 to 7.

Hopkins, *Life Among the Piutes* (cited in Chapter II), 106-111, 114, 116-117, 123, 135.

Copy of personal diary of Mrs. W. W. Johnson (from Archie McGowan).

Ms. and notes by J. J. Donegan.

Letter from Sam B. Parrish to Commissioner of Indian Affairs, April 26, 1875 (enclosure, report of H. R. Clum to Secretary of Interior, May 13, 1875), Office of Indian Affairs.

Report of Sam B. Parrish to Commissioner of Indian Affairs, Nov. 25, 1875, O.I.A., *Oregon*, P 1/1875. See also Parrish's report of April 4, 1876, O.I.A., *Oregon*, P 154/1876.

Letter (with enclosure) from James K. Kelley, U. S. Senate, to Commissioner of Indian Affairs, Dec. 24, 1875, O.I.A., *Oregon*, K 315/1875. See also report of D. F. Thompson to Commissioner, Jan. 1, 1876, O.I.A., *Oregon*, T 2/1876.

Unofficial report of Sam B. Parrish to General O. O. Howard, April 27, 1876, O.I.A., *Oregon*, P 191/1876.

Report of W. V. Rinehart to Commissioner of Indian Affairs, July 1, 1876, O.I.A., *Oregon*, R 209/1876. See also Rinehart's report to Commissioner, July 24, 1877, O.I.A., *Oregon*, M 615/1877.

Letter from Joseph Scattergood, Philadelphia, Pa., to Commissioner of Indian Affairs, Dec. 21, 1876, O.I.A., *Oregon*, S 981/1876.

Correspondence and enclosures, Secretary of War to Secretary of Interior, Jan. 8, 1877, O.I.A., *Oregon*, W 57/1877.

Rinehart's reports to Commissioner, Sept. 10, 1877 (with report of W. M. Turner to Rinehart), and Jan. 5, 1878, O.I.A., *Oregon*, M 731/1877 and R 40/1878.

Letter from Senator John H. Mitchell to Commissioner, May 27, 1878, O.I.A., *Oregon*, M 936/1878. (This discloses amount of appropriation and that Turner, after riding horseback over alkali deserts in hot weather, had become blinded in one eye.)

Interview with Mrs. Minnie Allsup (daughter of W. N. and Elizabeth Bonham), Gervais, Ore., Jan. 16, 1946.

CHAPTER XVII

Arnold, *Indian Wars of Idaho* (cited in Chapter II).

Brimlow, *Bannock Indian War of 1878.*

Brimlow, *Cavalryman Out of the West.*

Fee, *Chief Joseph* (cited in Chapter XVI).

Hopkins, *Life Among the Piutes* (cited in Chapter II).

Russell, *103 Fights and Scrimmages* (cited in Chapter VII).

Annual Report of Brig.-Gen. Howard (cited in Chapter XIV).

Bedrock Democrat (Baker City, Ore.) 1878. Copy of embellished story of burning of Smyths' home; with letter from J. J. Donegan.

"Particulars of Col. Bernard's Battle With the Indians," in an extra edition of the *Statesman* (Boise City), June 27, 1878.

Brimlow, editor, mss., *Bannock War Diaries of Frederick Mayer and Lieutenant W. C. Brown, First U. S. Cavalry, 1878.*

Ms. by E. F. Albrecht, Troop A, First U. S. Cavalry, 1878 (the

Bannock War, with battlefield sketches, compiled from notes, Feb. 20, 1927).

Ms. by Maurice Fitzgerald, *Harney County, Its Early Settlement and Development*, 1940. (Copy from Frank Whiting, Burns, Ore.).

Ms., testimony of W. D. Kiger (cited in Chapter XI).

Ms., recollections of John Witzel, Burns, Ore., March 8, 1935. Copy from Archie McGowan to Brimlow.

Ms. and notes by J. J. Donegan.

Diary of Mrs. W. W. Johnson (cited in Chapter XVI).

Letters and copies of *Oregon Inn-Side News* from Phil Metschan.

Interview with Tea Pokibro, Bannock, Fort Hall Reservation, Idaho, July, 1939.

Interview with Schuyler Whiting, Burns, Ore.

Interview with Mrs. Minnie Allsup (cited in Chapter XVI).

CHAPTER XVIII

Arnold, *Indian Wars of Idaho* (cited in Chapter II).

Brimlow, *Bannock War of 1878, Cavalryman Out of the West;* edited diaries of Mayer and Brown (cited in Chapter XVII).

Hopkins, *Life Among the Piutes* (cited in Chapter II).

Russell, *103 Fights and Scrimmages* (cited in Chapter VII).

Col. Thompson, *Reminiscences* (cited in Chapter IV), 139-147.

Annual Report of Brig.-Gen. Howard (cited in Chapter XIV).

Statesman, extra edition (cited in Chapter XVII).

Ms., *History of Baker, Grant, Malheur and Harney Counties.*

Ms. by E. F. Albrecht (cited in Chapter XVII).

Ms. by J. J. Donegan, including copies of letters from J. H. Raley.

Ms. by Maurice Fitzgerald (cited in Chapter XVII).

Letters and copies of *Oregon Inn-Side News* from Phil Metschan.

Letters from L. V. McWhorter, Yakima, Wash., to Brimlow.

Interview with J. C. Cecil, Burns, Ore., June 14, 1947.

Interview with Tea Pokibro (cited in Chapter XVII).

CHAPTER XIX

Arnold, *Indian Wars of Idaho* (cited in Chapter II).

Brimlow, *Bannock War of 1878, Cavalryman Out of the West;* edited diaries of Mayer and Brown (cited in Chapter XVII).

Hopkins, *Life Among the Piutes* (cited in Chapter II).

Aaron F. Parker, *Forgotten Tragedies of Indian Warfare in Idaho,* pamphlet (Idaho County Free Press, Grangeville, 1925).

Annual Report of Brig.-Gen. Howard (cited in Chapter XIV).

Story of Dove's and Egbert's Fights on August 9, 1878, in *Morning Oregonian,* Aug. 12, 1878.

Letter signed by "Kitro" to editor, *Morning Oregonian,* Aug. 5, 1878 (letter dated at Yakima City. W. T., July 27, 1878).

Ms., thesis by Peterson (cited in Chapter VI).

Ms., thesis by Oliphant (cited in Chapter III).

Ms., *History of Baker, Grant, Malheur and Harney Counties.*

Ms. and notes by J. J. Donegan.

Letter from Secretary of Interior to W. V. Rinehart, July 1, 1878 (with varied information), O.I.A., *Oregon,* R 290/1880.

Annual Report of W. V. Rinehart to Commissioner of Indian Affairs, Aug. 15, 1879.

Letter of W. V. Rinehart to Secretary of Interior, Feb. 24, 1880, O.I.A., *Oregon,* R 290/1880.

Letter of W. V. Rinehart to Commissioner of Indian Affairs, Oct. 14, 1880.

Chapter XX

Anne Shannon Monroe, *Feelin' Fine* (Doubleday, Doran, Garden City, N. Y., 1930), 37, 77, 88, 110-111.

J. R. Keith, "When the Long Horned Cattle of Texas Came to Idaho Territory" (cited in Chapter VIII), 49.

E. D. Smith, Jr., "Communication Pioneering in Oregon," in *Oregon Historical Quarterly,* XXXIX (December, 1938), 371.

Item on Rattlesnake Jack in *Evening Gazette* (Reno, Nev.), Nov. 3, 1882.

Item on death of Chief Winnemucca in *Silver State* (Winnemucca, Nev.), Sept. 27, 1882.

On William Hanley in *Times-Herald* (Burns, Ore.), Sept. 16, 1935.

Fred Lochley, "Impressions and Observations of the Journal Man," in *Oregon Journal* (Portland), Oct. 2, 1936.

M. Leona Nichols, "The Saga of William (Bill) Brown," in *Sunday Oregonian,* Oct. 23, 1932.

Letters and copies of *Oregon Inn-Side News* from Phil Metschan.

Letter from E. C. D. Marriage, State Librarian of Nevada, Carson City, May, 29, 1940.

Minutes of First School Meetings, Silvies River District 13 (cited in Chapter XI).

Ms., thesis by Oliphant (cited in Chapter III), 113, 170, 247.

Ms. and notes from E. M. Rowland, Eugene, Ore.

Ms., affidavit of Martin H. Brenton, Burns, Ore., in testimony in hearing of Federal Government v. State of Oregon in regard to Malheur Lake lands.

Ms., recollections, by Alphena Venator, Burns, Ore. (Copy to Brimlow, June 12, 1949).

Ms. and notes by J. J. Donegan.

Ms. and notes by Maurice Fitzgerald.

Interview with Martin H. Brenton, June 11, 1947.

Interview with Schuyler Whiting, Burns, Ore., June 12, 1947.

Interviews with Robert D. Baker and Archie McGowan, Burns, Ore., June 14, 1949.

Interview with Mrs. William Hanley, Burns, Ore., June 13, 1949.

Interview with Mrs. T. J. (Julia Garrett) Shields at Silver Creek ranch, June 15, 1949.

CHAPTER XXI

Dan E. Clark, *The West in American History* (cited in Chapter IV), 623.

Treadwell, *The Cattle King* (cited in Chapter XIII), 116-132.

W. J. Ghent, "Sarah Winnemucca," in *Dictionary of American Biography*, XX, 391.

Bright, "Auburn—The Story of an Oregon Ghost Town" (cited in Chapter VI), 68-70.

John T. Ganoe, "The Pacific Far West One Generation After the Frontier," in *Pacific Historical Review*, IX (June, 1940), 211-212.

Mills, "A History of Transportation in the Pacific Northwest" (cited in Chapter X), 292.

Wentworth, "Eastward Sheep Drives From California and Oregon" (cited in Chapter VIII), 522-529.

Journal of Hartman K. Evans (edited by Robert H. Burns), "Sheep Trailing From Oregon to Wyoming," in *Mississippi Valley Historical Review*, XXVIII (March, 1942), 581-592.

Letter from Oswald Garrison Villard to editor, *Saturday Evening Post* (Philadelphia), June 26, 1948, p. 6.

Letter from Maurice Fitzgerald to Ernest Haycox of Portland, Ore. (copy of—no date).

On Dr. Hugh Glenn in *Silver State* (Winnemucca, Nev.), Feb. 17 and 20, 1883, and March 24, 1883.

Ms., thesis by Oliphant (cited in Chapter III), 127-128, 141, 160, 165, 168, 172-173, 181, 298, 303, 334, 338.

Ms. and notes by Maurice Fitzgerald.

Ms. and notes from E. M. Rowland.

Miscellaneous notes, Harney County Historical Society.

Interview with Martin H. Brenton, June 12, 1947.

CHAPTER XXII

Carey, *History of Oregon* (cited in Chapter VII), 771.

J. D. Ferguson, *Pride and Passion, Robert Burns, 1759-1796* (Oxford University Press, 1939).

Turnbull, *History of Oregon Newspapers* (cited in Chapter IX), 417-418.

Lewis A. McArthur, *Oregon Geographic Names* (Binfords & Mort, Portland, Ore., 1944), 2nd edition, revised, 67.

Max Eastman, "Poet of the People," in *Reader's Digest*, XLVIII (June, 1946), 59-63.

Powers and Finke, "Survey of First Half-Century of Oregon Hotels" (cited in Chapter VI), 244.

"Death Takes Fred Racine, 1884 Pioneer," in *Times-Herald*, Oct. 22, 1948.

Letter from Jay Powell, Newport, Ore., to editor, *Morning Oregonian*, Feb. 10, 1948.

Diary of Mrs. W. W. Johnson (cited in Chapter XVI).

Account book of Dr. Samuel B. McPheeters, Burns, Ore.

Minutes of First School Meetings, Silvies River District 13 (cited in Chapter XI) , and photo in Goodman-McGowan files.

Records of Burns Post Office, prepared by Darrell L. Howser, postmaster, June, 1947. (All references to this post office's business hereafter are from this source.)

Letters and copies of *Oregon Inn-Side News* from Phil Metschan.

Ms., Brenton's affidavit (cited in Chapter XX) .

Ms. and notes by J. J. Donegan.

Ms. and notes by Maurice Fitzgerald.

Mss., recollections, by George McGowan at Tigard, Ore., March 17, 1917, and undated.

Ms. by Alphena Venator (cited in Chapter XX) .

Ms. and notes from E. M. Rowland.

Ms. and letter from Archie McGowan, Dec. 30, 1948.

Interviews with Schuyler Whiting and Mrs. T. J. Shields.

CHAPTER XXIII

McArthur, *Oregon Geographic Names* (cited in Chapter XXII) 173-174.

On Sarah Winnemucca in *Morning Call* (San Francisco) , Jan. 22, 1885. See also *Silver State* (Winnemucca, Nev.) , Sept. 7, 1883.

On businesses in Harney, *East Oregon Herald* (Burns, Ore.) , May 23, 1888.

Items on Connie Moffett and Denio, *Times-Herald,* March 19, 1948

Ms. and letter from John E. Loggan, Burns, Ore., Jan. 14, 1948.

Ms., A. McGowan, Dec. 30, 1948.

Ms. by A. Venator.

Ms. by J. J. Donegan.

Ms. by Maurice Fitzgerald.

Letters and copies of *Oregon Inn-Side News* from Phil Metschan.

Miscellaneous records (medical) , Harney County Historical Society.

Interview with Mrs. T. J. Shields.

CHAPTER XXIV

Mack and Sawyer, *Our State: Nevada* (cited in Chapter VII) , 177.

Treadwell, *The Cattle King* (cited in Chapter XIII) , 96--115, 137-146, 152.

Oregon, American Guide Series (cited in Chapter X) , 422-424.

Biggs, *Devine Monument Dedication* (cited in Chapter XIII) .

Keith, "When the Long Horned Cattle of Texas Came to Idaho Territory" (cited in Chapter VIII) , 45-46.

Nichols, "The Saga of William (Bill) Brown" (cited in Chapter XX) .

Item on Devine's brand, in a Burns paper, Nov. 15, 1888.

Letter signed "Harney" in *East Oregon Herald,* April 11, 1889.

On "Del Norte," *Times-Herald,* June 5, 1931.

Ms., thesis by Oliphant (cited in Chapter III) , 181, 271, 340, 342.

Mss. by Donegan, Fitzgerald and Venator.
Interviews with Robert D. Baker, Alphena Venator, Mrs. T. J. Shields and Martin H. Brenton.

CHAPTER XXV

History of Baker, Grant, Malheur and Harney Counties, 637, 640.
Brimlow, "Goings-on in Canyon City, Oregon" (cited in Chapter VI).
"Best Whip on the Road," in *East Oregon Herald,* June 27, 1888.
Items from a Burns newspaper, Jan. 4, and May 16, 1888.
Items in *East Oregon Herald,* May 9 and 16, Dec. 6, 1888; April 25, Nov. 14, 1889.
Letters and copies of *Oregon Inn-Side News* from Phil Metschan.
Ms. and notes by J. J. Donegan.
Interview with Mrs. Minnie Allsup, Gervais, Ore.

CHAPTER XXVI

MacLeod, *The American Indian Frontier* (cited in Chapter XV), 538-539.
Turnbull, *History of Oregon Newspapers* (cited in Chapter IX), 417-419.
O. K. Armstrong, "Set the American Indians Free," in *Reader's Digest,* XLVII (August, 1945), 48.
Ganoe, "The Pacific Far West One Generation After the Frontier" (cited in Chapter XXI), 216.
On Sarah Winnemucca, *Silver State* (Winnemucca, Nev.), Sept. 27, 1887.
"The Piute Princess," in *Daily Herald* (Helena, Mont.), Nov. 4, 1891.
"Mask," in *East Oregon Herald,* Nov. 23, 1887.
"Journalism from Dame Rumor," in *East Oregon Herald,* May 9, 1888.
Items in *East Oregon Herald:* Nov. 30, Dec. 14, 1887; Jan. 4, May 16, Oct. 3 and 25, 1888; April 11 and 25, July 4 and 18, Nov. 7 and 28, Dec. 5 and 26, 1889.
Items in *Times Herald,* June 5, 1931.
Minutes of First School Meetings, Silvies River District 13 (cited in Chapter XI).
Ms. by A. McGowan, Dec. 30, 1948.
Ms. and notes by J. J. Donegan.

CHAPTER XXVII

History of Baker, Grant, Malheur and Harney Counties, 638.
Turnbull, *History of Oregon Newspapers* (cited in Chapter IX), 418-420.
Items in *East Oregon Herald:* Jan. 30, Feb. 6, 13, 20, March 6, July 9, 1890; Nov. 28, 1891; May 25, Dec. 28, 1892; March 29, 1893; Aug. 26, 1896.

Clippings from a Burns newspaper, May 6, June 10 and 17, July 11, 1891; May 30, 1894.

Items in *Times-Herald,* June 5, 1931.

"Death Beckons Jasper McKinnon," in *Times-Herald,* March 12, 1948.

Harney County Records with photo of first group of county officers, 1890. See also Vol. A, p. 29, April 27, 1889; Marriage Record, Vol. A, p. 2, May 6, 1889; Vol. A, p. 14, Nov. 22, 1890.

Note of Nov. 8, 1888, Harney County Historical Society.

Ms. by A. McGowan, Dec. 30, 1949, and letter from same, March 6, 1950.

Ms. and notes by J. J. Donegan.

Interviews with Mrs. T. J. Shields, John W. Biggs and Martin H. Brenton.

CHAPTER XXVIII

Nancy Wilson Ross, *Farthest Reach* (Alfred A. Knopf, New York, 1941), 66-67, 77.

Examiner (Lakeview, Ore.), extra edition, Dec. 27, 1894.

Item clipped from a Burns newspaper, May 8, 1895, quoting the Baker City *Democrat.*

Items clipped from a Burns newspaper of 1895: March 27, April 10, May 1, 8, 29, Aug. 14, Sept. 4, 11, 18, Nov 15.

Items in *East Oregon Herald,* March, July, 3, 1895.

Times-Herald, July 22, 1896 (first issue under this name).

Items in *Times-Herald*: June 17, Aug. 12, 26, Oct. 6, 1896; Jan. 6, June 9, July 14, 1897; April 7, 1950.

Letter from Clara A. Marsden to the editor, *Times-Herald,* March 31, 1950.

Records of Burns Post Office.

Harney County Records of Incorporations, Vol. A, p. 25, April 1, 1897.

Ms., reminiscences, by Dennis R. O'Brien (true copy from Martin H. Brenton to Brimlow, June 14, 1949).

Ms., recollections, by John E. Loggan, Jan. 14, 1948.

Ms. and notes by J. J. Donegan.

Interview with Archie McGowan, April 6, 1950.

CHAPTER XXIX

Monroe, *Feelin' Fine* (cited in chapter XX), 128-125 ff.

Oregon, American Guide Series (cited in Chapter X), 434.

Ross, *Farthest Reach* (cited in Chapter XXVIII), 86-87.

"Bill Brown" (necrology), in *Oregon Historical Quarterly,* XLII (March, 1941), 108.

Strong, "Beef Cattle Industry in Oregon, 1890-1938" (cited in Chapter X), 253-255.

Nichols, "The Saga of William (Bill) Brown" (cited in Chapter XX).

Letter from Frank M. Neth, Lebanon, Ore., to editor, *Sunday Oregonian,* Dec. 11, 1949.

Earl N. Pomeroy, "Trumpets in the Tules: Wildlife Regains Famed P Ranch," in *Sunday Oregonian,* Sept. 1, 1946.

Items clipped from a Burns newspaper: May 3, 1893; March 27, July 24, Oct. 30, 1895.

Times-Herald, April 21, 1897.

Ms. by Dennis R. O'Brien (cited in Chapter XXX) .

Oregon's Meat Animals and Wool, 1867-1947, Extension Bulletin 684 (October, 1947, Oregon State College, 11.)

Ms. and notes by J. J. Donegan.

Interviews with John C. Scharff, Marvin H. Brenton, Alphena Venator, Robert D. Baker, Mrs. William Hanley.

Ms. and notes by J. J. Donegan.

Interviews with John C. Scharff, Martin H. Brenton, Alphena Venator, Robert D. Baker, Mrs. William Hanley.

CHAPTER XXX

Biggs, *Devine Monument Dedication* (cited in Chapter XIII) , 1, 3, 6.

R. C. Clark, "The Oregon Land Frauds," in *Dictionary of American History* (Charles Scribner's Sons, New York) , IV, 183.

E. H. MacDaniels, "Twenty-Five National Forests of North Pacific Region," in *Oregon Historical* Quarterly, XLII (September, 1941) , 247, 249, 251, 255.

Mills, "A History of Transportation in the Pacific Northwest" (cited in Chapter X) , 303.

J. Orin Oliphant, "History of Livestock Industry in the Pacific Northwest," in *Oregon Historical Quarterly,* XLIX (March, 1948) , 18.

Powers and Finke, "Survey of First Half-Century of Oregon Hotels" (cited in Chapter VI) , footnote, 245.

Wentworth, "Eastward Sheep Drives From California and Oregon" (cited in Chapter VIII) , 533, 537-538.

"Road Builder Honored," in *Sunday Oregonian* (undated clipping, 1925) .

Lochley, in *Oregon Journal* (cited in Chapter XX) .

Times-Herald, June 5, 1931.

Harney County Records, Docket B, p. 140 (about Jan. 29, 1904) . On hanging of Harry D. Egbert, alias John Frost.

Harney County Records of Incorporations, Vol. A, p. 36, April 6, 1900.

Letters from Archie McGowan, March 6, 7, 8, 1950.

Ms. and notes by J. J. Donegan.

Interviews with Martin H. Brenton, Mrs. W. Miller, and Archie McGowan, Burns.

Chapter XXXI

Monroe, *Feelin' Fine* (cited in Chapter XX), 160-167.

Ross, *Farthest Reach* (cited in Chapter XXVIII), 85-86.

Toynbee, *A Study of History* (cited in Chapter XII), 110-111.

Treadwell, *The Cattle King* (cited in Chapter XIII), Foreword, 366-367.

Turnbull, *History of Oregon Newspapers* (cited in Chapter IX), 421.

"Bill Brown," in *Oregon Historical Quarterly* (cited in Chapter XXIX), 108.

Randall V. Mills, "Prineville's Municipal Railroad in Central Oregon," in *Oregon Historical Quarterly,* XLII (September, 1941), 261.

Sprague, "Willamette Highway" (cited in Chapter VII), 248.

Strong, "Beef Cattle Industry in Oregon, 1890-1938" (cited in Chapter X), 260-262, 269, 281.

Richard L. Neuberger, "Hinterland Railroad to Star in Pacifiic Coast Freight Rivalry," in *Sunday Oregonian,* Feb. 12, 1950.

Nichols, "The Saga of William (Bill) Brown" (cited in Chapter XX).

Editorial on William Brown in *Bulletin* (Arlington, Ore.), Jan. 17, 1941.

Neth's letter (cited in Chapter XXIX).

Oswald West, "When I Slept With 'Bill' Brown of Wagontire," in *Times-Herald,* Nov. 18, 1949.

On death of William Brown, *Times-Herald,* Jan. 17, 1941.

Items in *Times-Herald,* August-September, 1924; June 5, 1931; Sept. 16, 1935.

Ms. and notes by J. J. Donegan.

Interviews with Mrs. William Hanley, June 13, 1949, and with Guy C. Willard and James S. Poteet of Bell A Ranch, June 15, 1947.

Interviews with Martin H. Brenton, Robert D. Baker, Alphena Venator, Archie McGowan and Mrs. Pearl Smyth, Burns, Ore.

Chapter XXXII

Turnbull, *History of Oregon Newspapers* (cited in chapter IX), 421.

Oswald West, Review of book, *The Wild Horse of the West* (Wyman), in *Oregon Historical Quarterly,* XLVI (September, 1945), 278-279.

Lochley, in *Oregon Journal* (cited in Chapter XX).

Items in *Times-Herald,* Sept. 25, 1924; clipping, 1928.

"Forty Years in the Wilderness," in *Times-Herald,* Sept. 24, 1924.

Herrick Timber Contract, Malheur National Forest, Oregon. Hearings Before the Committee of Public Lands and Surveys, U. S. Senate, 69th cong., 2nd sess. (Jan. 28 and Feb. 11 to 24, 1927). U. S. Govt. Printing Office, Washington, 1927.

Ms. and notes by J. J. Donegan.

Letters and notes from Archie McGowan, March 6 and 8, 1950.
Interview with Alfred R. Dewey, general manager, Edward Hines Lumber Co., Hines, Ore., April 5, 1950.

CHAPTER XXXIII

Bulletins of the Malheur National Wildlife Refuge, 1945-46.
Pomeroy, "Trumpets in the Tules" (cited in Chapter XXIX).
Letters and copies of *Oregon Inn-Side News* from Phil Metschan.
Ms., "History of the Experiment Station in Harney County Near Burns, Oregon," by Supt. W. A. Sawyer of the station, April 3, 1950.
Ms. and notes by J. J. Donegan.
Interviews with Supt. John C. Scharff, Malheur National Wildlife Refuge, June 15, 1947, and April 7, 1950.
Interviews with Mrs. William Hanley, Guy C. Willard and James S. Poteet.

CHAPTER XXXIV

Matton, *Baptist Annals of Oregon, 1887-1910,* 104-105.
Edwin V. O'Hara, *Pioneer Catholic History of Oregon* (St. Anthony Guild Press, Paterson, N. J., 1939), 219.
Rev. Vincent C. Egan, "History of the Holy Family Parish," in *Holy Family Parish Monthly,* XXVII (November, 1938).
Items in *Times-Herald,* June 17, Aug. 12, 26, 1896.
Ms. by the Rev. Arthur Beckwith, Burns, Ore., April 7, 1950.
Interviews with Rev. Vincent C. Egan, Julian Byrd, Rev. Fred L. Swanson, Rev. G. A. Johnson, Lelah McGee, Mrs. A. Davis, Rev. John H. Koch, Rev. Arthur Beckwith, all of Burns, April 5-10, 1950. Notes taken from church records.

CHAPTER XXXV

MacLeod, *The American Indian Frontier* (cited in Chapter XV), 540-541.
O. Larsell, *The Doctor in Oregon* (Binfords & Mort, for Oregon Historical Society, Portland, Ore., 1947), 542.
Randolph C. Downes, "A Crusade for Indian Reform, 1922-1934," in *Mississippi Valley Historical Review,* XXXII (December, 1945), 332-353.
Items in *Times-Herald,* May 3, 1924.
Letter from Mrs. Clara Marsden to editor, *Times-Herald,* March 31, 1950.
Letter from Friends to editor, *Times-Herald,* March 31, 1950.
"Dial Phones Come to Burns," in *Times-Herald,* April 7, 1950.
Burns City Hall Records, on first electric plants, waterworks, movies, and fire-bell tower.
Records of Burns Public Library.
Records of Harney County Clerk's office.
Ms. by Grover N. Jameson on beginnings of electric power in Burns, April 7, 1950.

Ms. by Mrs. John Biggs on history of Ladies' Library Club and library movement in Burns.

Ms. and notes by J. J. Donegan.

Letters and notes from Archie McGowan, March 6, 1950.

Interviews with Mrs. John Biggs and Harney County Clerk William Carroll at Burns, April 5-10, 1950.

Chapter XXXVI

Mack and Sawyer, *Our State: Nevada* (cited in Chapter VII), 187-190.

Anne S. Monroe, *Walk With Me, Lad* (Doubleday, Doran, Garden City, N. Y., 1934), 33.

Turnbull, *History of Oregon Newspapers* (cited in Chapter IX), 421.

Armstrong, "Set the American Indian Free" (cited in Chapter XXVI), 47, 51.

Strong, "Beef Cattle Industry in Oregon, 1890-1938" (cited in Chapter X), 281.

On William W. Brown's death and his career, *Oregon Historical Quarterly* (cited in Chapter XXXIV), 108. See also *Times-Herald,* Jan. 17, 1941, and *Bulletin* (Arlington), Jan. 17, 1941.

Item on town of Harney in *Oregonian,* June 19, 1938.

Lockley, in *Oregon Journal* (cited in Chapter XXV).

Item in *Times-Herald,* June 13, 1941.

On William Hanley's death and his career, *Times-Herald,* Sept. 16, 1935.

"Rites Today Will Honor C. W. Frazier," in *Times-Herald,* July 30, 1948.

"Burns Postoffice Established on January 22, 1884," in *Times-Herald,* Jan. 23, 1948.

Records of Burns Post Office, compiled by Darrell L. Howser.

Records of Harney County Clerk and Harney County Court.

Records of Harney County Post No. 63, American Legion.

Records of Burns-Hines Post No. 1328, Veterans of Foreign Wars.

Notes on records from Supt. J. W. Elliott, Warm Springs Indian Agency, Warm Springs, Ore.

Ms., poem, "Town of Burns," by George McGowan.

Ms. and notes by J. J. Donegan.

Letters and notes by Archie McGowan, March 6, 7, 8, 1950.

Interviews in June, 1947, with Pat Donegan, Darrell L. Howser, Rev. Vincent Egan, Mrs. Teresa F. Guinee, Mr. and Mrs. Clarence Young, Guy C. Willard and James S. Poteet, all of Burns.

Interviews in June, 1949, with Harry Williams, Mrs. William Hanley, Robert D. Baker, and Alphena Venator, all of Burns.

Chapter XXXVII

E. R. Jackman, "Burns, Oregon," in *The Saturday Evening Post* (Jan. 31, 1948), 20, 21, 50, 52, 56.

Richard L. Neuberger, "Where There's No Place Like School," in *The Saturday Evening Post* (April 8, 1950), 17.

Letter from W. L. Lowe to editor, *Times-Herald,* March 5, 1948.

"Million Dollar Harney Pay Roll Gain Indicated," in *Times-Herald,* May 7, 1948.

"Bardwell is 1949 Pioneer President," in *Times-Herald,* June 18, 1948.

"Explore New I.O.N. Highway Improvement," in *Times-Herald,* July 30, 1948.

"Unique Designs Mark History On Brief Case," in *Times-Herald,* Aug. 6, 1948.

Items on Harney County Livestock Association in *Times-Herald,* March 24, April 14, 1950.

"Harney County Trade Volume Up 200 Per Cent Since 1939," in *Times-Herald,* April 14, 1950.

Items on new Harney County Hospital in *Times-Herald,* April 14 and 21, 1950; also in *Sunday Oregonian* (April 23, 1950), 10.

Items in *Times-Herald,* Nov. 24, Dec. 1, 1950.

Douglas McKay, "Governor McKay Looks at Oregon's Future," in *Sunday Oregonian Magazine* (April 23, 1950), 6.

Ilda O. Thompson, Harney County assessor, *Statement of County Budget and Taxes* (summary of assessment roll for 1949).

Records of Burns Branch of U. S. National Bank of Portland, Ore., 1950-51.

Ms. by Harley S. Hotchkiss on Harney County Livestock Association.

Letters and notes from Archie McGowan, March 6, April 19, 1950.

Interview with C. L. Dalton, Burns, Ore., April 10, 1950.

INDEX

305